D0941053

CENTRAL WYOMING COLLEGE
LIBRARY
RIVERTON, WY 82501

Women Pioneers in Television

Women Pioneers in Television

Biographies of Fifteen Industry Leaders

by CARY O'DELL

with a foreword by SALLY JESSY RAPHAËL

McFarland & Company, Inc., Publishers
Jefferson, North Carolina, and London

CENTRAL WYOMING COLLEGE
LIBRARY
RIVERTON, WY 82501

PN
1992.8
W65
O34
1997

British Library Cataloguing-in-Publication data are available

Library of Congress Cataloguing-in-Publication Data

O'Dell, Cary.
    Women pioneers in television : biographies of fifteen industry
leaders / by Cary O'Dell. ; with a foreword by Sally Jessy Raphaël.
      p.   cm.
    Includes bibliographical references and index.
    ISBN 0-7864-0167-2 (library binding : 50# alkaline paper) ∞
    1. Women in television broadcasting—United States—Biography
I. Title.
PN1992.8.W65034   1997
791.45'028'082—dc20
[b]   96-46132
                                            CIP

©1997 Cary O'Dell. All rights reserved.

*No part of this book, specifically including the index, may be reproduced or
transmitted in any form or by any means, electronic or mechanical, including
photocopying or recording, or by any information storage and retrieval system, without permission in writing from the publisher.*

Manufactured in the United States of America

*McFarland & Company, Inc., Publishers
  Box 611, Jefferson, North Carolina 28640*

ACKNOWLEDGMENTS

How a man in his twenties came to write about the history of women in television is a story too long and involved to go into here. Nevertheless, it was not, by any means, a quest undertaken alone.

My greatest thanks to the literally hundreds of individuals who opened up their libraries, scrapbooks, file cabinets, and hearts to assist me in gathering the data necessary to write this book. I would especially like to acknowledge the libraries and collections of the Academy of Motion Picture Arts & Sciences, the Academy of Television Arts & Sciences, the Museum of Broadcast Communications in Chicago, Illinois, the Museum of Television & Radio in New York City, the UCLA Film and Television Archive, the New York City Public Library, the Broadcast Pioneers Library, Syracuse University, and WMAQ-TV, Chicago.

Personal thanks to Dr. Anna Paddon, Phylis Johnson, and, especially, Dr. Joe Foote, who were there for guidance and suggestions at the inception of this project.

Thank you also to Lisa Habiger, Jane Wilson, Wendy Maulding, Lora Ellegood, Beth Speer, and Keisha Smith. Most especially love and thanks to Marilyn Lingle. They were my "office mates" at the start of this book; then, as now, they are also my friends.

Thank you to Dr. Mary Ann Watson and to Michael Keith.

Unending love and gratitude to my very dear friend Karmon Runquist who has been a faithful, patient, and supportive companion on every step of this trip, beginning to end.

Finally, my eternal gratitude and appreciation to the fifteen extraordinary women whose life stories are detailed herein, women who lived lives of incomparable energy, accomplishment, and personal vision and who were always a joy to read about, write about, and rediscover.

TABLE OF CONTENTS

*Many women are singing together of this:
… one is anywhere and some are everywhere and all
seem to be singing, although some cannot
sing a note.*

—ANNE SEXTON

FOREWORD
by Sally Jessy Raphaël

I sometimes think I got into broadcasting because I didn't know any better.

No one told me it would be harder for a woman to succeed than a man! I began to get the picture as a student at Columbia University, when I took one of the earliest courses in media history. There wasn't one woman mentioned. When I graduated, I went to Pat Kelly, the great old dean of announcers at NBC, who had been one of my teachers. I wanted to become an NBC page. "Sorry," he told me, "you're a woman."

"I'm the 'A' student in the class," I sputtered. "What does this mean—that I can't get a job right out of college?" And he said, "That's right. We don't hire women!"

I became a disc jockey, because they said nobody would listen to a woman's voice. Men felt women at home must be so sex-starved that they would only listen to a male voice.

So I went to Puerto Rico, where I had spent much of my childhood, and started working at Channel 18. It was common knowledge that broadcasting in South America and Europe was a far different picture for women than in America. Puerto Rican shows were geared towards being resold to Latin America, where, for some farsighted reason, women seemed to be equally accepted on air. I had a career there that I couldn't have had in the states. For some of us, leaving the country was the only way to get started.

I emerged on the scene somewhere in between those wonderful Faye Emersons and Pauline Fredericks and before the girls with blonde hair and flip hairdos. It was an awful period! You never read about women in television, even in trade magazines. No matter who you were, you couldn't get them to write about your business exploits.

I was lucky enough to meet Dorothy Fuldheim a number of years ago, when I went out to St. Louis to launch *Sally*. When I heard there was a woman who had been doing a show for almost forty years, I said, "Impossible." It was like hearing there was another Eskimo on the face of the earth when you thought you were the only one! I spent an afternoon with Dorothy, and there's a lesson to be learned from her life. Even other women in broadcasting didn't know who she was. She was never given an article in a magazine.

1

You had to be in her listening area to know who she was. And the lady only had a forty-year career.

Ida Lupino, Lucille Ball, and Gertrude Berg, because they were in front of the camera as well as behind the scenes, were able to attract the limelight for their efforts. But both Ball and Berg played down their other respective talents—a brilliant business mind and writing talent—because of the tenor of the times.

That's why I'm so grateful to Cary O'Dell for this important book on women in television. We may have come a "long way," but we're not completely there. There is still not a woman at the helm of a top network. If he hadn't presented these brilliant women in an historical perspective, we still might not have a history at all.

INTRODUCTION

Before cable and celestial satellites interconnected the world, television was a rickety system of weak electronic signals moving from antenna to antenna. Each of these signals was an attempt to communicate, to be heard. Each signal was an innovation. Each innovation an idea. Each idea a voice.

This is a book about fifteen of those voices, voices not always heard— fifteen important women in the history of television, a medium that, for its relative youth, has had its story told and retold many times. Barnouw, Brown, Keith, Sterling, Head, and others have documented the formation of the world's greatest communication marvel. Similarly, the stories of some of television's major players like William S. Paley, Frank Stanton, and Edward R. Murrow have also been extensively studied and recorded. However, after reading these fine (and relatively comprehensive) studies one is often struck with a question they inexplicably and unintentionally ask: Where are the women?

True, the contributions of some women, like Lucille Ball and Joan Ganz Cooney, simply cannot be ignored. Nor are these two women ignored in these books, though they do often find themselves relegated to little more than a quick mention at an end of a chapter or placed in a short, fleeting footnote.

A survey of the fifteen-page index to Head and Sterling's 642-page tome *Broadcasting in America*, an instructional industry survey with historical overtones, reveals in its discussion of important people and contributors the presence of only nine women's names. Of those nine only FCC Commissioner Frieda Hennock and newswoman Barbara Walters rate more than a single page reference.[1] More women are mentioned throughout Erik Barnouw's epic trilogy of broadcasting history, *A Tower in Babel*, *The Golden Web*, and *The Image Empire*, but of those names scattered about, only Hennock and Lucille Ball emerge as notable figures.[2] The absence of women from media histories can even be seen in some of their titles; note radio historian Tom Lewis's *Empire of the Air: The* Men *Who Made Radio* (emphasis mine).

More attention to women has been paid in certain specialized histories. Edward R. Bliss's 1991 history of broadcast journalism, *Now the News*, devoted a special chapter to female news anchors and reporters. Yet, while Bliss's book summarized the overall progress of women, from the likes of Pauline Frederick

3

through Barbara Walters to the present day, it did not contain biographical data on any of them. Books on the evolution of children's television, such as Kate Moody's *Growing Up on Television* (1988) and Edward L. Palmer's *Children in the Cradle of Television* (1987), have made mention of the accomplishments of Joan Ganz Cooney and Peggy Charren. Similarly, histories of daytime dramas like Robert LaGuardia's *Soap World* (1983) and Robert C. Allen's *Speaking of Soaps* (1985) have included substantial discussion of the work of Irna Phillips, the undisputed queen of the soaps. And Charles Montgomery Hammond's tome on the television documentary, *The Image Decade* (1981), devoted space to the work of Lucy Jarvis.

In women's literature, Judith Gelfman summarized women's progress in the area of broadcast journalism and evaluated their current state in the business in her 1976 book, *Women in Television News*. Following in her footsteps, Marlene Sanders' and Marcia Rock's *Waiting for Prime Time* appeared in 1988 and documented Ms. Sanders's own career, while placing it in a context of previous and current female correspondents.

Women from the world of television comedy have been placed in books like Linda Martin's and Kerry Segrave's *Women in Comedy* (1986), a study examining women from many disciplines, including theater and cinema. Contributions by women in journalism and film have been documented through books such as Madelon Golden Schilpp's and Sharon M. Murphy's *Great Women of the Press* (1983) and Louise Heck-Rabi's *Women Filmmakers* (1984).

In rare cases entire books have been devoted to a single woman who has made her greatest impact through television. Dorothy Kilgallen and Barbara Walters have both had books written about them. A 1974 book by Richard Polsky told the story of the development of *Sesame Street* and its creator Joan Ganz Cooney. Not surprisingly, Lucille Ball has been the most frequent subject of books, most notably in works by Charles Higham (1986), Joe Morella and Edward Z. Epstein (1990), and Kathleen Brady (1994).

In some cases women have spoken for themselves. TV newswomen Liz Trotta, Nancy Dickerson, and Jessica Savitch all authored autobiographies. Celebrated television actresses like Carol Burnett, Eve Arden, and Audrey Meadows also penned memoirs. Longtime television regulars like Arlene Francis, Kitty Carlisle Hart, and Virginia Graham also published their life stories. As for women profiled in this work: actress/writer Gertrude Berg wrote an autobiography in 1961; newswoman Dorothy Fuldheim wrote two memoirs during her lifetime, the first in 1966, the second in 1974; and Betty White published *Here We Go Again: My Life in Television* in 1995.

Despite this library of works, however, a collective, cross-sectional, detailed study celebrating women and their place in the history of television has never been written. Hence, women have seldom found themselves—individually or as a group—in the canon of media history education.

Why? By and large, histories, wars, and battles are told in terms of their generals, seldom through the stories of their foot soldiers. Unlike Paley and others, none of the women included in this study ever founded a television network or single-handedly ran one; yet all were dedicated women, making definitive contributions and creating a far-reaching influence in the medium of television. They were doing this at a time when few other women were able to carve out a place for themselves in the medium. It should also be noted that the contributions these women were making were usually in areas and genres where few, if any, men had yet succeeded or even made attempts. In that sense, these women were pioneers not only in terms of their gender but in terms of their vision for an entire industry.

Choosing which women to include in this biographical work (history's "stream of souls" as Yeats has called it) was not an easy decision. Some names (Ball and Cooney) leapt quickly (and deservedly) to mind. Others took more deliberating. Most beneficial in determining which individuals belonged in a work about important women in television were Les Brown's *The New York Times Encyclopedia of Television*[3] and editor Lois O'Neil-Decker's colossal undertaking, *The Women's Book of World Records and Achievements*.[4] Each devoted special attention to prominent women who have worked in television and communications-related fields. In choosing which women to write about, an attempt was made to represent the diversity of the television landscape, to encompass every field of the television medium, showcasing women and women's accomplishments in a variety of endeavors.

The women who were finally selected were chosen for any number of reasons: accomplishment, longevity, innovation, fame, influence, vision. Additionally, each of the women chosen was selected as a symbol of other women in her same area. For example, Pauline Frederick represents here all newswomen, past and present. Dorothy Fuldheim exemplifies not only female news anchors but also women who have had substantial impact on local rather than national levels. The same is true for Judith Waller. Gertrude Berg, Faye Emerson, and Betty White offer dynamic examples of female talent in front of the camera, while Mildred Freed Alberg and Ida Lupino do the same for women behind the scenes. Frieda Hennock speaks for women in government and telecommunications policy. And Peggy Charren speaks for women trying to create change and improvement in the medium through interest groups and specialty organizations.

After each of the women were chosen, information on their lives and careers was gathered from a wide variety of places: newspaper and magazine articles, scripts, television programs and films, encyclopedias, government documents, theses and dissertations, books and journals. Interviews with assorted family, friends, and coworkers of each of these women were conducted to fill in some of the gaps and to round out general impressions. Finally, when possible, interviews with the subjects themselves were conducted.

These chapters, once pooled, evolved into fifteen distinct portraits of fifteen distinct individuals—all of whom shared as many dissimilarities as similarities and each of whom, through her own talents and determination, excelled in her chosen field.

Lucille Ball and Joan Ganz Cooney have both become household names through their drive, talent, and achievements. Likewise, the history of the daytime drama as a genre cannot possibly be told without a lengthy discussion of the work of Irna Phillips. Neither can the great moments of the television documentary be evaluated without speaking of Lucy Jarvis.

But whether widely known or unknown, mentioned in other books or forgotten, all of these women belong in a book that hopes to record the accomplishments women have made over the years to the development of the television medium. Collectively, they constitute an integral part of television's vast, rich, and diverse history. They belong as part of a larger family of accomplishments that together, and individually, illustrate the finest qualities television is capable of producing. These women succeeded before others, but their stories do not end here. Their stories are the history of television. Their stories are the stories of all women, of all people who speak to be heard.

NOTES

1. Sydney W. Head and Christopher H. Sterling, *Broadcasting in America* (Boston: Houghton Mifflin, 1982).

2. Erik Barnouw, *The Golden Web* (New York: Oxford, 1968); *The Image Empire* (New York: Oxford, 1970); *A Tower in Babel* (New York: Oxford, 1966).

3. Les Brown, *The New York Times Encyclopedia of Television* (New York: Times Books, 1977).

4. Lois O'Neil-Decker, *The Women's Book of World Records and Achievements* (Garden City, NY: Anchor Press/Doubleday, 1977).

Mildred Freed Alberg

Few producers in any medium have the honor of having their names become synonymous with quality and prestige. One of those who does happens to be a woman. Esteemed British actor Maurice Evans once said of her: "Where others take something popular and make it good, she takes the good— the great classics of literature and history—and makes it popular."[1] She is a producer of such extraordinary accomplishment, pedigree, and recognition that a summary of the many honors she has received contains the names of all of television's major prizes. For her work behind the scenes during her thirty-plus years as a producer, overseeing the production of dozens of *Hallmark Hall of Fame* productions and other programs for television, she has been the recipient of two George Foster Peabody Awards, seven Sylvania Awards, six Christopher Awards, the *McCall's* Golden Mike, four Radio-Television Daily Awards and five Emmys. All of these are inscribed with one name: Mildred Freed Alberg.

The daughter of Harry and Florence Freed, Mildred Freed was born on January 15, 1921, in Montreal, Canada, the third of four children, three girls and one boy. Her father founded the Freed Paper Box company in Montreal, a dangerous business in those days because of the flammability of the product and primitive fire-fighting methods.[2]

Alberg was born in a house facing Fletcher Field, where she often joined the boys for various sports, including when the kids needed another "man," tackle football games. Also, across from the house was a 600-foot "mountain" that Mildred climbed many times over the course of her childhood. From that hill and its plush surrounding foliage Alberg acquired a lifelong love of nature.[3]

Though Alberg has referred to her childhood as "ideal," it was not always easy. Her older sister died of pneumonia at age 13 while at Ottawa Ladies College. That same year her father died at age 45, also from pneumonia. It was 1931 and the Depression was still new; money for the family quickly became scarce. Alberg's brother took on responsibility for the family and later was able to earn a college degree by attending night school. Alberg's chance for a university degree, though, never materialized. A voracious reader, she has since said that the lack of a college education never affected her life: "It didn't matter. I'll have to admit I never missed it."[4]

MILDRED FREED ALBERG

Along with her much-loved books, Alberg had an early "abiding love of and interest in the theater."[5] Since early childhood she had dreamed of taking herself (and her interest in the written word) to New York City and the world of well-produced English theater. She arrived there on a Saturday night in 1939 and, in near storybook fashion, landed a job with a writer the next day after reading an ad for a typist in the Sunday *New York Times*.

When Alberg arrived for work, she found that she had been hired by two of George Abbott's ghost writers who were working on a new play. Mildred remembers the early days of the job as "typing for an hour, hour and a half as these mad men handed me pages."[6] "Being young," as she said, Alberg finally looked up from her keyboard one day and asked, "Do you want me just to type or to tell you what I think?" Alberg remembers, "I had both of them at my feet in no time as we discussed the play."[7] She remained a ghost writer for about a year, but that role came to an end when she refused to follow the other two writers to California, preferring to remain in New York. Before they left for the West Coast, though, they found Mildred a job typing novels for a New York publisher; Alberg remembers, "I got so I could type a novel—if I stayed up all day and all night—in a day or day and a half."[8] She filled the rest of her time by attending theater school and the New School for Social Research, "taking what I felt was interesting at the time."[9] Whatever time was left was spent "going to plays, plays, plays."[10]

Not long after arriving in New York, Mildred Freed had a second occurrence of good luck. Through a mutual friend, she met the man who would become her husband. Somer Alberg was a well-respected Shakespearean actor from Montreal; he and Mildred had both arrived in New York within one day of each other.[11] In the beginning Mildred tried to set Somer up with a friend of hers and had arranged a double date consisting of Mildred, the friend, their friend Harry, and Somer. On the day of the date, only Mildred and Somer showed up. They hit it off well enough and were married on January 28, 1940.

Mildred Freed Alberg's next job took her into the world of radio. She assisted in the production of a series of half-hour debates organized by a group of "young, ultra conservatives ... just spoiled college kids really."[12] That job, like her previous one, finally called for her input: "One day I suddenly said, 'Don't you think you should have two sides if you call it a 'debate'?" Alberg was invited onto the next broadcast.[13] She recounts her early days in the big city: "I just loved it. I had a friend whose family rented out a guest bedroom; it was available and I became their 'star border'.... I had fun."[14]

Alberg's radio career continued to evolve. She remembers:

> When World War II broke out, I was busy writing radio public service announcements and radio dramatizations. That was when I discovered that actors were the most generous people in the world. If there was a cause they believed in they contributed time and talent gladly: Helen Hayes, Burgess Meredith, Paulette Goddard, to name a few.
>
> After the war, I took a job as a writer for the newly-formed relief organization CARE. It had been formed by the leading American relief organizations to solve a problem—sending relief packages from the U.S. to an individual who had written desperately for help. [Unfortunately], relief packages at that chaotic pace were usually pilfered or lost.[15]

Eventually CARE formulated a system to store boxes in various recipient countries abroad; representatives would then carefully distribute the packages from there. What was lacking in the plan was making known to the American public the European need for humanitarian aid.[16] To help solve this problem, Alberg was promoted to CARE Director of Information in 1947; she immediately approached ABC radio. She wanted to produce dramatizations based on several CARE case histories, using Hollywood and theater celebrities, to raise money for the organization. The premiere show, produced by Mildred Freed Alberg, had Meredith and Goddard (married at the time) donating their time. Douglas Fairbanks, Jr. also made several appearances during the program's run.[17] Later Alberg traveled to Europe giving press conferences for the American and European press. Alberg remained with CARE until 1951.[18]

Mildred Freed Alberg's life changed forever one evening in the early 1950s after the viewing of a television performance of *Julius Caesar*. Though she considered the production, starring a young Charlton Heston, good, she was "furious" over its length. In order to meet the timetable of television, the entire three-hour play by William Shakespeare was cut down to run only one hour. To speed things up the network had rewritten dialogue and sliced many of the soliloquies, leaving little but action sequences and death scenes.[19]

Alberg's viewing of that program coincided soon after with another significant event in her life. In 1950, taking a break from her radio career, producing shows on and off for CARE, Alberg had accompanied her husband on a road company tour of *The Devil's Disciple* starring Maurice Evans, the great British Shakespearean actor renowned for his performance in the lead of *Hamlet*. Mildred took a walk-on part in some of the play's crowd scenes.[20] Observing Evans's craft, Alberg struck on the idea of bringing the actor's genius to its widest audience ever, by taking Evans to television. After introducing the idea to Evans and convincing him to take his first look at the TV medium, Evans responded to Alberg's request, "I'd sooner sell tickets to a sideshow than appear on that monstrosity."[21]

Alberg, though, would not give up. She finally convinced Evans that a television *Hamlet* would be wonderful. She and colleague Tom Sand presented him with a *Hamlet* TV script, based on Evans's own *GI Hamlet*. The *GI Hamlet* was a shortened version of the play that Evans had performed around the world during the war to entertain military troops; that version condensed the four-hour play to two. Maurice Evans eventually said "yes" but on one condition: he had to have a full two hours for the performance.[22] Alberg remembers, "Maurice didn't think I had a chance."[23] Later Evans told her he only agreed to do the two-hour production "because he was sure it never would be sold. He thought they'd throw me out."[24]

Soon after getting Evans's okay, Alberg marched into the offices of NBC television with an "exciting, new idea" and tried her best to get to the highest ranking person in programming: "I finally walked up to this man and said, 'Do you have power of authority to make program decisions?'" He did. And Alberg began to "sell" her idea, "Why don't we take the greatest play in the world and do it as if it were the greatest play and give it two hours?"[25] NBC executive John Rayle asked, "Such as?" Alberg responded "*Hamlet*, with Evans."

To Alberg's delight the network was interested. NBC executive director Al McCleery was then given the assignment of acquiring the interest, and sponsorship, of Joyce Hall, head of the Hallmark Card Company, whom NBC thought might be interested.[26] Hallmark had been the sponsor of a well-received perennial production of *Amahl and the Night Visitors* for the network.[27]

Alberg assumed the role of associate producer and helped adapt the final script; NBC did not object because Alberg had a history producing for radio and had asked for very little money from the network to stage the production. The budget was a calculated move on Alberg's part:

> I figured if I promised to keep the budget down I could ask for total artistic control. And that's what happened.... I didn't see any reason why we should go to advisers or producers; it just seemed if you wanted control, you had to learn by doing it. We had to. No one else was doing two-hour television drama at that time.[28]

Joyce Hall, the sponsor, and NBC supported Alberg totally. Still, all was not smooth sailing. Alberg remembers walking down the hallway behind two NBC vice presidents one day only to overhear their conversation which began: "My God! *Hamlet?*"[29] Another early nay-sayer told her, "You're out of your ever-lovin' mind. The customers won't hold still for two hours, and for Shakespeare, yet."[30]

Despite a few hurdles and a few critics, work on the program continued—often well into the night. Meetings with Evans, who was appearing on Broadway in *Dial M for Murder*, had to fit in with his theater schedule. Alberg and George Schaefer, their stage director (and a longtime associate of Evans's) would arrive at Evans's home at eleven at night, after the play's performance, and discuss the show until one or two in the morning.[31]

Hamlet, starring Maurice Evans and Ruth Chatterton, aired under the sponsorship of Hallmark on NBC-TV on April 26, 1953. More people that night saw *Hamlet* than had ever previously seen it in centuries of the theater.[32] The production was an unqualified success, attracting such reviews as "brilliant" and "spectacular."[33]

Nineteen fifty-three also saw the founding of Mildred Freed Alberg's production company. It was christened Milberg Enterprises, Inc., a name she hated (her lawyer dreamed it up one day while she was out of town).[34] Based on the success of *Hamlet*, the willing talents of Maurice Evans, and the guiding hands of Mildred Freed Alberg and NBC, Hallmark agreed to sponsor an ongoing series of Shakespearean plays for television starring Maurice Evans. In 1954 they produced *Richard III* and *Macbeth*, each starring Evans in the lead roles.[35] In 1955 the *Hallmark Hall of Fame* became a long-term, regular feature on NBC. Mildred Freed Alberg was named executive producer, overseeing nearly all aspects of the presentations from the budget, to the script, to the music selection and casting.[36] Alberg determined that six productions a year could be staged, no more or the quality would go down. This number was fine with Hallmark since it would allow each of them to air near or on a major holiday, a plus for the greeting card business.[37] Alberg remained with the *Hall of Fame* as executive producer for six years, overseeing the production of more than twenty different presentations, including *The Taming of the Shrew*, *Dial M for Murder* (both starring Maurice Evans), *Born Yesterday*, *There Shall Be No Night*, and a production of *Ah, Wilderness!* in 1959, with Helen Hayes.[38]

While producing some of the shows, Alberg sometimes ran into unforeseen complications, many of them technical and unique to television. During the live presentation of *Hamlet*, an overhead boom became visible, and just after actor Evans started his recitation of a soliloquy beginning "Now I am alone…," a stagehand wandered in front of the camera and stayed there a full minute. Later that week, comic Milton Berle invited the man on his show as "TV's most famous celebrity."[39]

In 1956, while preparing for a production of *The Little Foxes*, it was noticed that immediately after the climactic scene in which lead character Regina Giddens watches unemotionally as her husband dies in his futile attempt to reach his heart medication, a commercial reminding the audience to "remember their loved ones at Christmas" was scheduled to air.[40] Fortunately, this sudden change in tone was discovered and this comical juxtaposition was averted. Later, during a 1957 production of *The Lark*, starring Julie Harris, the back of the camera fell off just before the final shot. "That created a little problem," Mrs. Alberg said.[41]

Another time, while Maurice Evans was performing live on the air and Mildred was in her usual position in the control booth, watching the clock and giving hand signals to him (stretch, on the nose, etc.), she found the program was running far too long. Alberg excused herself from the booth, went down to the studio floor, looked directly at Evans, and simulated cutting her throat. He got the idea, and the program finished on time.[42]

In February 1958 the *Hall of Fame*'s musical production of Mary Mapes Dodge's *Hans Brinker, or the Silver Skates*, starring Tab Hunter and directed by Sidney Lumet, necessitated bringing a little bit of Holland to a Brooklyn television studio. Along with building sets of the Brinker home and an Amsterdam town square, a working windmill and a small island had to be constructed. Most difficult of all was the ice needed for the skating portions of the show. Alberg oversaw the construction of a canal, 80 feet by 45 feet, down the middle of the studio; and she supervised the delivery of sodium chloride, "miles of tubing," and two compressors—the second one just in case the first did not work.[43] She told reporter J.P. Shanley, "After the program ends we have to be sure the ice is broken up and removed before it melts. Otherwise there would be a flood in the studio."[44] She said of it later, "I grew up in Canada and always went ice skating, [but] I never knew how cold you could be on an indoor ice rink. It was petrifyingly cold."[45]

Sets once before had been a major concern on the *Hall of Fame* when, in

1955, Alberg took on the task of creating the difficult dreamscapes of Lewis Carroll's *Alice in Wonderland*. This production starred Elsa Lanchester and Eva Le Gallienne.[46] Alberg remembers, "A first-class writer and scenery designer were invited to join the [preproduction] meetings and the production won high praise."[47]

Other problems, though, were less easy to solve. A 1956 production of George Bernard Shaw's comedy of manners, *Man and Superman* encountered network opposition because of a speech in the play's second act. The speech was a tirade delivered by the main character, a confirmed bachelor, against a young woman with designs on marrying him, her scheming mother, and the nature of motherhood as a whole. Not only did the network object to the depiction of mother as monster, but it feared that the sponsor, Hallmark Greeting Cards—whose third-largest sales after Christmas and Valentine's Day took place for Mother's Day—would absolutely forbid the speech. Though NBC stood firm, Alberg was undeterred. She approached Joyce Hall directly. He wanted it kept in. When *Man and Superman* (starring Maurice Evans) aired on November 25, 1956, it attracted a national audience of twenty million with no angry phone calls or correspondence.[48]

Greater controversy occurred when Alberg and Hallmark attempted to stage a production of the Pulitzer Prize–winning *The Green Pastures* by Marc Connelly. In the play a group of African-American children, unfamiliar with biblical history, reconstruct the story of Christ in terms of their own lives: there is a fish-fry for the angels in heaven, the lord is referred to as "De Lawd," and evil is represented by crap games and knife fights.[49] A play dealing with race and religion (in 1957) drew debate from many sides early on. Some Southern affiliates refused to carry the program, and Hallmark, Inc., received threats of lost business. Black publications attacked the program for perpetuating "Uncle Tom"–like stereotypes.[50] Fanning the flames of the controversy was the real-life drama taking place in Little Rock, Arkansas, where nine black students were refused enrollment in an all-white high school and the Governor was forced to call in the National Guard. To quiet things down, Alberg called dozens of prominent black leaders to assure them that the program was not a satire and brought in members of the clergy and community leaders (northerners and southerners, black and white) to go over the script. After months of work and peacekeeping, the show aired on October 17, 1957, receiving only an 18.7 rating. The show had been aired opposite an all-star party in Madison Square Garden celebrating Mike Todd's film *Around the World in Eighty Days*. Despite the original ratings disappointment, overwhelming critical reaction to *Green Pastures*—the *New York Times* called it "one of television's most glorious evenings"—allowed for an encore production on March 23, 1959.[51] *The Green Pastures* remains one of Mildred's favorite *Hall of Fame* productions.[52]

Although the *Hall of Fame* specials did not always garner the highest ratings of the week, their prestige and quality of production enticed some of America's biggest stars to appear in them.[53] Alberg attracted high-caliber performers (and kept the budget low in spite of it) by offering the performers opportunities to play roles they were not usually offered. That is how Mary Martin, Robert Redford, Charles Boyer, and others were cast.[54] That is also how Alberg was able to get Greer Garson for the most un–Mrs. Miniver–like role of Regina Giddens in Lillian Hellman's *The Little Foxes*.[55]

After six years with Hallmark, Alberg decided to move on. She was hoping to indulge a long-standing interest in archeology—producing archeology films and archeology-based dramas—when a phone call from William Morris sent her in a different direction. "Someone had a problem," she remembered. "They had bought a series for Fred Coe and Fred had become ill. William Morris asked if I would meet with them."[56] "Them" were representatives of the Equitable Life Assurance Societies and the editors of *American Heritage Magazine*. The series, to be titled *Our American Heritage*, was a number of specials dramatizing crucial, representative events in the lives of famous Americans.

At first Alberg was leery. She was Canadian, and what business did a Canadian have retelling American history? She plunged into reading about as many leaders as possible: Hamilton, Jefferson. "I loved it," she said and agreed to produce the series.[57]

Our American Heritage—now a Milberg production—premiered on Sunday, October 18, 1959, with a program on Thomas Jefferson titled "Divided We Stand."[58] Later shows dealt with the lives of Ulysses S. Grant, Eli Whitney, and Andrew Carnegie.[59] The show garnered an Emmy and was named the "most outstanding educational program of 1959."[60] The series ran until 1961, with Mildred Freed Alberg producing around fifteen hour-long specials. (Contrary to many reports, Mrs. Alberg did not work on *Playhouse 90* at this time; in fact, she was never at any point in her career affiliated with that show.)[61]

In 1960 Alberg took a stab at producing for the stage. An original script by James Costigan titled *Little Moon of Alban*, the story of a young Irish nurse, had remained in her mind since she produced it for the *Hall of Fame* in 1958. The play, starring Julie Harris, opened on December 1, 1960, and ran for several months.[62] Although Alberg enjoyed the experience, she found it "frustrating.... [T]hings I could do in television I couldn't do in the theater."[63]

Alberg spent the next several years at work on her first motion picture. She had come upon a St. Clair McKellway short story in the *New Yorker* and had it turned into a script by Ira Wallach titled *Hot Millions*. She talked actor Peter Ustinov into taking the lead role. In typical Alberg fashion, she convinced MGM, in 1965, to finance the project. The film premiered in 1968.[64] Though an enjoyable experience, film, like theater, held little interest for

Alberg: each required greater sums of money and, with those larger sums, more investors and bosses, limiting her creative control.[65]

Alberg returned to television and the idea of archeologically accurate dramatizations based on Biblical narratives. Alberg said, "I wanted to start with Moses, but I couldn't find enough material that could be [historically] proven." Her first film was *The Story of Jacob and Joseph*, shot on location in the Middle East with a careful eye for historical accuracy. There was also a careful eye for personal safety: Alberg and her crew were filming in the state of Israel when war broke out.[66] Despite a few complications and close calls, the production finished on time. *Jacob and Joseph* ran on ABC in 1974.[67] That two-hour telefilm was followed by another Milberg production, *The Story of David*, costarring Jane Seymour, in 1976.[68]

The following year, on May 31, 1977, Mildred suffered the death of her husband Somer. Somer, since retiring as an actor, had found a second successful career in insurance.[69] He and Mildred had been married for thirty-seven years.

After a few films produced for the Television Academy of Arts & Sciences, Mildred Freed Alberg embarked on yet another new challenge—her first documentary. Once again in the interests of archeology, Alberg traveled to Syria for PBS to produce a remarkable film titled *The Royal Archives of Ebla*. The discovery in the 1970s of a "library" of 17,000 stone fragments and tablets that contained the first evidence of a written language in that part of the world caused an extraordinary sensation in the history and archeology communities. It also peaked Alberg's interest. In typical Alberg fashion, she approached PBS with the idea for the film, not the other way around. The film premiered at the Smithsonian in Washington and aired on PBS in October of 1980. Later it won the Gold Medal for best TV documentary at the International Film and TV Festival in New York City.[70]

There were a few more projects for the Television Academy of Arts & Sciences, but after that Mildred Freed Alberg retired from television production.

She moved to Florida in 1984 and, today, between extensive travels around the world, she indulges her passionate creativity as an artist in oil painting.[71]

Throughout her career, Mildred Freed Alberg has defined in relatively simple terms what makes a good producer: "A good producer is just someone who really wants to do something and will take the time to study it and do it well."[72] The matter of her gender, in her mind, has never stood in the way of doing what she wants to do (or in doing it well):

> The fact that I am female has been neither blessing nor handicap. There's nothing up my sleeve. Women in business should forget that they're women. Don't make a mental hurdle of it. Go after what you want—not as a woman, but as a creative person.[73]

As a "creative person," Mildred Freed Alberg has set one of the highest standards for quality television in the medium's history. That which she helped create, the *Hallmark Hall of Fame*, and her other many films for television remain as jewels in television's crown and bold, bright examples of what television can be. The *Hall of Fame*—though different now from what she began—continues to produce programs that draw an intelligent audience, one comprised of viewers who want to be respected, entertained, and enlightened.

Mildred Freed Alberg's achievements speak for themselves. And they speak very loudly today to an industry that too often favors money over quality, the popular over the classic. The types of films that Alberg chose to produce do not appear on the four main television networks anymore. They are now the hallmark of PBS and Arts & Entertainment. Television, especially network television, is not as open to sharp people with controversial ideas as it was when Mildred Freed Alberg marched into NBC headquarters and asked for two hours of primetime to stage something special. Would she (or anyone, for that matter) be able to do something like that today, to create something different out of the norm, to give audiences what they did not know they really wanted? It could be remotely possible for a few. For someone of Mildred Freed Alberg's caliber, though, it would be the only possibility. She said in 1992, "I did what I did because I never compromised or was asked to…. [I just said] this I want to do, I can do, and I will do."[74]

Mildred Freed Alberg

January 15, 1921	Born in Montreal, Canada.
June 1939	Arrived in New York City to begin career.
January 28, 1940	Married Somer Alberg, actor.
1940-43	Worked as producer for radio, New York City.
1944	Worked as radio producer/writer for AFL-CIO Community Services Committee, New York City.
1946	Ended radio producing career.
1947-1951	Worked as Director of Information for CARE.
April 26, 1953	*Hamlet*, starring Maurice Evans, aired as a *Hallmark Hall of Fame* presentation. Television's first two-hour dramatic special.
January 24, 1954	*Richard III*, produced by Mildred Freed Alberg, aired as *Hall of Fame* production.
November 28, 1954	*Macbeth* aired as *Hall of Fame* production.
January 1955	*Hall of Fame* named regular series of television specials sponsored by Hallmark, Inc. Mildred Freed Alberg named producer of series.
October 23, 1955	*Alice in Wonderland* aired.

March 18, 1956	*The Taming of the Shrew* aired.
October 28, 1956	*Born Yesterday* aired.
November 25, 1956	*Man and Superman* aired.
December 16, 1956	*The Little Foxes* aired.
February 10, 1957	*The Lark* aired.
March 17, 1957	*There Shall Be No Night* aired.
April 10, 1957	*Yeoman and the Guard* aired.
October 17, 1957	*The Green Pastures*—after long delays and controversy—aired as *Hall of Fame* presentation.
November 17, 1957	*On Borrowed Time* aired.
December 15, 1957	*Twelfth Night* aired.
February 9, 1958	*Hans Brinker, or The Silver Skates* aired.
March 24, 1958	*Little Moon of Alban* aired as *Hallmark Hall of Fame* presentation starring Julie Harris.
April 25, 1958	*Dial M for Murder* aired.
October 13, 1958	*Johnny Belinda* aired.
November 20, 1958	*Kiss Me Kate* aired.
December 14, 1958	*The Christmas Tree* aired.
February 5, 1959	*Berkeley Square* aired.
April 28, 1959	Presentation of *Ah, Wilderness!,* Mildred Freed Alberg's last *Hall of Fame* production, aired.
October 18, 1959	First production of *Our American Heritage* television specials aired.
December 1, 1960	Mildred Freed Alberg's production of *Little Moon of Alban* opened on Broadway stage; play starred Julie Harris.
August 1965	Began preproduction work on first feature film, *Hot Millions,* for MGM.
August 1968	Film *Hot Millions* opened.
April 4, 1974	*The Story of Jacob and Joseph,* produced by Mildred Freed Alberg, aired.
April 9 and 11, 1976	*The Story of David* miniseries aired.
May 31, 1977	Somer Alberg, husband, passed away in Pound Ridge, New York.
October 1980	Documentary *The Royal Archives of Ebla* aired on PBS. First documentary produced by Mildred Freed Alberg.
1984	Retired from television and film producing.

NOTES

1. "Mildred Freed Alberg," NBC News Release (20 September 1960), p. 1.
2. Interview with Mildred Freed Alberg (9 December 1991). All other information and quotes from Mrs. Alberg in this chapter were taken from this interview.

3. Ibid.
4. Ibid.
5. "Mildred Freed Alberg," p. 1.
6. Alberg interview.
7. Ibid.
8. Ibid.
9. Ibid.
10. Ibid.
11. Ibid.
12. Ibid.
13. Ibid.
14. Ibid.
15. Ibid.
16. Ibid.
17. Ibid.
18. Ibid.
19. Ibid.
20. "Mildred Freed Alberg," p. 1.
21. Mildred Freed Alberg, "Our Fight Against TV Taboos," *Saturday Evening Post* (21 March 1959), p. 58.
22. "Mildred Freed Alberg," p. 2.
23. Ibid.
24. J. P. Shanley, "Distaff TV Executive: Mrs. Mildred Alberg Talks of 'Hans Brinker' and a Studio Canal," New York Times (9 February 1958), p. 13.
25. Alberg interview.
26. Frank Sturcken, *Live Television* (Jefferson, NC: McFarland, 1990), p. 59.
27. "Hallmark Hall of Fame: The First 40 Years," UCLA Film and Television Archive (1991), p. 32.
28. Alberg interview.
29. Ibid.
30. Alberg, "Our Fight Against TV Taboos," p. 59.
31. Alberg interview.
32. "Mildred Freed Alberg," p. 1.
33. Sturcken, p. 59.
34. Alberg interview.
35. "Hallmark Hall of Fame: The First 40 Years," p. 32.
36. Alberg, "Our Fight Against TV Taboos," p. 59.
37. Alberg interview.
38. "Hallmark Hall of Fame: The First 40 Years," p. 32.
39. Alberg, "Our Fight Against TV Taboos," p. 59.
40. Ibid.
41. Alberg interview.
42. Ibid.
43. Shanley, p. 13.
44. Ibid.
45. Alberg interview.
46. "Hallmark Hall of Fame: The First 40 Years," p. 32.
47. Alberg interview.
48. Alberg, "Our Fight Against TV Taboos," p. 29.
49. Ibid., p. 50.
50. Ibid.
51. Ibid., p. 51.
52. Alberg interview.
53. Ibid.

54. Ibid.

55. Ibid.

56. Ibid.

57. Ibid.

58. "She Takes the Good and Makes It Popular, Rather Than Taking the Popular and Making It Good," NBC Feature (22 October 1959), p. 2.

59. "Mildred Freed Alberg," p. 2.

60. "Mildred Freed Alberg," Screen Gems Biography (1973), p. 2.

61. Alberg interview.

62. Ibid.

63. Ibid.

64. Louis Pelegrine, *Hot Millions*, *Film and Television Daily* (5 September 1968).

65. Alberg interview.

66. Ibid.

67. Alvin H. Marill, *Movies Made for Television* (New York: Baskin, 1987), p. 401.

68. Ibid.

69. "Somer Alberg," *Variety* (15 June 1977).

70. Alberg interview.

71. Ibid.

72. Ibid.

73. "She Takes the Good and Makes It Popular, Rather Than Taking the Popular and Making It Good," p. 1.

74. Alberg interview.

Lucille Ball

She is one of only a few individuals in history to be on a solely first name basis with the world: Marilyn, Elvis, Lucy. She was a national treasure. She remains a world icon, recognizable from Tallahassee to Timbuktu, from Paducah to Peru. No other performer in any medium or of either sex has inspired the devotion and generated the international love and appreciation that she has. Said one admirer: "Lucy ... [is] a common denominator for nations, continents, and hemispheres, doing in entertainment what others have not accomplished in professional diplomacy."[1]

By all standards Lucille Ball is the Queen of Television, the medium's one universally known figure, its classiest clown, its single greatest claim to fame. And while this Lucy (Ricardo, Carmichael, Carter, whatever) is known to three generations, to hundreds of millions, few know the other Lucy. That other Lucy has the distinction of cofounding one of the most important production facilities in history, of being the first woman president of a major Hollywood studio, and of being one of the finest, sharpest show business minds in history. Of course, she also has the distinction of being a great comedian.

Lucille Desiree Ball was born on August 6, 1911, in Celoron, New York, just outside Jamestown.[2] Ball said many years later of her humble origins, "I am from a suburb of Jamestown, New York. Not Jamestown itself, but a suburb, yet. *Yet*."[3] Her mother was Desiree Ball, a former concert pianist. Her father was Henry D. Ball, an electrician and telephone lineman. He died of typhoid fever when Ball was four. Ball's mother remarried, and Lucy and her brother Fred were housed for a time with her step-grandparents.[4] Ball remembered her early years this way:

> Most comedy success stems from long-standing inferiority complexes, and I had mine.... My step-grandparents had stern, old-country ideas.... It gave me a feeling of frustration and of reaching-out-and-trying-to-please. I found the quickest and easiest way to do that was to make people laugh.[5]

Ball was a wild, energetic child, so much so that once, to keep her from running off, her step-grandparents put her in a dog collar wired to an overhead cable.[6] To deal with her smalltown boredom, Ball made up an imaginary friend named Sassafrassa. Sassafrassa assured Ball she would one day

21

LUCILLE BALL

grow up and be a famous star. Ball believed her.[7] From her earliest memory, Lucy wanted to be in show business:

> I was always stage-struck. I would recite speeches at the drop of ... anything. I'd sing, I'd dance, I'd perform all the time. But I was always interested in being *of* the business. *Of the business.*[8]

Ball was so in love with show business that she made a yearly attempt to run away to New York (and to the big time).[9] Someone usually found her at the city limits and brought her back home. Finally, after Ball's continual begging, her mother agreed to send her to New York to study at the John Murray Anderson-Robert Milton Dramatic School. Lucille Ball was fifteen.[10]

It was 1926 when Ball arrived for her first bite of the Big Apple. Classes at John Murray were tough. One star pupil took most of the limelight, leaving Ball feeling "terrified and useless," alone in the shadows.[11] That star pupil was a lightning quick, hard-as-nails dynamo named Bette Davis.[12] Ball's one semester of enrollment was enough for the school to decide she had no talent as an actress. They cabled her mother and said she was wasting her money and Ball was wasting her time.[13]

Kicked out of drama school, Ball would still not give up. She started to work on and off as a model to support herself. But money was tight. To make ends meet, she had to steal tips from tables in coffee shops,[14] and to eat, she had to make soup from ketchup and hot water.[15] Often, she hung around lunch counters—where two donuts were sold for a nickel—looking for a "one donut man"; when he left, Lucy would slide onto his stool to eat the leftovers. On dates, she chose restaurants where baskets of rolls would be served; she stuffed extras into her handbag when no one was looking.[16]

Between modeling assignments and a few chorus line jobs, Ball had a succession of jobs that read like *I Love Lucy* scripts: her brief career as a soda jerk came to an end when she forgot to put a banana in a banana split.[17]

Figuring she was having no luck as Lucille Ball, Ball decided to change her name. For a short time in the early 1930s, she became Diane Belmont. *Diane* she chose after the legendary Goddess of the Hunt, and *Belmont* she borrowed from the famous New York racing track. Said Ball, "It was such a glamorous name. A real model's name."[18] Surprisingly, the switch brought her good fortune. Her modeling work picked up, and Ball had her biggest success to date when dress designer Hattie Carnegie chose her to be one of the showroom models in the designer's downtown salon.[19]

Ball, at that time, bore a resemblance to film actresses Joan and Constance Bennett, two Carnegie clients, and to continue the illusion Ball dyed her brown hair platinum blonde.[20]

Lucille Ball's successful modeling career came to an abrupt halt one day on the runway when she collapsed to the floor unable to move. Carnegie rushed her to the hospital where she was diagnosed with severe rheumatoid arthritis.[21] Many specialists believed Ball would never walk again. For the next three years, after returning to her mother's house in upstate New York, Ball remained largely bedridden, visiting doctors, enduring experimental procedures and attempting to walk again. Finally, and quite unbelievably, an experimental treatment of injections from pregnant horses proved successful. Ball was back on her feet.[22]

As soon as she was strong enough, she headed back to New York. Carnegie gave Ball her old job back, and in 1933 she also got the biggest break of her young career: she was chosen to be Chesterfield Cigarette's newest "Chesterfield Girl." The Chesterfield company was huge, and its yearly ad campaigns featuring different models were exceptionally successful. By 1934 Ball's face was peering up from dozens of magazine and newspaper ads and looking down from roadside billboards all over the country.[23]

Ball's biggest break, though, came a little later and quite by chance. "I seldom use the word luck, but in 1933 when I became a Goldwyn Girl it was pure luck," she said.[24] During an oppressive heat wave in New York City a woman came up to her on the street and asked, "How'd you like to go to California?" Ball's response: "I'd go anywhere to get out of this heat."[25] Soon, she was taking the place of a fellow model who could not make the trip west to become a "poster girl" in the Goldwyn Studio's Eddie Cantor comedy *Roman Scandals*. Her salary: $50 a week.[26]

Ball remembered her early days in Hollywood this way:

> I was a Goldwyn Girl, but was the least attractive. So I'd do whatever had to be done—mud pies in the face, running, jumping, screaming things. It was ... part of getting started.[27]

In her first meeting with Goldwyn, Ball was forced to line up with the fellow "girls" in bathing suits to be sized up by the new boss. To set herself apart from the other women, Ball stuffed the upper part of swimsuit with toilet paper, gloves and socks. Not only did she stuff it, she over stuffed it to near comical proportions. Ball remembers, "Some of the toilet paper was still trailing out of the top when Mr. Goldwyn came by. If nothing else, they certainly noticed me."[28]

Though Ball was brought out to Hollywood especially for *Roman Scandals*, her first screen part was not in that film since preproduction on the picture was continuously delayed. Instead, the studio put Lucy to work in several small roles in films like *Broadway Thru a Keyhole* and *Blood Money*.[29] Ball received her first screen credit in RKO's *Carnival* in 1935.[30]

After a few more thankless walk-on parts, and a few parts where she was little more than an extra, Ball's salary was raised to $150 a week. After eighteen months, Ball left Goldwyn and jumped over to Columbia Pictures to become part of its resident stock company.[31] She took a cut in pay (down to $75 a week) but considered her chances of improvement good enough that she cabled her family (mother, grandfather, cousin Cleo) to come live with her in the booming state of California. Unfortunately, California did not boom for long. The day after sending the telegram, Ball was part of a group of Columbia contract players let go by the studio.[32] Ball remembered, "I stood there crying [after being fired] thinking that was the end of my career."[33]

Ball's unemployment was short-lived. A friend at the time informed her that Columbia's rival, RKO Studios, located just down the street, was having an actor's "cattle call" that very day. Ball promptly got herself hired at $50 a week.[34] In an atypical life for an actor, these two to three hours of joblessness were the only period of unemployment Lucille Ball ever encountered during her long career.[35] Ball would remain with RKO Studios for the next seven years, from 1935 until 1942. At RKO, Ball found some work in "A" pictures. She was in three Astaire-Rogers musicals *Top Hat*, *Roberta*, and *Follow the Fleet*. Mostly though, she worked along in grade "B" efforts.[36]

In dozens of "B" movies ("B plus actually, I was queen of the B-pluses," she said later) Ball played the hero's girlfriend and a few times comedy foil to some legendary male comics: Buster Keaton, Laurel and Hardy, and the Three Stooges.[37] By and large though, Ball was passed over for comedy roles: "Comedy wasn't my strong suit. I was known for more dramatic or glamorous parts."[38] And for Lucille Ball, there were a lot of parts. She was one of Hollywood's hardest driven work horses during the 1930s and 1940s. From 1933 to 1937, she starred or costarred in more than twenty-five different motion pictures, eleven in 1934 alone.[39]

Gradually, Ball began to climb the movie-star ladder. In 1937 Ball had her best role yet costarring with such heavy-hitters as Ginger Rogers and Katherine Hepburn in RKO's *Stage Door*, the story of a group of struggling young actresses all living together in a melting pot of a boarding house.[40]

But after this brief flirtation with the frontlines, Ball was back to her backlot programmers. At least now, however, she was headlining them. She had substantial success starring in two screwball comedies, *The Affairs of Annabel* and its sequel, *Annabel Takes a Tour* both in 1938.[41] In 1940 she popped up in director Dorothy Arzner's *Dance, Girl, Dance* playing a burlesque queen.[42]

For audiences familiar only with Ball's television work—and therefore her small-screen persona—Ball's earlier film work can be rather jarring to watch. Gone is the scatterbrained, wide-eyed innocent; in her place is a brassy, seen-it-all "dame." During her many years as a film actress, Ball specialized in playing "been-around" showgirls—tough-talking, no-nonsense gals usually from the wrong side of the tracks. Though the roles were typically comic in nature, the "Lucy humor" was very different; often in her roles she dropped quick, acidly funny asides in a style her friend Eve Arden would later make famous.

It was during the making of *Dance, Girl, Dance* that Ball first laid eyes on a young (age 23) Cuban musician who had previously scored stage successes in New York and had introduced the latest dance craze to America, the conga line. He was now making his first film in Hollywood.[43] Said Ball many years later, "It was, for me at least, love at first sight."[44] His name was Desi Arnaz.

To her delight, Ball's next film, *Too Many Girls*, starred the young Latin with whom she had hit it off. Ten days after the film's New York premiere, Lucy and Desi were married on November 30, 1940. They soon set up house on a ranch outside of Los Angeles, christening their new home Desilu—a hybrid of their two names.[45]

Though fan magazines and studio press releases painted the Arnaz marriage as a fairy tale, things were seldom easy. Arnaz's career as a bandleader took him touring all over the United States, and Ball's acting career kept her firmly in California. To keep in touch, the couple amassed more than $29,000 in phone bills during their first three years together.[46] The physical distance began to take a toll on their relationship. Also contributing to Ball's growing disenchantment was Arnaz's unwavering roving eye.[47]

To keep her mind off her struggling marriage, Ball kept working. Writer James Agee once described Lucille Ball as an actress who "tackles a role like it was sirloin and she didn't care who was looking."[48] At no time was this comparison more noticeable than in 1942, when, after a considerable amount of campaigning on her part, Ball was awarded a costarring role opposite Henry Fonda in Damon Runyon's *The Big Street*.[49] In the film Ball plays "Her Highness," a pompous, selfish showgirl who has been crippled by an accident and who dominates and takes advantage of the kindness of a young man played by Fonda. At no time before or since was Ball less like her later Lucy characters and more the dramatic actress: she stripped the character of any playful or soft qualities and let no sentiment seep in. Her role was recognized at the time as the best of her career and critics heaped on the praise: "superb," "the girl can really act."[50]

RKO, though, was not so easily impressed; it continued to assign her to mediocre films. Ball balked at some of the roles and was put on suspension by the studio. A favor by an old friend, however, got her quickly hired away by MGM, the classiest studio in town.[51] Besides the change in employer, Ball also adopted another major change in her life: she became a redhead. Ball started out with her hair color mousy brown, then went platinum blonde for her late modeling jobs and early film roles, and then found her greatest fortune in a bottle of Egyptian henna rinse. An MGM hairdresser took one look at her when she arrived at the studio and ordered a change: "The hair is blond but the soul, it is *fire*. We will dye the hair red," the stylist supposedly said.[52] Ball's new coloring earned her a place in many MGM color extravaganzas (*DuBarry Was a Lady* in 1943 and *The Zeigfeld Follies* in 1946); it also earned her a new nickname, Technicolor Tessie.[53]

In 1947, Lucille Ball began what was to become the second, and much more successful, phase of her career. Ball signed on to play the role of Liz Cooper, the wacky wife of a midwestern banker played by Richard Denning in the radio series *My Favorite Husband*. Liz Cooper, in many episodes, was simply an early Lucy Ricardo. The radio show (and her part in it) was an unqualified success.[54]

Soon, Ball's new persona as comic rather than glamour girl got Hollywood's attention. Her next few films (at various studios) were some of the best received of her career. She was a slapstick marvel in *The Fuller Brush Girl* (1950) and held her own opposite Bob Hope in *Sorrowful Jones* (1949) and *Fancy Pants* (1950).[55]

Despite her radio fame, her few good parts, her "B pluses," and her supporting of various stars, top-of-the-line roles had eluded Ball since her beginning in films. By 1948 Ball was still an actively employed, and employable, actress but she was also 37 years old and had been a Hollywood fixture for almost twenty years. First-rank stardom had passed her by. Ball knew she would be able to continue in dozens of "B" films and, perhaps, the occasional

"A," but the chance to pick and choose her parts, to acquire the fame and prestige of a Ginger Rogers or a Bette Davis, was now, in all probability, beyond reach.[56] She accepted her plight, saying she would be happy "just to be a part of show business."[57]

Ball was not able to soften the career hurt by taking solace in her marriage. Arnaz continued to tour the country with his orchestra, one-night stand after one-night stand. The distance between husband and wife was proving too much. The idea of staying in the same town together, and thereby saving their marriage, was one of the factors that led to the idea of starring in their own situation comedy on television. A second factor was CBS. CBS believed that Ball's radio success in *My Favorite Husband* would translate well to the new medium of TV. When the network approached the actress with the idea, Ball jumped at the chance. Yet there was one condition: Arnaz would have to have the role of her husband.

Bart Andrews, the world-renowned expert on *I Love Lucy*, recounts the early negotiations this way:

> The idea [for the show] was just to do a TV version of *My Favorite Husband*. Denning was this nice white-bread Midwestern actor. Desi was a Cuban bandleader who couldn't act, so you understand CBS's dilemma. But Lucy insisted it be Desi or no show.[58]

Lucille Ball said about the CBS opposition to Desi, "They thought he was just a bongo player."[59]

The couple went to great lengths to help sell the network on the idea of Arnaz as Ball's on-screen husband. Their first step would be a stage show to prove to CBS that America would buy a Hollywood redhead and a Cuban bandleader as a married couple. Ball and Arnaz toured the country with their show consisting half of Arnaz and his orchestra and half of comedy skits with Lucy impersonating a comical cello player, "the Professor," who, during his offbeat and off-key audition, takes a few moments to impersonate a seal.[60] The Ball-Arnaz on-stage collaboration proved a crowd pleaser.

In 1950 Lucy and Desi formed Desilu Productions to finance the making of a pilot to show to CBS.[61] The seal skit from their stage revue was incorporated into the un-aired, March 1950 pilot. In the program, there were no Fred and Ethel Mertz; there were not even any "Ricardos." Ball and Arnaz played characters named Lucy and Larry Lopez.[62]

The pilot—which did not air for more than twenty-five years—helped not only to get CBS's approval but also gained the show a sponsor, cigarette manufacturer Phillip Morris. From the beginning, CBS knew this show was going to be different, but the network was not always happy about it. After CBS picked up the pilot, some fine-tuning took place. Friends (and landlords) of the couple were added—their names, Fred and Ethel Mertz.[63] More revolutionary though was where the show would be produced: Hollywood,

California. CBS had expected the Arnazes to produce the show in New York, like all other TV programs at that time. But the Arnazes were happy in California. They owned their own ranch there and had no intention of moving to New York. Additionally, Arnaz hated the canned laughter used on many network comedy shows and the poor quality of kinescope recordings. Ball wanted to work in front of a live audience to get instant feedback. Both Ball and Arnaz wanted to have films of the program to show someday to their children.[64]

There was only one solution. The show would have to be performed live with a studio audience and with three film cameras all simultaneously recording the action. Nothing like this had ever been attempted before. Remembered Ball about the early days of the series:

> There was a lot to be scared about. We were innovators. I liked being an innovator, but people told us we were crazy, that we were committing career suicide. I didn't listen.... I liked creating a show from scratch.[65]

Ball's fear did not let up until the evening she had a dream about actress Carole Lombard, an old friend who died in 1942. In the dream, Carole said to Lucy, "Take a chance, honey. Give it a whirl."[66]

By giving the show "a whirl" and photographing the show on film, Ball and Arnaz had accidently stumbled onto television's greatest money-making byproduct: the rerun. After the original broadcasts of the *I Love Lucy* episodes, each could be run again and again, raking in millions of dollars for the show's two owners, Ball and Arnaz.

To photograph the show successfully required the genius of cinematographer Karl Freund (whom Ball had known back at MGM and whom she insisted be hired) and producer/showman Jess Oppenheimer. Together they formulated an expensive but flawless method of lighting, shooting, and editing. Finally, though, to get the show from planning board to screen would take more than those talented people (and some eighty others); it would also take a $5,000 loan taken out by the Arnazes.[67]

But before the camera (or the three of them) could roll on the show, the Arnazes had some personal business to take care of. Ball had suffered several miscarriages during the course of the marriage; just as the new TV project began to take form, Lucy found herself pregnant again. She continued to tour in the couple's stage show (wearing large, loose men's jackets to hide her pregnancy) and to plan the pilot while expecting. Lucie Arnaz ("Little Lucie" as she was usually called) was born on July 17, 1951.[68]

I Love Lucy premiered a few months later on Monday, October 15th.[69] From that day forward, America followed the adventures of the residents of Apartment 4-A at 623 East 68th Street in Manhattan, New York. The Ricardos and their landlords, the Mertzes, became part of America's extended family, part of American popular culture.

Ball compared her theatrical and television careers:

> I'd been in pictures for years and made more than forty or fifty, and most
> people hardly knew who I was. Then after three months on TV, everybody
> in the country knew us and felt so close to us.[70]

As with much of show business, however, all was not as it appeared.
Lucy and Desi's marriage had always been touch and go and the added pressure of working together all day led to numerous confrontations. Costars
William Frawley and Vivian Vance despised each other from the start and
would remain that way throughout the entire run of the series.[71] Even Ball
and Vance, the best of friends on the air, did not hit it off well. After several
years of acting together and sharing pain resulting from unfaithful husbands,
however, the two women found a deep and lasting bond. After Vance's death
in 1979, Ball often broke down in tears during interviews when remember-
ing her old friend and costar.[72]

I Love Lucy gained extraordinary national attention. By the end of the
show's first season it was ranked number one, beating out such longtime TV
successes as *Your Show of Shows* and Arthur Godfrey.[73] Soon, the show was
recognized as television's biggest hit ever.[74] It even received the respect of the
TV industry itself—as did its leading lady. When comic Red Skelton received
an Emmy Award for outstanding comedian of the year, he began his acceptance speech by saying: "I don't deserve this. It should go to Lucille Ball."[75]

Soon the show became a merchandising bonanza as well. Ball and Arnaz
were soon showing up in their own daily comic strip, in coloring books, in
recipe books, in sheet music, on cigarette lighters, as paper dolls, even on
cufflinks. One business even licensed *I Love Lucy* linoleum.[76]

I Love Lucy became a national phenomenon unlike anything before it. Stores
noted drops in sales on Monday evenings (some closed down completely). Movie
theaters reported a noticeable drop in attendance. Even the telephone company
noted a significant drop in calls during the half-hour the show ran.[77]

In trying to understand the popularity of *I Love Lucy* and its star Lucille
Ball, dozens of critics over the years have offered a wide variety of theories.
Mostly though, the theories fall flat by looking too small, too minutely for
some unnoticed detail. What made Lucille Ball special was not anything
small but something very large, something all-encompassing. The Lucy
Ricardo character (or the Lucy Carter or Lucy Carmichael characters for that
matter) consisted of a variety of simultaneous opposites. While Ball's character could not be considered extremely smart, she was never dumb; she was
highly inventive and, at times, down right ingenious. While Ball on screen
was never mean-spirited, she was never anyone's doormat, never a victim.
And while Ball never lost her child-like enthusiasm, she never came across
as the overgrown baby or the pitiful fool.

During *I Love Lucy*'s second season, the show's dominance continued. Its popularity reached a peak when actress Lucille Ball and TV character Lucy Ricardo each delivered baby boys on January 19, 1953. Lucille's was born, by cesarean section, in Cedars of Lebanon Hospital and Lucy's was born in practically every living room in America. The episode of the birth of "Little Ricky" on *I Love Lucy* drew an audience larger than any previous media event. More than forty-four million people watched that episode, roughly seventy-one percent of all people who owned a television.[78] The inaugural of President Eisenhower was televised the next day, but its ratings were a significant step down: only twenty million tuned in. Desi Arnaz said about the difference, "[Lucy's] as important as Ike. I wonder if we could run her for President in fifty-six?"[79]

The colossal success of *I Love Lucy* soon set the stage for the success of Desilu Studios. Desilu's revolutionary three-camera method caught on like wildfire, and it signaled the move of the television industry out of New York and to the West Coast where film facilities were located. With the money coming in from *I Love Lucy* and skilled TV craftsmen at their disposal, Desilu began to produce other hit TV series: Eve Arden's *Our Miss Brooks*, Ann Sothern's *Private Secretary*, and Danny Thomas's *Make Room for Daddy*.[80] Later, *The Untouchables*, starring Robert Stack, became another Desilu success story; it premiered in 1959.[81]

Additionally, Ball and Arnaz parlayed their TV fame into feature films. They costarred in two big-screen comedies: *The Long, Long Trailer* in 1954 and *Forever, Darling* in 1956.[82]

After six seasons of *I Love Lucy*, and two children to raise, Ball decided to cut back on her work load. From now on there would be only the occasional *Lucy-Desi Comedy Hour* specials. These programs began in November 1957. The *Comedy Hour*s ran until April of 1960.[83]

Though on-screen life in the Ricardo living room continued in its usual wacky fashion, things were completely different off screen. Ball said:

> Those last five years [of the show] were sheer, unadulterated hell. I'm afraid I didn't cope too well. We both knew it was over. But we had commitments to fill, so we stayed together.[84]

Or, at least they stayed together in public. In private, they had taken to separate bedrooms in their home. Often they chose only to speak through third parties.[85]

Though the public thought they were still the "happy-go-Lucy" Ricardos, coworkers and intimates knew that divorce was unavoidable. Arnaz's workload was overwhelming, and he had begun to drink too much as well. Actress Ann Sothern, a longtime friend of Ball's, remembers: "When Desi was drinking a lot, she'd call me in the middle of the night and say, 'Get the priest. Do something, Ann, do *something*.'"[86]

Actress and longtime friend Shelley Winters, a woman well known for speaking her mind, believed the Ball-Arnaz marriage was doomed from the start, "He just couldn't take it that she was so much more important than he was. Nobody ever called her Mrs. Arnaz."[87]

While the Ball-Arnaz marriage continued to disintegrate, the Ball-Arnaz business partnership continued to expand. In September 1957, to keep up with the expanding needs of their TV empire, Ball and Arnaz bought the facilities of RKO Studios—lock, stock, and barrel. By acquiring RKO Studios, Desilu enlarged its holdings to thirty-five sound stages and a forty-acre backlot. The buyout also gave Ball a bit of personal revenge: she now owned the company that had once fired her when she was a young, struggling actress. The facilities not being taken up by Desilu productions were quickly leased out to other film and TV producers.[88] When the company went public on the New York Stock exchange in 1959, it took in more than $26 million for its owners.[89]

With Arnaz now Hollywood's newest tycoon and Ball busy acting and raising two children, little time was left for their marriage. Knowing that they were entering the last season of *Lucy*, Ball and Arnaz decided to stick it out until the last show was shot.

The divorce became official in 1960, almost immediately after the last Lucy/Ricky Ricardo show was aired. The divorce was uncontested; Ball received half of Desilu Productions, the Beverly Hills house, two station wagons, and a burial plot in Forest Lawn.[90]

Ball immediately ran to the New York stage to take the starring role in the musical *Wildcat* where she gave 171 performances and introduced the song "Hey, Look Me Over." She kept busy working in motion pictures as well. She had success working with Bob Hope in the feature film *The Facts of Life* in 1960.[91]

While appearing in *Wildcat*, Ball was introduced to stand-up comic Gary Morton. She liked his easygoing style and the fact that he was not intimidated by her; Morton said, "*I Love Lucy* was just something I'd heard about. When it was on the air I was always on stage somewhere, working."[92] They were married on November 19, 1961, by the Reverend Doctor Norman Vincent Peale, whose doctrine of positive thinking Ball had been following for many years.[93] Their marriage would endure for more than twenty-five years, longer than the Lucy-Desi match.

Lucille Ball returned to weekly television with a bang in her hit solo comedy, *The Lucy Show* costarring friend Vivian Vance in 1962. On better terms now that they had divorced, Desi Arnaz was the show's producer.[94] That same year saw Ball's entrance into the role of studio boss. Desi Arnaz, overstressed and ailing, relinquished the presidency of Desilu and sold his stock in the company to his ex-wife. She paid him just better than market value for his shares and immediately took control of what was at the time the largest film and television complex in the world, employing more than 5,000 people.[95] Ball was, by every estimation, the wealthiest, most powerful woman who had ever worked in show business.

But Ball's role as Madame President was conditional on her part. She had only one goal from the day she took over: get the business back on its feet and sell it at a good price.[96] It would not be an easy task. During the last years and months of Desi Arnaz's leadership, Desilu had fallen on hard times, a result of Arnaz's years of overwork and too much alcohol. Studio production was down, contracts had lapsed and expired, fresh ideas for programs had come to a near halt.[97] Lucille Ball has said, "Desi's nature is destructive. When he builds something, the bigger he builds it, the more he wants to break it down. That is the scenario of his life."[98]

As a way of achieving her business goals, Ball wasted no time or expense in surrounding herself with the top names in the business. Oscar Katz, an old friend of Ball's and a former CBS executive, was brought in as her chief advisor.[99] Ball's business style was twofold. On the set of her TV programs she yielded to no one, following only her own creative vision; the title of director on a Lucille Ball show by this time was basically just that, a title. In business affairs, however, Ball regularly deferred to her pool of company advisors. Still, the Lucille Ball presence was felt everywhere. People management was a Ball specialty. She said, "Anytime one of my people is unhappy, he or she is free to go; if a person is unhappy, you have nothing."[100] Business contracts were often passed over in favor of a handshake. With Ball and her new staff at the helm, Desilu soon meant (show) business again. Ball had sole final project approval, green-lighting which scripts were to go before the cameras. During her term in the president's office, Desilu Studios was responsible for creating such now classic TV fare as the original *Star Trek* and *Mission: Impossible*.[101]

The two roles of Madame President and company top-earner (via her own Lucy sitcoms) were sometimes difficult to mesh. Stockholder and board of directors meetings were usually scheduled only when Ball's filming schedule would allow it. Sometimes Ball would have to run straight from the set to the board room. "I remember one time sitting there with my front teeth blacked out," Lucy recalled.[102]

Ball as actress or as Lucy Ricardo bore no resemblance to Ball as businesswoman. She was tough and shrewd. Said a CBS employee, "She's not the childlike 'Lucy' character she plays. She's diamond-hard, extremely bright and cautious with people."[103] Said Tony Randall, a frequent costar:

> A lot of people found her tough to work with. She bossed everybody around and didn't spare anybody's feelings. But I didn't mind that because she knew what she was doing. If someone just says, "Do this!," it's awful when they're wrong. If they're right, it just saves a lot of time. And she was always right.[104]

In 1967, Ball had obtained the goal she set when she took over Desilu in 1962. The company was now solvent and a major player in the film production world. When Gulf + Western offered her $17 million for the Desilu facilities, Ball was willing to listen. She sold the company that year.[105] That same year, *The Lucy Show* ceased production.[106]

Gulf + Western's deal solidified Ball's place as Hollywood's richest woman. She was still taking in residuals from *I Love Lucy* when her sale of Desilu netted her roughly $10 million.[107] Soon, the addition of her next prime-time series, *Here's Lucy*, brought in between $20 and $40 million annually. Ball said, "Money has never mattered that much to me, and in fact, much of what I have made has gone back into the business. The real reward is being able to enjoy my work."[108]

After the sale of Desilu, life with Lucy took on a less hectic pace. She did, however, immediately form another company, Lucille Ball Productions. Ball was named president, Gary Morton vice-president.[109] The firm's early projects revolved around producing Ball's TV comedy *Here's Lucy*, which ran from 1968 until 1974. Later, Ball's company would expand into producing non-Lucy vehicles like a 1984 TV remake of *Sentimental Journey*, starring Jaclyn Smith, and the Tom Cruise theatrical film *All the Right Moves* one year earlier.[110] In 1981, the company began to develop properties for Home Box Office and other pay-cable channels. Ball said, "Like it or not, that's where the future is."[111]

As an actress Ball made sporadic television appearances throughout the 1970s and 1980s, usually in one-hour specials and in guest spots. In 1974 she had the starring role in the big budget, big-screen musical extravaganza *Mame*.[112]

In 1985 Lucille Ball received one of the highest honors of her career. Because of her overwhelming longevity and solid track record of success and her personal impact on television, she was chosen to be one of the first inductees—and the first woman—inducted into the Television Academy's Hall of Fame.[113] Also in 1985 Ball had one of the most serious acting roles of her career in the sensitive TV drama *Stone Pillow*. She played a homeless woman attempting to readjust to a normal life.[114]

In 1986—not happy resting on her laurels, playing backgammon, doing the occasional show, and drinking in standing ovations—Ball, at age 75, decided to return to regular network television. *Life with Lucy*, filmed at the old Goldwyn Studios where Ball had her very first job fifty years earlier, ran for only a handful of episodes on ABC. It was a largely misconceived venture for a now elderly Lucy character. The show drew scathing reviews and low ratings.[115] (Later, unaired episodes, however, show a Lucy funny and back to her classic form.)[116]

Ball put the blame for the show's failure on herself. She said:

> People see me one way—as Lucy [Ricardo]—and they shouldn't have to think about that character's getting old. People should think things stay the same, even though they don't.[117]

Many believe Ball never completely recovered from the letdown of this last, unsuccessful small-screen venture. Close friend Lillian Winograd remembers:

> The failure of her last TV show hurt her more than anything, but not for herself. She kept saying, "My God, these people are going to be out of work." One headline in an LA newspaper read THE QUEEN IS DEAD. That hurt her more than anyone can know.[118]

No one blamed her for long, however, and she was soon drinking in standing ovations and tributes all over again. Lucy was too well loved to be so easily forgotten or dismissed. When she died on April 26, 1989, of cardiac arrest, a nation mourned. [119]

In June of 1989 she was posthumously voted to receive the Television Academy of Arts & Sciences's Governors Award, their highest honor. She remains, to date, the only woman ever to receive this tribute.[120]

With years of distance and perspective, most writers agree that Ball's best moments as a performer came with the original *I Love Lucy* series. Most have been unkind to her later series work, some ignoring it completely. Ball's post–*Love Lucy* efforts were less finely tuned and based much more on exaggerated situations than the earlier Lucy/Desi programs. Yet, they fit perfectly alongside the other comedy products of that era. During the 1960s and early 1970s, Ball's shows were all part of that time's less-than-realistic, slightly obvious, over-the-top comedies. These shows included *Get Smart*, *Green Acres*, *I Dream of Jeannie* and *The Monkees*.

The Lucy character (and, at times, Ball herself) has also drawn criticism from women's groups and feminists. Women have objected to Ricky's domination of Lucy in *I Love Lucy*. Ricky was the one who controlled the house, who held the checkbook, who spanked her like a child when she got out of hand. Still, in many ways Lucy Ricardo was the personification of the pre-feminism feminist. She was the oppressed housewife yearning for greater economic power and her own career, held back by her husband, by dominant sex roles and social norms.[121]

Additionally, and almost poetically, Ball's different incarnations in the different Lucy shows have mirrored the progress of women during the latter part of the twentieth century. In *I Love Lucy*, she was a stay-at-home wife and mother. In her next show, she was a widow raising two kids and trying to make it on her own. Later, she was a working woman. Finally, in her last two series, she was the co-owner of her own business. Bart Andrews and Thomas Watson, in their book *Loving Lucy*, crystalize Ball's everywoman appeal:

> [She] created her own, unique brand of chaos in New York, Los Angeles, Europe, Florida, Cuba, Connecticut and points in between.... She was a wife, a neighbor, the mother of one, a widow, the mother of two, the mother of none, a secretary, a sister-in-law....

She dearly loved her husband and became overly jealous when another female came near. She waited up when her daughter went out on dates and went to work to buy her boy a bike. She bawled like a baby when her daughter announced she was leaving home.

She cared for her friends and neighbors and wept openly when it was time to move away. She lived in a bustling metropolis but fought to keep a small town on the map.

She was one part henna, one part illogic, three parts beauty.

She was love. She was "Lucy."[122]

That love and that everywoman appeal made Lucille Ball one of the world's best-liked and best-known citizens, a timeless icon. A few years back, *TV Guide* made a startling estimate. By totaling Lucille Ball's hours on television, as viewed all over the globe, they came to the conclusion that the face of Lucille Ball had been seen by more people, more often than any other individual in history[123]—more than George Washington, Abraham Lincoln, Mahatma Ghandi, Queen Elizabeth II, or anyone else. All in all, not a bad achievement for a girl from Celoron, New York. And while it seems highly unlikely that Lucille Ball ever set out to obtain such a goal, at the same time, this record could not be considered simply a happy accident. Any individual's image could have—and could be—broadcast enough times over the televised airwaves to become known worldwide. But only Lucille Ball's was. Only her presence was demanded enough by the three generations of audiences necessary to set such a record. Ball's ability to hold such an honor, such a place in history, lies not in the mass communications capabilities of television but in the mass appeal of the artistry of Lucille Ball. For her, television was only a tool, a means to an end—like a musician using an instrument, or a writer using a pen, or a painter, her brush.

Lucille Ball

August 6, 1911	Born in Celoron, New York.
Autumn 1926	Arrived in New York City to study acting.
1929	Returned to New York, after illness, to resume career.
Spring 1933	Chosen as Chesterfield Cigarette Girl model.
July 1933	Signed to become "Goldwyn Girl" chorus girl; moved to California.
Autumn 1933	Had first film role, a bit in *Broadway Thru a Keyhole*.
February 1935	Received first on screen credit for role in *Carnival*.
May 1940	Began work on film *Dance, Girl, Dance*; had chance meeting with Desi Arnaz.
November 30, 1940	Married Desi Arnaz.
August 6, 1942	Signed contract with MGM studios; changed hair color to red.

1947	Signed to play role of Liz Cooper in *My Favorite Husband* on radio.
July 5, 1948	First broadcast of *My Favorite Husband.*
June 2, 1950	First performance of Lucy/Desi stage show.
December 1950	Formed Desilu Productions with husband Desi Arnaz.
March 2, 1950	Filmed pilot for *I Love Lucy.*
July 17, 1951	Gave birth to first child, a daughter, Lucie Arnaz.
October 15, 1951	First episode of *I Love Lucy* aired.
January 19, 1953	Lucille Ball and TV character Lucy Ricardo both have baby boys. Lucille Ball's named Desi Arnaz, Jr. Evening's broadcast of *I Love Lucy* one of the highest rated in television history.
September 1957	Desilu Studios purchased facilities of RKO studios.
April 1, 1960	Final *Lucy-Desi Comedy Hour,* "Lucy Meets the Moustache," aired.
May 4, 1960	Received divorce from Desi Arnaz.
December 16, 1960	Debuted in *Wildcat* on Broadway.
November 19, 1961	Married Gary Morton.
October 1, 1962	*The Lucy Show* premiered. Ball starred as widow with two children living in New England.
November 1962	Bought out Desi Arnaz's shares in Desilu Productions; assumed presidency of studio. First woman in history to obtain such a position.
September 1965	First episode of continuing *Lucy Show* with new format aired: Ball's character moved to San Francisco.
July 1967	Finalized sale of Desilu Productions to Gulf + Western; formed Lucille Ball Productions.
September 16, 1968	Last episode of *The Lucy Show* aired.
September 23, 1968	First episode of rechristened *Lucy Show, Here's Lucy* aired. Ball costars with her two real-life children, Lucie Arnaz and Desi Arnaz, Jr.
March 1974	Film version of *Mame* starring Ball released. Ball's final motion picture.
1984	Inducted into Academy of Television Arts & Science's Television Hall of Fame. First woman inducted.
December 1985	*Stone Pillow* aired. Ball's first full dramatic role on television.
September 20, 1986	*Life with Lucy* premiered. Ball's final series.
November 15, 1986	Final episode of *Life with Lucy* aired.
March 1989	Made final television appearance, with Bob Hope, on Academy Awards telecast.
April 26, 1989	Passed away at Cedars-Sinai Medical Center in Los Angeles.

June 1989   Posthumously awarded Governors Award by the Academy of Television Arts & Sciences.

NOTES

1. Howard Rosenberg, "She Set the Standard for Situation Comedy," *Los Angeles Times* (27 April 1989), sec. 6, p. 1.
2. *Current Biography* (1978), p. 32.
3. Lynn Hirschberg, "I Love Lucy," *Rolling Stone* (23 June 1983), p. 28.
4. Linda Martin and Kerry Segrave, *Women in Comedy* (Secaucus, NJ: Citadel, 1986), p. 263.
5. Ibid.
6. Brad Darrach, "All the World Loved This Clown, Lucille Ball," *People* (8 May 1989), p. 50.
7. Ibid.
8. Hirschberg, p. 28.
9. *Current Biography* (1978), p. 34.
10. William A. Henry, "A Zany Redheaded Everywoman," *Time* (8 May 1989), p. 101.
11. *Current Biography* (1978), p. 32.
12. Warren G. Harris, *Lucy & Desi* (New York: Simon & Schuster, 1991), p. 26.
13. *Current Biography* (1978), p. 32.
14. Jack Kroll, "Everybody Loved Lucy," *Newsweek* (8 May 1989), p. 75.
15. Tony Velocci, "The Real Lucille Ball," *Nation's Business* (October 1981), p. 76.
16. "Lucy: The Life Behind the Laughter," *People* (14 August 1989), p. 67.
17. Darrach, p. 50.
18. Hirschberg, p. 29.
19. *Current Biography* (1978), p. 32.
20. Bart Andrews and Thomas J. Watson, *Loving Lucy* (New York: St. Martin's Press, 1980), p. 29.
21. Darrach, p. 50.
22. Hirschberg, p. 28.
23. *Current Biography* (1952), p. 35.
24. Hirschberg, p. 29.
25. Ibid.
26. Velocci, p. 76.
27. Fred Robbins, "Who Me? Funny?," *Redbook* (December 1986), p. 121.
28. Hirschberg, p. 29.
29. Andrews and Watson, p. 43.
30. Lucille Gilbert, "World's Best-Loved Redhead Lucille Ball Is Dead at 77," *Variety* (27 April 1989), p. 10.
31. Andrews and Watson, p. 44.
32. *Current Biography* (1952), p. 35.
33. Velocci, p. 76.
34. *Current Biography* (1952), p. 35.
35. Andrews and Watson, p. 44.
36. Ibid., p. 47.
37. Hirschberg, p. 31.
38. Ibid.
39. Ephraim Katz, *The Film Encyclopedia* (New York: Perigee, 1979), p. 73.
40. Andrews and Watson, p. 55.
41. Gilbert, p. 10.
42. *Current Biography* (1952), p. 35.

43. Harris, p. 68.

44. Hirschberg, p. 31.

45. Harris, p. 94.

46. *Current Biography* (1952), p. 36.

47. Harris, p. 99.

48. "We Love Lucy," *US News & World Report* (8 May 1989), p. 14.

49. Gilbert, p. 10.

50. *Current Biography* (1952), p. 36.

51. Harris, p. 107.

52. Hirschberg, p. 31.

53. Ibid.

54. Ibid.

55. Gilbert, p. 10.

56. Harris, p. 139.

57. Velocci, p. 75.

58. Ray Richmond, "In the Beginning There Was the Tube, and On the Tube Was Lucy," *Los Angeles Herald Examiner* (2 March 1986), sec. E, p. 10.

59. Hirschberg, p. 31.

60. Harris, p. 152.

61. *Current Biography* (1952), p. 36.

62. Richmond, p. 10.

63. Ibid.

64. Velocci, p. 76.

65. Hirschberg, p. 32.

66. Ibid.

67. Velocci, p. 75.

68. "The Real Story of Desi and Lucy," *People* (18 February 1991), p. 87.

69. *Current Biography* (1978), p. 33.

70. "Lucy Has Grown Up a Lot," *US News & World Report* (22 September 1986), p. 80.

71. Richmond, sec. E, p. 11.

72. Gilbert, p. 19.

73. Richmond, p. 11.

74. Hirschberg, p. 32.

75. *Current Biography* (1952), p. 37.

76. Richmond, p. 10.

77. Ibid.

78. Martin and Segrave, p. 273.

79. Rick Mitz, *The Great TV Sitcom Book* (New York: Perigee, 1983), p. 46.

80. Harris, p. 199.

81. Tim Brooks and Earle Marsh, *The Complete Directory to Prime Time Network TV Shows* (New York: Ballantine, 1981), p. 791.

82. *Current Biography* (1978), p. 34.

83. Ibid., p. 253.

84. Richmond, p. 10.

85. "Lucy: The Life Behind the Laughter," *People* (14 August 1989), p. 69.

86. Ibid.

87. "The Real Story of Desi and Lucy," p. 92.

88. Gilbert, p. 11.

89. Kathleen Brady, "The CEO of Comedy," *Working Woman* (October 1986), p. 98.

90. Hirschberg, p. 92.

91. Andrews and Watson, p. 169.

92. Fred Robbins, "Life With Lucy Gets Better ... and Better," *Fifty Plus* (December 1986), p. 46.

93. Kroll, p. 75.

94. "The Death of Lucille Ball," *Broadcasting* (1 May 1989), p. 40.

95. Velocci, p. 75.

96. Brady, p. 92.

97. Velocci, p. 77.

98. Hirschberg, p. 92.

99. Harris, p. 275.

100. Velocci, p. 76.

101. Harris, p. 282.

102. Velocci, p. 77.

103. "The Immortals," *TV Guide* (Commemorative Edition) (July 1991), p. 20.

104. "Lucy: The Life Behind the Laughter," p. 70.

105. Hirschberg, p. 94.

106. Brooks and Marsh, p. 447.

107. Hirschberg, p. 96.

108. Velocci, p. 76.

109. Hirschberg, p. 95.

110. Ibid.

111. Velocci, p. 78.

112. Andrews and Watson, p. 219.

113. Harris, p. 325.

114. Ibid., p. 316.

115. Robbins, p. 45.

116. Unaired episodes of *Life with Lucy* can be viewed at the Museum of Broadcast Communications in Chicago, Illinois.

117. Hirschberg, p. 93.

118. "Lucy: The Life Behind the Laughter," p. 75.

119. Darrach, p. 50.

120. "ATAS Votes Lucille Ball 1989 Governors Award," ATAS Press Release (June 1989), p. 1.

121. Martin and Segrave, p. 271.

122. Andrews and Watson, pp. 11–12.

123. *Current Biography* (1978), p. 32.

Gertrude Berg

Though she looked nothing like the stereotypical show-business executive, Gertrude Berg—with her doe-like eyes and plumpish figure—was, in every sense of the term, a media mogul. A prolific writer/producer, a smart, savvy, and sometimes very tough businesswoman, she was the creator of a multimedia entertainment empire, the Goldberg dynasty. Gertrude Berg was one of television's first sitcom moms and the star and creator of one of the medium's earliest hits. Writer Gilbert Seldes, in his 1956 *Saturday Review* article, "The Great Gertrude," remembered just how early it was:

> The first time I saw Mrs. Gertrude Berg on television was so long ago that you had to lift the lid of your receiver, exposing a mirror, which then reflected the image on the tube. The program was a grab-bag of bits and pieces of radio programs, [used by TV networks] to demonstrate, I believe, to sponsors what their shows would look like in the new medium. None of the half-dozen people watching the show expected too much and none of us, I am sure, expected the sudden excitement when an excerpt from *The Rise of the Goldbergs* came on—and everyone of us knew that this was it! This was television and nothing else.[1]

But before Berg could make it big in TV, and on Broadway, she had already made it big in radio, where the Molly Goldberg character, her make-believe family and opening show cry of "Yoohoo, Mrs. Bloom!" were already a national institution. And so was she.

Gertrude Edelstein was born on October 3, 1899, the only child of Jacob and Diana Edelstein in the cosmopolitan district of Harlem.[2] She was raised surrounded by a large group of assorted family. "We didn't have Tennessee Williams problems," she once said, "It was more George Kaufman."[3] Especially close to her was her Grandfather Mordecai, who told her repeatedly as a little girl, "This is your America."[4] Gertrude's father divided his career between New York City theater owner and, in the summer, running hotels in the Catskill Mountains. She began her writing career as a teenager writing skits to amuse the hotel guests on rainy days and to keep the children of the guests busy. Some later scripts for *The Goldbergs* had their idea origins in these sketches.[5]

Gertrude attended Wadleigh High School but never graduated, and her only college education consisted of playwriting and acting courses at Columbia

GERTRUDE BERG

University. Around this time, 1918, she met and married Lewis Berg, then an engineering student at Brooklyn Polytechnic Institute. Two weeks after his graduation he found work as a sugar technologist on a plantation in Reserve, Louisiana. While there Mrs. Berg found little to do during the day but read.

She gave birth to two children while in Louisiana, Cherney in 1922, and Harriet in 1926.[6]

Life for the Bergs in the South, however, came to an end in 1929, after a fire destroyed the plantation, and the family returned to New York City where the Depression had left few opportunities for employment. To support her family, Berg, on the advice of a friend, decided to put her playwriting talents to work and sell scripts to local radio stations.[7] Though the

WMCA executive she auditioned for did not care for her first script ("It has about as much entertainment value as the telephone book," he told her), he liked her voice well enough to pay her five dollars to translate a gasoline commercial into Yiddish.[8] Thus, Gertrude Berg began her radio career.

Afterward, she occasionally earned an extra five dollars by reading recipes in Yiddish. Since she did not speak the language herself, she read them with proper inflections from phonetic translations.[9] Berg's first attempt at regular radio scriptwriting came when she created a show for CBS called *Effie and Laura*, about two working class salesgirls. Berg played one of the two roles. Considered too advanced in their views on love and marriage, *Effie and Laura* lasted only one airing.[10]

Undeterred, Berg drew on the inspiration of her Jewish grandmother and dialect comedian Milt Gross and drafted a gentle and warm family comedy. Titled *The Rise of the Goldbergs*, it centered around daily life for a Jewish family living in New York. Molly, the mother, was the center of the show, and she was joined by husband, Jake (originally played by James R. Waters), children Rosalie (Roslyn Siber) and Sammy (Alfred Ryder and later Everett Sloane), and live-in Uncle David (played by well-known Yiddish actor Mensha Skulnik).[11] The show had a basic format. Mrs. Goldberg, though not really a busybody, did spend a lot of her time interfering in the lives of her family and friends and a lot of time leaning out of her window shmoosing with her neighbors.[12]

Berg presented the audition script for the show to NBC in an entirely illegible handwriting, knowing she would be forced to read it aloud and therefore be able to add the tone and vocal inflection she thought it needed. The radio executive was so impressed he offered her a job of writing the show, and playing the lead.[13] *The Rise of the Goldbergs* premiered on the air on November 20, 1929.[14] The station paid Berg $75 a week to write and star in the show. Out of that sum she was also expected to pay the cast and crew. Program genres were less defined in those days, and Berg's daily serialized stories were considered soap opera (or, as they were also known, "washboard weepers"). Authors Madeline Edmondson and David Rounds believed that, despite humorous situations and character-led laughs, the show was a soap at heart:

> The series reflected a quintessential domesticity, presided over by a powerful and benevolent woman; its subject matter was human relations, and its surface was resolutely realistic.[15]

Though the story was continuous and it ran six times a week, it never dealt with such soap staples as amnesia, crime, or "other women."[16]

Whatever it was, it was popular. During its radio run, *The Goldbergs* picked up an underwriting sponsor, Pepsodent, and spawned several vaudeville skits and a comic strip. Once, when Berg had a sore throat and another actress filled in the role of Molly, the station received 30,000 letters of complaint. Fans were so loyal to the show that a group of nuns from Libertytown, Maryland, once sent Berg the following letter:

> One of the pleasures that the sisters have given up for Lent is listening to *The Goldbergs*. We would all be deeply grateful, however, if you could send us the scripts of the Goldberg serials we missed—after Lent is over.[17]

A later letter came from a refugee: "Coming from Germany, I could not believe to hear such a program, but today I know that this country really means freedom....[18]

Besides making Berg popular, the series also eventually made her very rich. During *The Goldbergs* radio heydays, Berg was receiving a weekly salary of $7,500, making her the highest paid woman in the medium. Soap opera writer Irna Phillips came in a very close second.[19] At this time, *The Goldbergs* ran on three different networks at once: NBC at 11:30 A.M., CBS in the afternoon, and WOR-Mutual early the next morning. Part of Berg's salary also came from writing the daily radio serial *Kate Hopkins*, the "exciting story of a visiting nurse."[20]

Such wealth allowed Berg and husband, Lewis, and their two children to split their time between a ten-room Park Avenue duplex in Manhattan and a twelve-room house in Bedford Hills, New York (next door to flamboyant actress Tallulah Bankhead).[21] Son Cherney later became a television producer, first for *The Goldbergs* and then for other programs. Daughter Harriet later married an army physician, whom Berg always introduced as "my son-in-law, the doctor."[22] Between the two of them, they eventually made Gertrude a six-time grandmother.[23]

After the demise of the first incarnation of *The Goldbergs* in 1934, to take the show to the stage on a national tour, Gertrude Berg returned to regular radio comedy in 1935, in a second, self-written, self-starring vehicle for the NBC network, *House of Glass*. Set in a Catskill Mountain resort hotel (drawn from memories of her childhood), the show featured Berg as Sophie, the cook. The show never caught on, mostly because as *Variety* wrote in 1966:

> She [Berg] is no longer the kindly, philosophical Jewish mother and housewife ... but a cold, matter-of-fact businesswoman whose major concern is the success of her summer resort.[24]

The program lasted less than a year.[25]

In the winter of 1936, Berg traveled to Hollywood to try her hand at screenwriting.[26] Only one of her features was ever produced. It was a small RKO comedy titled *Make a Wish* and starred Basil Rathbone and boy singer Bobby Breen.[27]

The Goldbergs, show and family, were revived for radio in early 1938 when

Berg was offered a contract worth one million dollars to come back to New York and pick up where she left off. *The Goldbergs* ran once again on both NBC and CBS until 1945. All told, *The Goldbergs* ran on radio (in one form or another) for seventeen years, more than 4,500 episodes, second only to *Amos 'n' Andy* in terms of longevity.[28]

To write so many scripts, Berg relied on working habits which were both rigid and legendary. She rose at 6:00 A.M. to write scripts (usually three weeks in advance) in a longhand cursive legible only to her and her daughter, who usually typed the finished product.[29] Gradually her scripts grew more detailed, but in the beginning they were often little more than outlines which Berg and cast improvised live on the air.[30] Once, when a key actress failed to show up for the show, Berg devised a new script in eight minutes.[31] At ten, her morning writing done, she would leave for the studio to rehearse the day's program.

By the end of her career, Berg had written more than 10,000 *Goldberg* scripts, more than fifteen million words.[32] Her scripts, though funny, never leaned towards silly. Like many other modern-day sitcoms, her stories often dealt with exaggerated circumstances—crash diets, problems with income tax. Still, the majority of their humor came straight out of character and, more often than not, out of Molly's mouth. Though Berg was American-born and spoke unaccented, perfect English, she gave Molly such a troubled tongue that her frequent misconstrued statements became known as "Mollyisms" or "Goldbergisms." Some of the best remembered: "Enter, whoever!," "If it's nobody, I'll call back later," and "I'm putting on my bathrobe and condescending the stairs."[33] Often, Molly also offered up some friendly, motherly advice (sometimes ad-libbed): "Better a crust of bread and enjoy it than a cake that gives you indigestion."[34]

Berg said, "Molly's humor comes ... out of life";[35] "... ours was never a show that made jokes about people. The humor came from the love and warmth of the characters. Molly was never a joke."[36]

Once the script was written, Berg took to the task of putting the show on the air. She called the shots there too. She was a stickler for detail and accuracy; Berg allowed no "faked" sound effects on radio. For the sound of eggs breaking into a frying pan, she broke two eggs into a frying pan. When the script required Molly to give daughter Rosalie a shampoo, Berg lathered up the hair of actress Roslyn Siber.[37] And when son Sammy Goldberg (and the actor playing him) was drafted into the Army, Berg arranged for the family goodbye scene to be played in the middle of Grand Central Station.[38] She was also picky about line readings. Once she made an actor repeat a line eighteen times in rehearsal before she got the effect she wanted.[39]

Berg did the same for casting. Local elevator operators, grocery clerks, and delivery boys were often recruited by Berg to play characters with similar jobs on her show. She also had a good eye (or ear) for talent. Such performers as

Eartha Kitt, Joseph Cotten, Van Heflin and Anne Bancroft all had early roles on radio's *Goldbergs*.[40]

In 1948 Gertrude Berg moved the Goldbergs to a new venue: the Broadway stage. On February 26 her play *Me and Molly* opened at the Belasco Theater and received good to mixed reviews. The family's radio popularity allowed for a strong Broadway run of 156 performances.[41]

It was while appearing in the play that Berg struck upon the idea of moving the family into the then new medium of television.[42] Television, though still very new, was nevertheless all the rage; Berg decided *The Goldbergs* should be part of the newest trend. After setting her mind to it, she went about trying to sell the show to the networks. It took a little work. NBC-TV turned her down, not believing the show would translate well to the small screen. On her second attempt, this time at CBS, Berg, after meeting with opposition from lower executives, arranged a meeting with William Paley, head of CBS. He set up an audition for her and the show in front of a group of CBS executives and possible sponsors. The audition went so well that immediately afterward, Berg and crew received a Monday night, half-hour timeslot and General Foods as its first sponsor.[43] (Sanka coffee took over sponsorship of the program in late 1949; Mrs. Goldberg's windowsill was thereafter graced with a flower growing out of an empty Sanka coffee can.)[44]

The Goldbergs began on television on January 10, 1949. The show's cast consisted of Gertrude Berg as Molly, Philip Loeb as Jake, Larry Robinson as Sammy, Arlene McQuade as Rosalie, and Eli Mintz as Uncle David.[45] From its earliest broadcast, the show was a hit. Over the course of its run, it attracted an average weekly TV audience of forty million. Usually, it ranked second in the ratings, between Milton Berle and Arthur Godfrey.[46] Berg was soon being showered with awards from various groups, including the U.S. Treasury Department, for helping the sales of savings bonds; the Girls Clubs of America, for "setting an outstanding example of motherhood"; and from the National Conference of Christians and Jews. In 1950 Berg received an Emmy Award for best actress in a continuing performance, the first ever winner of that award.[47]

The love of the Molly Goldberg character, and *The Goldbergs*, was easy for Berg to explain:

> The answer always comes out that it's because we are the same.... In school ... my teacher talked of the universality in literature and drama.... There are surface differences [but] to me the really interesting and beautiful thing is that these surface differences only serve to emphasize how much alike most people are underneath.[48]

The show was praised by critics and religious leaders at the time for its portrayal of Jewish culture and gentle home life and for being a tool for ethnic understanding; it was said of Berg that "she speaks a universal language with a Yiddish accent."[49]

On television, conflicts in the Goldberg household (played out at the imaginary address of 1038 East Tremont Avenue, Apt. 3-B, the Bronx) were relatively minor and easily fixed by mother Molly; off screen, though, things could not have been more different. In June 1950 *Red Channels*, a paperback book with lists of names of entertainment figures with alleged Communist ties, came out. One of the names on the lists was actor Philip Loeb, husband Jake to Berg's Molly.[50]

Boss and friend, Gertrude Berg, refused to fire him and came to his defense: "Philip Loeb has stated categorically that he is not a Communist. I believe him."[51] Nevertheless, she was later forced by the show's sponsor to fire him. Though he was no longer on the show, Berg kept Loeb on salary at a personal cost of $85,000 for two years. Later, unable to find work or support himself, Loeb committed suicide by overdose on September 1, 1955.[52] A new Jake, actor Harold Stone, was hired, but no sponsor could be found for the show and *The Goldbergs* was off the air from June 1951 to February 1952.[53]

Just prior to leaving the air, and before the dismissal of Loeb, Molly took on the movies. In a script penned by Berg and N. Richard Nash and titled, not surprisingly, *Molly*, Molly and family hit the big screen for Paramount studios. The film, which starred, besides Berg, the usual stable of actors, received good reviews and earned back its money at the box office as well. Turning a profit on the film was not that difficult since the film was shot using television rehearsal and production techniques rather than standard motion picture techniques.[54]

The Goldbergs came back to TV in 1952 and ran until October 1954.[55] In 1955 the show returned once more in an off-network, syndicated form. For thirty-five more episodes, Molly/Gertrude and her brood lived again, this time in suburban bliss. Berg said:

> I felt the series needed a change, so I moved the family out of the city to the mythical Haverville. And from live television to film. Of course, the money from repeat showings was no small consideration.[56]

In 1959 Berg shook off the Molly character (or at least her name) and took to the Broadway stage in a triumphantly received production of *A Majority of One*. In the play by Leonard Spigelgass, directed by Dore Schary, Berg worked opposite British actor Sir Cedric Hardwicke. Berg played a Jewish, Brooklyn-based widow whose son had died in World War II. She goes to Tokyo and falls in love with a Japanese diplomat (Hardwicke), whose daughter died at Hiroshima. Along the way she does more for international relations than her State Department son-in-law.[57] The role, tailor-made for the actress, garnered Berg nothing but rave reviews:

> The qualities [of her performance] that make it endearing are, one feels, extensions of herself—her simplicity of manner, her nobility of soul.[58]

She received the Antoinette Perry Award (the "Tony") for best actress in a play that year, beating out competition from Lynn Fontanne, Kim Stanley, Maureen Stapleton, and Claudette Colbert.[59] The play ran for two years.[60]

In 1961 Berg returned to weekly television in a series titled *Mrs. G. Goes to College* (also known as *The Gertrude Berg Show*). Though her character's last name was Green and a widow, she was still basically Molly Goldberg. Berg created the self-explanatory show herself which costarred her former stage companion Cedric Hardwicke, who played a visiting British professor.[61] Though the majority of the writing was handled by others, there was little doubt about who was boss. As the *Los Angeles Examiner* reported, "nothing leaves the set on film without her considered approval."[62] The show failed, however, to gain an audience. It lasted only a year.

In 1963 Berg returned to the Broadway stage in a play based on one of her ideas and written again by Leonard Spigelgass. *Dear Me, the Sky is Falling* was an offbeat comedy-drama about a domineering mother whose daughter enters psychoanalysis. Berg played the mother and it ran for six months.[63]

Also in 1963 Berg wrote her bestselling autobiography with her son Cherney. The book's title, *Molly & Me*, continued Gertrude's association with her world-famous and much-loved alter ego.

Berg worked until the end of her life in guest spots on television and in the dramatic anthologies of the period. She was preparing for a return to the Broadway stage in *The Play Girls*, a play based on one of her ideas, when she died of heart failure in New York City on September 14, 1966. She was sixty-six.[64]

The appeal of Gertrude Berg (and therefore Molly Goldberg) has been a subject of great speculation among fans and critics alike. William Leonard in a 1961 article for the *Chicago Tribune* saw her this way:

> She can be herself ... and in being herself she pleases individuals who find comfort in seeing in her old fashioned common sense and serenity that they sense too seldom in a world racked with insecurity and indecision.[65]

Gertrude Berg also had the luck of totally looking her most famous part: five feet four inches tall and admittedly overweight (she often said she started a diet every Monday and quit every Tuesday). All together, Gertrude Berg looked just like everyone thought Molly sounded. Besides looking the part, she lived it. Fans addressed her only as "Molly" and finally so did friends and coworkers. Frequently her "autographs" were inscribed "Molly Goldberg."[66] Basically, though, Berg was an actress, and Gilbert Seldes in 1956 considered her one of the nation's finest:

> She never plays to us and never to the camera.... [She has] the capacity to entrance, to absorb us until we reach the point of total belief.... She is a great

force in whatever she does and in this, the primary business of giving life to imagined people, she is incomparable.[67]

The early episodes of *The Goldbergs* have not been in wide syndication for more than twenty years. Gertrude Berg's accomplishments as a TV comic have been slightly overshadowed by the incredible work of some of her contemporaries like Lucille Ball, Audrey Meadows, and Imogene Coca. Nevertheless, Berg was there—acting, writing, and producing her own program. Her work as both main star and primary writer of a weekly television show has not been repeated by anyone in television, male or female. No one has had that much creative vision or that much personal drive. Berg's career is remarkable not because she happened to be a woman but because she was able to do it all.

In the early 1990s, after a strong influx of female creative talent behind the scenes and in the driver's seat occurred in the television industry (Diane English with *Murphy Brown*, Linda Bloodworth Thomason with *Designing Women*), many media watchers seemed to have forgotten all about Gertrude Berg as they heralded the "new trend" of assertive women in television. *Newsweek* and others explored the recent breed of "networking women" who were writing strong roles for women in television comedies and were, as producers and writers, taking on strong roles for themselves as well.[68] While this trend of powerful female characters was refreshing, it was not—in regard to TV history—a new idea: fans of Molly Goldberg and her alter ego, Gertrude Berg, knew the truth.

Gertrude Berg

October 3, 1899	Born in Harlem, New York.
December 1, 1918	Married Lewis Berg.
1922	Birth of son Cherney.
1926	Birth of daughter Harriet.
1929	Returned to New York City from Louisiana; began in radio with once aired show *Effie and Laura*.
November 20, 1929	First episode of *The Rise of the Goldbergs* aired on radio.
1934	End of first incarnation of *The Goldbergs*; toured in stage play based on program.
April 17, 1935	Berg radio show *House of Glass* premiered.
Winter 1936	Moved to Hollywood to work as studio script writer.
June 1937	Berg written film, *Make a Wish*, opened.
January 1938	*The Goldbergs* returned to radio on the CBS network.
June 1941	*The Goldbergs* began being broadcast by NBC in addition to its airing on CBS.
March 1945	Final incarnation of *The Goldbergs* on radio aired last broadcast.

February 26, 1948	Stage version of *The Goldbergs*, *Molly & Me*, premiered on Broadway.
January 10, 1949	First episode of *The Goldbergs* aired on television.
November 1950	Theatrical film version of *The Goldbergs*, *Molly*, premiered.
June 1951	In the wake of scandal, first incarnation of *The Goldbergs* ceased television production.
February 1952	Resurrected *Goldbergs* television series premiered.
October 19, 1954	Most recent television incarnation of *The Goldbergs* ended on network television.
Fall 1955	Episodes of the last incarnation of *The Goldbergs* began being aired in first-run syndication.
February 1959	Debuted in Broadway play *A Majority of One*.
October 4, 1961	First episode of *Mrs. G. Goes to College* (a.k.a. *The Gertrude Berg Show*) aired.
April 5, 1962	Last episode of *Mrs. G. Goes to College* aired.
1963	Published autobiography, *Molly & Me*.
September 14, 1966	Passed away, Doctor's Hospital in New York City.

NOTES

1. Gilbert Seldes, "The Great Gertrude," *Saturday Review* (2 June 1956), p. 26.
2. *Current Biography* (1960), p. 26.
3. "Milestones," *Time* (23 September 1966), p. 97.
4. Gertrude Berg, *Molly and Me* (New York: McGraw-Hill, 1961), p. 7.
5. James Poling, "I'm Molly Goldberg," *Redbook* (August 1950).
6. Barbara Sicherman and Carol Hurd Green, *Notable American Women: The Modern Period* (Cambridge: Belknap, 1980), p. 73.
7. Linda Martin and Kerry Segrave, *Women in Comedy* (Secaucus, NJ: Citadel, 1986), p. 159.
8. Poling.
9. Sicherman and Green, p.73.
10. Joe Franklin, *Joe Franklin's Encyclopedia of Comedians* (Secaucus, NJ: Citadel Press, 1979), p. 54.
11. Jim Harmon, *Great Radio Comedians* (New York: Doubleday, 1970), p. 60.
12. Episodes of "The Goldbergs" can be viewed at the Museum of Broadcast Communications, Chicago, Illinois.
13. Martin and Segrave, p. 160.
14. *Current Biography*, p. 26.
15. Madeline Edmondson and David Rounds, *The Soaps* (New York: Stein & Day, 1973), p. 37.
16. Harmon, p. 60.
17. William Leonard, "Molly Goldberg's 30 Wonderful Years," *Chicago Tribune* (29 October 1961).
18. Poling.
19. "The Inescapable Goldbergs," *Time* (23 June 1941), p. 55.
20. Ibid.
21. Morris Freedman, "The Real Molly Goldberg," *Commentary* (April 1956), p. 363.

22. "Gertrude Berg, Molly of 'The Goldbergs,' Dead," *New York Times* (15 September 1966), p. 43.

23. Robert J. Landry, "Gertrude Berg Dead at 66; 'Goldbergs,' Etc., Star Had 'Instinctive Showmanship,'" *Variety* (21 September 1966).

24. Ibid.

25. Ibid.

26. Sicherman and Green, p. 74.

27. "Make A Wish," *Variety* (25 August 1937), p. 17.

28. "Gertrude Berg, Molly of 'The Goldbergs,' Dead," p. 43.

29. *Current Biography*, p. 27.

30. Landry.

31. John Dunning, *Tune In Yesterday* (Englewood Cliffs, NJ: Prentice-Hall, 1976), p. 239.

32. Rick Mitz, *The Great TV Sitcom Book* (New York: Perigee, 1983), p. 14.

33. Poling.

34. Dunning, p. 239.

35. "The Unsinkable Molly Goldberg," *TV Guide* (25 November 1961), p. 24.

36. Hal Humphrey, "So What's New with Molly?," *Los Angeles Mirror* (9 September 1961), p. 9.

37. Dunning, p. 239.

38. Edmondson and Rounds, p. 38.

39. Dunning, p. 239.

40. *Current Biography*, p. 27.

41. "Gertrude Berg, Molly of 'The Goldbergs,' Dead," p. 43.

42. Berg, p. 233.

43. Ibid., p. 235.

44. Mitz, p. 16.

45. Tim Brooks and Earle Marsh, *The Complete Directory to Prime Time Network TV Shows* (New York: Ballantine, 1981), p. 290.

46. Poling.

47. *Current Biography*, p. 28.

48. Harmon, p. 60.

49. Poling.

50. Mitz, p. 16.

51. Ibid.

52. Ibid.

53. Ibid.

54. "Molly," *Look* (27 February 1951), p. 20.

55. Brooks and Marsh, p. 291.

56. Mitz, p. 16.

57. "Gertrude Berg Conquers Japan," *Life* (9 March 1959), p. 50.

58. *Current Biography*, p. 28.

59. Isabelle Stevenson, ed., *The Tony Awards* (New York: Crown, 1980), p. 57.

60. "Gertrude Berg, Molly of 'The Goldbergs,' Dead," p. 43.

61. Brooks and Marsh, p. 283.

62. Charles Denton, "Mrs. B. Comes to Hollywood," *Los Angeles Examiner* (1 October 1961), p. 5.

63. Gerald Bordman, *The Oxford Companion to American Theatre* (Oxford: Oxford University Press, 1984), p. 73.

64. "Gertrude Berg, Molly of 'The Goldbergs,' Dead," p. 43.

65. Leonard.

66. Freedman, p. 363

67. Seldes, p. 26.

68. Harry F. Waters and Janet Huck, "Networking Women," *Newsweek* (13 March 1989), p. 48.

Peggy Charren

Over the years a handful of individuals who have never produced a single television program, performed in front of a television camera, or founded a large television production facility have created powerful, long-lasting effects on the television industry. Since the late 1960s and early 1970s, consumer activist groups have made an impact by pressuring networks, stations, and regulatory agencies. Groups like the National Association for the Advancement of Colored People, the Gray Panthers, the National Gay Task Force, and others have all influenced industry decision-makers—mostly at the national network level—to present positive rather than stereotypical images.

Few citizens' groups, however, have equalled the success of a pro-children's television group founded in 1968 by a Boston-area housewife. Action for Children's Television (ACT)—a 10,000-member, nonprofit, grassroots organization devoted to better children's programming—forever changed the face, and the force, of television in children's lives. Most of these changes came about solely because of its female founder's determined zeal to make them happen. Even some of the ACT's biggest critics have been forced to recognize its founder's influence. Advertising executive and author Cy Schneider admitted, "She has accomplished more to change children's television than any other person."[1] The founder of ACT is known as the Ms. Fixit of kidvid, Peggy Charren.

Peggy Walzer was born on March 9, 1928, to Maxwell and Ruth Walzer of New York City.[2] Television being only in its most experimental stages at the time of her childhood, Peggy's main amusement, and first love, came in the form of books. An early favorite was *Little Women*. She dreamed of being Jo. After seeing the 1933 MGM movie version, she dreamed of being the screen's Jo, Katherine Hepburn.[3] Books by Dickens and Thackeray were also popular reading material.[4] As a child Charren suffered the usual childhood aliments—measles, mumps, even scarlet fever—and while recuperating in bed, she busied herself reading through *Compton's Pictured Encyclopedia*, beginning with volume "A."[5]

Peggy Charren has said of her childhood:

> The most important thing I got from my parents was a sense that you can go out there and fix how the world works. I don't remember a time I wasn't worried about the rights of others.... It got started young for me and it stuck.[6]

53

PEGGY CHARREN

That active reading and love of books took her to Connecticut College where she graduated with a bachelor's degree in English in 1949.[7] Afterward, she found her first job, oddly enough, working for a television station. For a brief period, beginning in 1949, Peggy was the head of the film department at WPIX-TV in New York City.[8] Before forming Action for Children's Television twenty years later, that job was the extent of her involvement with the television industry.

On June 17, 1951, Peggy Walzer became Peggy Charren when she married Stanley Charren. Then just beginning his career in engineering, Stanley Charren is now the chairman of Kenetech, the world's largest company in the field of wind energy.[9] The Charrens have two children, Deborah and Claudia. Also in 1951, after her brief career in television, Charren went to work for herself. She became a business owner, starting up a local gallery, graphics, and framing shop in Providence, Massachusetts. Called Art Prints, Inc., it existed until 1953.[10]

Peggy Charren would return to the world of sole proprietorship many years later in 1960 when she founded her second solo business enterprise, Quality Book Fairs. Quality Book Fairs organized children's books fairs in schools in the New England area. In the late 1960s, leaving private business behind, Charren closed Book Fairs and became a member of the Creative Arts Council of Newton, Massachusetts. She held that post from 1966 to 1968. While on the Council, Charren worked to incorporate theater and dance groups, artists, and poets into programs for city schools.[11]

In 1968 Peggy Charren's life would change forever. Motherhood got Charren started on activism, broadcasting, and Washington politicking. In 1968, unable to find adequate daycare for her daughters, Charren decided to become a full-time, stay-at-home parent. While at home viewing television with her children, Charren became incensed over the quality—or lack thereof—of televised children's fare. What she saw stunned her into action. She said of children's TV at the time, "All they had ... were wall-to-wall monster cartoons."[12] After comparing notes with a small group of other concerned mothers, Charren and the others began to meet for informal discussions in the sitting room of Charren's Newton, Massachusetts, home. They talked about what they could do about the sorry shape of children's television.[13] Those early members consisted of Charren, Evelyn Kaye Sarson, Lillian Ambrosino, and Judith Chalfen.[14] Charren said of the early days of her movement:

> Although concern about television and children was widespread there was no organized advocacy for change. I wasn't sure how to become a child advocate. I knew that I didn't want to use censorship tactics.... Censorship meant fewer choices. We needed more choice, not less. I knew that many of my friends felt the same way.[15]

What began as a local, short-term, evening circle of friends devoted to some changes soon became for Peggy Charren a passion, a mission, and a lifelong cause. She remembers:

> When I started ACT, my youngest daughter was four and I was thinking about careers—but I thought I'd first take one year to fix up children's television, and then go back to work.[16]

Twenty years later, Charren, by then a grandmother, would still be at the helm of ACT, fighting for more TV choices for children.

Action for Children's Television—a name Charren dreamed up one day while in the shower—was officially formed in early 1968.[17] Surprisingly, Charren was not the group's first president. Evelyn Sarson was appointed to that office; Charren took the title of chairman. There were no firm job descriptions for either role, however, and the two women split most of the leadership duties. Sarson held the title of president of ACT until 1972, the year

Charren took over.[18] Charren then became the group's driving force, mouth-piece, and cheerleader. Writer Robert B. Choate has said, "Under Peggy Charren's forceful leadership, the organization grew and developed as a national entity."[19] As President of ACT (and before) Charren waged a tough, unforgiving, take-no-prisoners campaign for better viewing choices for children.

Though ACT was formed, little happened immediately. The group sat quietly for a year without writing any letters or filing any court suits. Instead, they made plans, discussed aims and planned strategies.[20] Early concerns of the group dealt with TV violence, over-commercialization of children's television, and the lack of programming choices and programming alternatives for children. Attempts to rid the airwaves of "violence," however, brought with it too many legal restrictions and questionable definitions, bordering at times on censorship. Charren said, "ACT is very opposed to censorship as a way of dealing with issues of children in media. I think censorship is worse than all the junk."[21]

ACT's first opponent was the local production of TV's *Romper Room*. The show regularly engaged its host as commercial salesman, taking time during the program to promote different products, including a special line of *Romper Room* toys. In the spring of 1969, ACT sponsored a university study to monitor the *Romper Room* series for four weeks and catalog the acts of "host-selling."[22] On the completion of the study, ACT presented a legal petition, based on the study's findings, to the Federal Communications Commission. Before the FCC had time to take any action, however, WHDH, the *Romper Room* station, ceased its practice of host-selling in order to put an end to the onslaught of negative publicity it was receiving due to ACT's initiative.[23]

Despite this first victory, ACT was underfunded and understaffed; it could not change children's television by expending so much time and effort on each individual, local abuse. If it tried, ACT would find itself stuck on the treadmill that other activist groups had found themselves stuck on: just getting one abuse put out when another would suddenly flame up. Additionally, local television was only part of the problem. Dozens of hours of children's television were being aired nationally on the three major networks, usually in head-to-head competition on Saturday mornings.

To get their voices heard, ACT requested meetings with the programmers of each of the three major networks. CBS consented to a meeting but did it more for publicity reasons than for any real desire to change or alter its current children's programming; ABC and NBC simply refused to meet.[24]

Almost a deadend, ACT struck upon the idea of lobbying the FCC, the body which regulates the television industry. Said Charren, "We found that when the regulators make noise the industry takes action to keep the rules away."[25]

In the spring of 1970 Action for Children's Television became the first public interest group in history to ask for an audience with the Federal Communications Commission. By all accounts, the FCC said yes only because it was not sure how to say no.[26] Though the FCC was sympathetic to the group's concerns, the Commissioners chose not to adopt binding standards of conduct for television stations. Nevertheless, the attention caused by the ACT lawsuit and the vocal support by FCC Chairman Dean Burch created a public, pro-ACT outcry by citizens.[27]

In September 1971 the FCC created a permanent unit devoted to issues in children's television. By January 1973, after continuing activities by ACT—and fearful of government rulemaking—the National Association of Broadcasters created new standards for children's television. The guidelines prohibited host-selling—an issue ACT had been fighting since its *Romper Room* days—and trimmed the allowable time for commercials during children's television from sixteen minutes per hour to twelve.[28] A year later, in 1974, the FCC set down a highly similar group of (unenforceable) guidelines for broadcasters; these were titled the "Children's Television Policy Statement."[29]

Action for Children's Television has also been adamant in petitioning the Federal Trade Commission (FTC) to better regulate advertising directed at children. An early battle centered around children's chewable vitamins. Charren said:

> When we started out, one-third of the commercials [during children's programs] were for vitamin pills, even though the bottles said, "Keep out of reach of children" because an overdose could put them in a coma.[30]

In December 1971 ACT filed a complaint naming three major drug manufacturers. The three manufacturers of the vitamins pulled their ads before the FTC was able to make any rulings against them.[31] Four years later, however, vitamin advertising became an ACT issue once again when a drug manufacturing company introduced and began to advertise Spiderman vitamins. ACT refiled its petition and the FTC formally set down a consent order banning the commercials.[32]

In the early 1970s Charren and ACT took its cause beyond the halls of Washington, holding its first Symposium on Children and Television and sponsoring two studies on children's television effects and attitudes.[33] Over the years the ACT Symposiums frequently attracted hundreds of people from broadcasting, medical, and psychological fields.[34] In 1972 ACT began to present its annual Achievement in Children's Television Awards to programs and producers offering positive alternatives. Later, ACT established its own news magazine, *re: act*.[35]

For many years, ACT operated from "a second floor old frame house ... badly in need of a paint job."[36] Peggy Charren as president drew a yearly salary of $20,000 and supervised a staff of only three or, occasionally, four

employees.[37] Despite foundation endowments and donations from private citizens, taking on the major names in broadcasting was an uphill battle. "Eco-
nomically, it's a David and Goliath story," Charren has said.[38]

By the end of the 1980s Charren had logged more than 300 trips to
Washington, D.C.[39] On one visit to FCC headquarters, she shared an elevator with then FCC Commissioner Richard Wiley. He asked her, "What brings
you to Washington?"

Charren responded, "My lawsuit."

"And who are you suing?" he asked.

"You," she shot back.[40]

During most of the 1970s Charren and ACT continued to file suits
against the FCC and the FTC. Some of the more important cases dealt with
the proposed banning of candy and sugary cereal ads from children's television, the prohibition of endorsements and testimonials aimed at children,
and the possible banning of all advertisements to children during children's
programming.[41] ACT kept itself very busy. Kate Moody compiled a timeline
list of important dates from ACT's history for her book *Growing Up on Television*; the chronology ran for a full seven pages and even then only went up
to 1979.[42]

To further its causes, spread information, and augment expenses, ACT
continued to sponsor its annual symposiums and to publish pamphlets, book-
lets, and kits on a variety of subjects ranging from TV news and children to
incorporating the visual and performing arts into the lives of children.[43] ACT
has also provided teachers and parents with numerous devices to help children curb the TV habit—from time sheets for children to keep track of their
viewing to parental reminder tags that hang on TV sets and say "Too much
television can be harmful to your child."[44] Charren herself has coauthored
three books: *Changing Channels: Living (Sensibly) with Television* (1983), *Television, Children and the Constitutional Bicentennial,* and *The TV-Smart Book
for Kids* (both 1986).[45] Peggy Charren has also seen her ACT activities gain
her wide public acclaim. She serves on the boards of numerous charities and
children's organizations, has received numerous honorary degrees, and has
been asked to speak at several media group functions, including the British
Film Institute and the Gannett Center for Media Studies.[46]

Despite the possibility of spreading herself too thin, Charren has never
lost sight of her original purpose: making children's television better. As a
means to that end, Charren has developed a tough outer shell and a well-
oiled weapon to take on the "big boys" of broadcasting. "I have a very big
mouth," said Charren in 1988.[47] She has learned the ins and outs of Washington political circles and how to talk in her adversaries' sometimes foreign
tongue. She knows the bottom line of the television business is money, not
quality programming, and she has learned to go with the flow. "They respect
anyone who can play their games," Charren has said.[48]

Perhaps Peggy Charren's biggest battle took place in 1978, when, in response to ACT lobbying, the FTC held industry hearings on altering children's television. One of the major items on the Commission's agenda was the ACT-proposed ban on advertising candy and presweetened cereals. The FTC hearings were a qualified victory for Charren; she said at the time, "No ads has been my bottom line for ten years."[49] Charren has said regarding the subject of advertising to children: "We protect children in all kinds of ways in this country. We don't let them work in factories, sign contracts.... [C]hildren deserve special protection."[50]

Thirteen ACT members and lawyers were called on to testify during the FTC hearings. To counter any anti-ad testimony, advertisers and the national networks assembled a $2 million war chest in what was unofficially named "Operation: Stop Peggy."[51] Many members of Congress were also opposed to her group's tough stand. To stop Peggy many representatives attempted, without success, to withhold funds for the FTC hearings.[52] While the hearings shed new light on prominent ACT objectives and shook up the broadcast establishments more than just a little bit, little ground was gained in the fight for stricter children's TV guidelines.

Perhaps the greatest gain from the hearings was in the form of acquired public support for ACT and in renewed national interest in children's television issues. Still, broadcasters continued to view Charren as something of a necessary evil—a busybody angel hovering over their shoulders and saying, "Do the right thing." Industry insiders have said Charren does not understand the financial end of the television business;[53] members of the Reagan administration nicknamed her the "wicked witch of the east."[54] She was labeled a "do gooder" and an "ax grinder" by Cy Schneider in his tell-all, behind-the-scenes expose on the kidvid business, *Children's Television*.[55] He believed that Charren's real success came from promoting herself and her group's name, not by obtaining any real, substantial success.[56]

ACT was also the focus of several all-out frontal attacks from business journals and magazines. *Fortune* called Charren's group a "fountainhead of progressive indignation."[57] In the early days of the organization, *Broadcasting* dismissed ACT as a group of "militant mothers."[58]

Working in Charren's favor, however, was grassroots appeal. From its inception, ACT acquired the backing of such organizations as the PTA, the NEA, the American Academy of Pediatrics, and the National Catholic Education Association.[59] ACT also was wise enough to distance itself from "moral majority"-type movements and other groups that have tried to "make television clean again."[60]

The 1980s and the Reagan presidency were tough on Charren and ACT and even tougher on children's television. Charren said in 1988, "The Reagan Administration is wholly to blame for everything rotten that's happened to children's television. They've literally wrecked it."[61] During the 1980s Reagan deregulation chipped away at many earlier advances. Mark Fowler became chair of the FCC in 1981; his definition of television was that it was an average household appliance, "a toaster with pictures."[62] Under Fowler's rule the FCC retracted its earlier kidvid policies, adopting in their place a laissez-faire attitude. The Fowler Commission held that the needs of children's television were now being met by home video and pay channel services. Charren labeled the assumption, "Let 'em eat cable."[63]

The networks and local stations, free of government interference during the Reagan years, lessened their commitments to children's television. Many quality children's programs came to an abrupt end. CBS, which had been producing news shows and segments aimed at children—shows like *30 Minutes*, a teenaged spin-off of *60 Minutes*, and *In the News*, a series of between-Saturday-cartoons snippets that simplified current events for young people—ceased production. Twenty CBS staffers working on those programs were quickly fired or reassigned.[64]

Other children's TV developments also raised the ire of Charren and ACT during the 1980s. High on the list were so-called "thirty-minute commercials," cartoon shows based on popular toy lines, such as the animated *He-Man* and *Thundercats* programs. Some of these programs were even designed to be interactive, that is, to require the purchase of a compatible toy to be used by children during the actual viewing of the program.[65] ACT saw these shows as nothing more than marketing tools used by toy manufacturers to sell their products. Adding substance to this argument was the fact that many local stations, in return for airing the programs, would receive a cut of the profits generated by toy sales. Additionally, toy companies frequently footed the bill for the cartoon's production.[66] Charren said of the phenomenon of these series:

> The problem of program-length commercials exists only on children's television. Soap opera plots, for example, do not revolve around the virtues of Tide and All.[67]

Also on ACT's hit list during the decade was businessman Chris Whittle's plan to launch a news and information service called Channel One in public schools. This service would air once a day for twelve minutes bringing to classrooms news stories from around the world. For signing up for the satellite-delivered pilot program, Whittle Communications would donate thousands of dollars worth of free video equipment to the school. Such generosity would be very welcome by many financially strapped boards of education. The catch: along with the news programming would come intermixed commercials pushing everything from soft drinks to sneakers. "Horrendous," is what Charren called the proposed program. "It would be as if the school system were telling students what to go out and buy. Every school system in the country should fight this."[68] Charren said:

Whittle is masquerading as an educator. What it really is is an agency that sells audiences to advertisers in a creative way. That's the kind of sleazy companies that educators are getting into bed with.[69]

She later added:

This trojan horse [ignores] some basic educational, moral and legal tenets. Learning works best when you feel good about yourself. Teen counselors call it self-esteem. But advertising works when a felt need is created that only a product will satisfy. Advertising in a classroom emphasizes economic differences. It is outrageous to tell students to spend money on anything when so many live in poverty.[70]

(Channel One still exists today, airing in thousands of classrooms nationwide, though Whittle was removed as its chief in the early 1990s not long before the entire enterprise was sold off to K-III Communications for $300 million.)[71]

Yet another new, disturbing development in children's media emerged during the 1980s. Telephone 900 numbers aimed at children, where youngsters called to hear favorite TV characters, fairy tales, or bedtime stories, began to be advertised on television. Not aware of the cost of such services, great numbers of children called the numbers without parental consent. To many a parent's dismay, huge fees on monthly phone bills illustrated just how effective the televised ads for these phone lines were. ACT adopted a tough line against the ads and the phone services. In 1990 ACT filed a complaint with the Federal Trade Commission and the FTC began an investigation.[72] In 1991 the FTC took legal action against three companies that provided the children's telephone services and advertised them to children through television.[73]

In 1988 Charren and company celebrated the twentieth birthday of ACT with an all-star party. Among some 350 guests in attendance were Jay Leno (who served as master of ceremonies), Phylicia Rashad, Jane Pauley, Peter Jennings, and Mickey Mouse (actor and costume courtesy of Walt Disney).[74] Perhaps in the name of "love thy enemy" togetherness, or perhaps out of mutual respect, a large percentage of the partygoers consisted of top brass from the three major networks. Said Peggy Charren after being introduced, "I always wondered how many of you would actually pay money to have lunch with someone who keeps telling you to pull up your socks."[75]

One year later, 1989, ACT's success and influence began to be felt oversees. BACT, a British-based consumer group modeled on the American Action for Children's Television, was launched in Great Britain. Though inspired by Charren's ACT, BACT was not affiliated with the U.S. organization. To help them out, however, Charren crossed the Atlantic for the kickoff celebration.[76]

That same year Charren was toasted and celebrated by some of the people she is usually yelling at. She was awarded the Trustees Award by the National Academy of Television Arts & Sciences in recognition for her work on behalf of children's television reform.[77] A few years later, in 1992, Peggy Charren received a Peabody, an award usually given to programs and networks, for her lifetime achievements. Other winners that year included *Murphy Brown* creator Diane English and NPR for its Gulf War news coverage. Said Charren at the awards ceremony, "I didn't even know you could get a Peabody if you didn't have a program."[78]

Despite the setbacks of the 1980s and the new challenges they presented, the decade ended on a definite upswing for Charren and ACT. After many years of bitter, back-and-forth battling between the White House and the House of Representatives, the House passed the Children's Television Act of 1990, a bill created in the aftermath of an ACT lawsuit.[79] This bill, vetoed by Ronald Reagan during his term and allowed to pass into law by George Bush without his Presidential approval, has been one of the dreams of ACT since the group's beginning. The law limits advertising time during children's programming (twelve minutes per hour on weekdays, ten and one-half minutes on weekends). It also orders stations to produce evidence that they are serving the educational programming needs of children or face revocation of their broadcast licenses.[80] Peggy Charren and ACT could hardly have asked for more.

With the passage of the Children's Television Act, Charren believed that ACT's mission had been largely accomplished. With the act in place, citizens groups and local communities now had the law on their side; they could legally demand changes from their regional broadcasters. Said Charren, "Children's television is now in the hands of citizens and their local stations. They [stations] should worry whether their children's programming pleases their local communities, not if it pleases Peggy Charren."[81] In January 1992, in a surprise announcement, Peggy Charren disclosed that Action for Children's Television, the organization she had founded and had embodied for over twenty years, would disband at the end of the year.[82]

ACT folded with an impressive list of victories, the congressional bill just the latest in a long line. Host-selling, vitamin advertising to children, and runaway product-program tie-ins have all come to an end largely because of Peggy Charren's efforts. Still, Charren insists she lost more battles than she won.[83] *Newsweek* perhaps summed up her career better than anyone when in 1992 it wrote, "Children's TV may still be a long way from her goal [for it], but it is a lot closer than it would have been without her."[84] Said Judy Price, vice president for CBS's children's programming, "Peggy was a pain in the neck, but often a good pain in the neck."[85] Said Henry Geller, longtime legal counsel to ACT, "She's a fighter who won't give up. She shows that one person really can effect change."[86] Said Charren in the middle of a battle in 1990, "I've never had more fun in my life."[87]

Today, Peggy Charren is still very much in the public eye, in the industry's face, and on the frontlines. Besides holding the title of Visiting Scholar at Harvard, she is frequently sought out by children's media groups for her advice and expertise. She is also frequently sought out by journalists who want to know what she has to say about current children's TV issues or about proposed attempts at censorship. Ever the advocate, she willingly lends her voice to the cause of quality television once more.[88]

A 1988 *Newsweek* article likened Peggy Charren to everybody's doting mother or the incurable Ms. Fixit—walking into restaurants and figuring out a better way to take care of business or approaching the man in the Corduroy Bear suit at the ACT birthday bash and straightening his suspenders.[89] Whatever origins her desire to stir up controversy and to create change comes from, Peggy Charren's life has been a mission fueled by her personal passion for cleaning up kid's TV (and straightening out overgrown bears). Mother's work, it seems, is never done.

Peggy Charren

March 9, 1928	Born in New York City.
1949	Graduated from Connecticut College with degree in English; first job at WPIX-TV, New York.
June 17, 1951	Married Stanley Charren, engineer.
1951	Started first business, Art Prints, Inc.
1953	Closed Art Prints, Inc.
1960	Started second business, Quality Book Fairs.
1964	Had first child, Deborah. (Later had second daughter, Claudia.)
1966	Joined Creative Arts Council of Newton, Massachusetts; worked to integrate fine arts into public schools.
January 1968	Cofounded Action for Children's Television (ACT). Evelyn Sarson appointed first president; Charren named chair.
Spring 1969	ACT initiated and sponsored first study: local production of *Romper Room* monitored; findings presented to WHDH, Boston.
February 1970	ACT met with Federal Communications Commission (FCC); first advocacy group in history to request meeting with Commission.
March 1970	ACT's first symposium on children's television held.
September 1971	FCC set up permanent unit devoted to issues in children's television.
November 1971	ACT petitioned the Federal Trade Commission regarding vitamin advertising.
1972	Charren assumed presidency of ACT; first ACT awards given out for outstanding children's programming.

January 1973	NAB set down guidelines regarding amount of advertising allowed during children's programming.
March 1973	ACT filed petition with FTC regarding candy and cereal advertising.
November 1974	FCC set down (unenforceable) guidelines regarding appropriate amount of advertising during children's television.
March 1976	ACT filed brief with FCC critical of imposing "family hour" restrictions on broadcasters.
April 1977	ACT filed petition with FTC requesting ban on all candy advertising to children.
February 1978	FTC initiated rule making proceedings to consider ban on TV advertising towards children.
January–March 1979	FTC held hearings on television advertising directed at children.
September 1979	ACT filed letter with FCC requesting the adoption of commercial time limits during children's television.
January 1981	Ronald Reagan took office.
May 1981	Mark Fowler appointed head of FCC.
1983	Wrote and published first book, *Changing Channels: Living (Sensibly) with Television.*
August 1984	FCC repealed, in total, guidelines set forth in 1974.
June 1987	Based on ACT action, US court ordered FCC to review its 1984 decision to repeal 1974 rules.
January 1988	Action for Children's Television celebrated twentieth birthday.
June 1988	U.S. House of Representatives endorsed Children's Television Act.
February 1989	English organization, BACT, modeled on ACT, is founded in Great Britain.
October 17, 1990	Children's Television Act passed into law.
January 1992	Action for Children's Television dissolved by Peggy Charren.
1993	Named Visiting Scholar at Harvard University.

NOTES

1. Cy Schneider, *Children's Television* (Chicago, IL: National Textbook Company, 1987), p. 175.

2. *Who's Who in America* (Wilmette, IL: Macmillan, 1988), p. 532.

3. "Reflections," *Life* (Spring 1990), p. 73.

4. Noreen O'Leary, "ACT's Peggy Charren: A Mother's Work Is Never Done," *Adweek* (20 February 1989), p. 32.

5. "Reflections," p. 73.

6. Ibid.

7. "Peggy Charren," Action for Children's Television (1992), p. 2.

8. Ibid.

9. Interview with Peggy Charren (10 June 1992). All other information and quotes from Mrs. Charren in this chapter were taken from this interview unless otherwise noted.

10. *Who's Who*, p. 532.

11. "Peggy Charren," p. 1.

12. Carol Lawson, "Guarding the Children's Hour on TV," *New York Times* (24 January 1991), sec. C, p. 1.

13. Edward L. Palmer, *Children in the Cradle of Television* (Lexington, MS: Lexington Books, 1987), p. 25.

14. Edward L. Palmer and Aimee Dorr, *Children and the Faces of Television* (New York: Academic Press, 1980), p. 241.

15. Peggy Charren, "What's Missing in Children's TV," *World Monitor* (December 1990), p. 4.

16. Kate Moody, *Growing Up on Television* (New York: Times Books, 1980), p. 182.

17. Paul Harris, "Charren's 20-Year Fight for Children's TV Rights Nears Finish Line," *Variety* (30 July 1990), p. 9.

18. Palmer, p. 26.

19. Palmer and Dorr, p. 326.

20. "A Harsh Critic of Kid's TV," *Business Week* (29 May 1978), p. 52.

21. "Champion of Children's TV," *NEA Today* (October 1990), p. 9.

22. Moody, p. 213.

23. Charren interview.

24. Palmer and Dorr, p. 242.

25. "A Harsh Critic of Kid's TV," p. 52.

26. Moody, p. 186.

27. Palmer and Dorr, p. 242.

28. Palmer, p. 32.

29. Ibid.

30. Lawson, p. 1.

31. Schneider, p. 176.

32. Moody, p. 95.

33. Ibid., p. 213.

34. Palmer, p. 32.

35. Moody, p. 96.

36. Ibid., p. 11.

37. "A Harsh Critic of Kid's TV," p. 52.

38. Moody, p. 11.

39. Harry F. Waters, "The Ms. Fixit of Kidvid," *Newsweek* (30 May 1988), p. 69.

40. Harris, p. 9.

41. Moody, p. 213.

42. Ibid.

43. "Peggy Charren," p. 2.

44. "A Harsh Critic of Kid's TV," p. 52.

45. "Peggy Charren," p. 1.

46. Ibid.

47. Waters, p. 69.

48. Ibid.

49. "A Harsh Critic of Kid's TV," p. 52.

50. "Ban TV Ads Aimed at Children?," *US News & World Report* (16 January 1978), p. 48.

51. "A Harsh Critic of Kid's TV," p. 52.

52. Ibid.

53. Ibid.

54. Waters, p. 69.

55. Schneider, p. 175.

56. Ibid., p. 178.

57. Daniel Seligman, "The Commercial Crisis," *Fortune* (14 November 1983), p. 39.

58. Leonard Zeidenberg, "FCC's Puzzler: Should It Move on Children's TV?," *Broadcasting* (20 November 1972), p. 52.

59. "Champion of Children's TV," p. 9.

60. Richard Zoglin, "Ms. Kidvid Calls It Quits," *Newsweek* (20 January 1992), p. 52.

61. Waters, p. 69.

62. "Champion of Children's TV," *NEA Today* (October 1990), p. 9.

63. Schneider, p. 177.

64. "Champion of Children's TV," p. 9.

65. Joseph Dominick, Barry L. Sherman, and Gary Copeland, *Broadcasting/Cable and Beyond* (New York: McGraw-Hill, 1990), p. 441.

66. Ibid., p. 398.

67. Seligman, p. 39.

68. "Barring the Schoolhouse Door," *Advertising Age* (23 January 1989), p.16.

69. O'Leary, p. 32.

70. Charren, "What's Missing in Children's TV," p. 4.

71. "A Media Empire is Whittled Away," *US News & World Report* (22 August 1994), p. 14.

72. "Champion of Children's TV," p. 9.

73. "If a Bunny Answers, Hang Up," *US News & World Report* (20 May 1991), p. 13.

74. Waters, p. 69.

75. Ibid.

76. O'Leary, p. 32.

77. Ibid.

78. Charren interview.

79. Waters, p. 69.

80. Zoglin, p. 52.

81. Charren interview.

82. "For the Record," *Advertising Age* (13 January 1992), p. 41.

83. Zoglin, p. 52.

84. Ibid.

85. Doug Halonen, "Charren Draws Praise as ACT Plans to Fold," *Electronic Media* (13 January 1992), p. 2.

86. O'Leary, p. 34.

87. Harris, p. 9.

88. Interview with Peggy Charren (20 October 1994).

89. Waters, p. 69.

Joan Ganz Cooney

From the beginning of television through the nineteen-fifties, television for children, with few exceptions, was a collection of cheaply made cartoons, recycled reruns, and pie-throwing clowns. Bob Keeshan's *Captain Kangaroo* and Judith Waller's and Dr. Frances Horwich's *Ding Dong School* both broke the norm by providing entertaining, diverting, and educational alternatives for children and parents. Though Keeshan's program would become a national institution, changing network priorities and a tighter competitive market eventually led to its cancellation. For many of the same reasons, *Ding Dong School* did not survive past 1961.[1] By and large, children's television was in a sad state when a bright, innovative, and determined television show for children hit the airwaves in the late 1960s. Titled *Sesame Street*, it was the brainchild of a former New York documentary filmmaker and her talented staff, who together had formed a production unit called the Children's Television Workshop (CTW). The CTW would go on to become the dominant voice in children's television and an important tool in early childhood education. The visionary behind this voice was one woman—Joan Ganz Cooney.

Joan Ganz was born on November 30, 1929, in Phoenix, Arizona. She was one of three children of Sylvan and Pauline Ganz. Her father worked for a bank and the family had a strong Roman Catholic center.[2] Joan Ganz has described her childhood as an "upper middle class, country club atmosphere":[3]

> I was raised in the most conventional way, raised to be a housewife and mother, to work in an interesting job when I got out of college, and to marry at the appropriate time, which would have been twenty-five.[4]

One of the earliest influences on Joan, however, took her away from that preset destiny. Father James Keller, the founder of the Catholic-based Christopher Movement, encouraged Christians to become involved in communication industries. Ganz said, "Father Keller said that if idealists didn't go into the media, nonidealists would."[5] Lucky for Joan, she was a self-described "driven, idealistic kid."[6] A second strong influence was a course in her North Phoenix High School taught by Bud Brown. The class engaged in active dialogues about poverty, the free press, and anti-Semitism in Germany. Joan Ganz said, "He [Brown] was concerned with poverty when it was not fashionable...."[7]

In 1951, after beginning her college career at the Dominican College of San Rafael, Ganz emerged from the University of Arizona with a bachelor's degree (cum laude) in education and the nickname "Guts."[8] Ganz said:

> I majored in education in college, but I really wasn't interested in teaching. It was something that girls of my generation did because teaching was very acceptable.[9]

After graduation, Ganz worked for the government in Washington for one year before moving back to Arizona and into journalism.[10] Her first reporting job was for the *Arizona Republican*.[11] After just one year, Ganz decided to move to New York City to pursue a career as a public relations woman.[12] It was a move not supported by her mother. Ganz remembers:

> When I left Arizona, she said, "You know you are a big fish in a little pond in Phoenix; why do you want to be a little fish in a big pond?" I said, "How do you know I won't be a big fish in a big pond?"[13]

With an education, great drive, and the Christopher mission all in tow, Ganz arrived in New York in 1953 at age 23. One evening at a party in New York, Ganz was introduced to RCA chief David Sarnoff, who was impressed enough by her to find her a job in the RCA information department.[14] Those duties soon led Ganz to a job with NBC writing soap opera summaries for $65 a week. "Just what I asked for," Ganz would later quip.[15] Nevertheless, it was a good stepping stone to her next major assignment one year later at the US Steel Corporation generating publicity copy for the highly acclaimed CBS dramatic anthology *The US Steel Hour*. She remained with that series until 1962.[16]

During this time, Ganz also fell in with a literary set of young writers and editors who gathered at the West Side apartment of *Partisan Review* editor William Phillips. Some of the notable group included Jason Epstein and Norman Mailer.[17] Ganz also became deeply involved in Democratic reform politics, gradually moving herself closer to prominent names in politics.[18]

Sometime during 1961 Ganz became aware of a legal struggle taking place in New Jersey. WNDT, a PBS station, was attempting to take control of Channel 13 in New York. Ganz has said, "If they [WNDT] won, I knew my future would be with them."[19] Earlier, she had tried for executive positions with the three major networks only to be turned down.[20]

WNDT won its battle, rechristened itself WNET, and Joan quickly applied for the job as the station's publicity director. The general manager told her he did not need publicity but did need producers. "I can produce," Joan bluffed.[21] She was hired in 1962. She would say later, "I've never been qualified for any job I've been hired for."[22]

The station, new and short of money, could put little on its air but daily

JOAN GANZ COONEY

talk shows and locally produced documentaries. One of the reasons they hired Joan was because of her ties with important names in the political and entertainment communities whom they hoped to interview. Ganz's first task was to coordinate a weekly live debate program titled *Court of Reason*.[23]

With time, Ganz began to produce documentary films for the station. She produced *A Chance at the Beginning*, one of the first films on the then experimental Head Start program. Later, in 1966, she produced *Poverty, Anti-Poverty, and the Poor* a three-hour documentary on the plight of the poor. It won her a local Emmy Award.[24]

In 1964, at age 34, Joan married Tim Cooney, a member of New York Mayor Wagner's staff. Joan Ganz Cooney remembers, "My first husband made me a feminist. He was very supportive and encouraged me."[25] Later, Mr. Cooney would drop out of the political arena and become an unpaid advocate for the urban poor. Joan Cooney became the family breadwinner.[26] Though the couple had no children of their own, they did take on the responsibility of fostering a young, inner-city African-American boy in 1969.[27]

In February 1966, at a now famous dinner party in her home, Cooney began talking to one of her guests, Lloyd Morrisett, then the vice-president of the Carnegie Corporation, a longtime funding source of educational research. He asked Cooney about her thoughts on the feasibility of using television to educate large numbers of preschoolers. Cooney remembers telling him, "I don't know, but it would be interesting to find out."[28]

Morrisett called a few days later asking Cooney to devise a study on the subject. Excited by the challenge, Cooney mapped out a plan of study.[29] She submitted the finished plan, a short paper, to Morrisett on May 13, 1966, and by June, Carnegie had awarded her funds to finance the project with Cooney as chief investigator.[30] She believed at the time that the project would take four months. She said of the task:

> I could do a thousand documentaries on poverty and poor people that would be watched by a handful of the convinced, but I was never really going to have an influence on my times. I wanted to make a difference.[31]

From June until September of 1966 Joan Cooney criss-crossed the United States and Canada gathering information about her study and talking to leading educators, pediatricians and psychologists.[32] Her degree in education (and her minor in psychology) began to pay off.

Cooney handed the finished report, titled "The Potential Uses of Television in Preschool Education," over to Morrisett in October of 1966.[33] In her report Cooney made mention of many entertainment and educational techniques that a show for preschoolers could utilize. They included the use of short videotaped spots, puppets, and a permanent host.[34] She also made note that a truly successful children's show for that age group would have to consist of different elements, among them a strong visual style, fast-moving action, humor, and music.[35] She suggested the show be produced in color instead of black and white, unusual for children's shows even in the mid-sixties.[36] Cooney also examined children's viewing habits. She determined that children often preferred commercials with catchy music and fast action within TV programs to the actual programs themselves.[37] She reported:

> Hearing every child in America singing beer commercials certainly suggested to me that television was teaching willy-nilly. Kids are just like little sponges. They pick up everything.
> I suggested we have a format of different things interrupted with these "commercials" to teach letters and numbers. For example, we would have a commercial just for the letter "A."
> What was different was that we used commercial techniques—such as puppets, animation, live action, and music—for our own purposes, which were educational.[38]

Some of Cooney's other findings and recommendations included the use of several short twelve- to ninety-second spots (the teaching "commercials") and the repetition of important concepts during the show, and throughout the day. To achieve this goal, Cooney advised that the proposed show be one-hour and that it be run twice a day, Monday through Friday.[39]

As the idea of creating an innovative and successful show for preschoolers gained momentum, WNET examined the feasibility of actually producing such a program. Gradually, it became apparent that to incorporate all the different elements from the study into an actual show would require greater resources than those of just one station. Gaining additional interest and funding for the program became the next order of business.[40]

Sponsors who added additional funds, along with Carnegie, included the Ford Foundation and the U.S. Office of Education.[41] Said Cooney, "We had decided from the first that we wouldn't go around begging for pennies. Either we would get full funding to do the show right or would drop it."[42] The Office of Education donated half of the first year's budget of $8 million.[43] But even with that amount, money was tight. A single half-hour cartoon program cost $50,000 to produce; Cooney could budget her animation segments at only $30,000.[44]

In May of 1967 Joan Ganz Cooney officially broke ties with WNET to concentrate full time with Carnegie on what was about to become the Children's Television Workshop.[45] To gain further direction and build up support for the new show, Cooney and her colleagues—Morrisett and experts from the fields of education and psychology—arranged a meeting with television consultants, including representatives from CBS and NBC.[46] Out of these meetings they constructed specific goals for the program, from recognition of simple letters and numbers to social and moral development for children.[47]

Additional seminars to find direct methods of teaching these subjects followed the next year. All totaled, *Sesame Street* was researched and developed for over two full years before the cameras began to roll.

On the creative end Cooney attracted former *Captain Kangaroo* producers Dave Connell, Jon Stone, and Sam Gibbon, who were experienced in the production of high-volume shows. Joe Raposo came aboard as musical director and songwriter. And they hooked up with a young puppeteer named Jim Henson, who had created a hybrid marionette and puppet called a "muppet." Recognizing his talent, they gave him a medium for his magic.[48]

Once the Children's Television Workshop was funded, it became necessary, in the minds of the contributing foundations, to install someone as the project's overall boss. Names of top educators and media moguls were tossed about. Naming a well-known name to the top position would gain press attention and, hopefully, additional funding. Joan Cooney, in this scenario, would remain with the production and be able to see to the day-to-day business as "project coordinator." Cooney's husband Tim did not agree with this idea. He told his wife: "Tell them you're not available for the second spot. They know you're the only one with the whole thing in your head."[49] Cooney stuck to her husband's advice and gained the company's top seat as chief executive.

As the show came towards its starting production date, Cooney and an associate once again traveled the United States "selling" the show to National Educational Television affiliates. Not only were they attempting to get the show aired on those stations but, preferably, aired sometime between the hours of nine and eleven in the morning—after households had quieted down from the morning rush and before older children came home from school and took control of the television from their siblings.[50] From the beginning this children's show was going to be different from anything on television. To appeal to the group the show most hoped to attract, inner-city children, the setting would be a realistic city street, complete with peeling paint, alleys, front stoops, and metal trash cans along the sidewalk. Cooney insisted that the regular performers for the series be made up of an ethnic mix of white and African-American men and women. (Asian and Hispanic actors were added in later years.) The same would be true for the rotating collection of children who appeared on the show. This was done to create a reproduction of the viewing child's own neighborhood.[51]

A title was hit on one day when someone saw the parallels between the show's opening of opportunities for children and the magical command for opening shut doors: "Open Sesame!" Because it was already determined that the setting would be a city street, the show adopted the name *Sesame Street*.[52]

Even before the show went on the air, enthusiasm was mounting. To gain early audience reaction, pilots of *Sesame Street* were previewed on a UHF channel in Philadelphia and in daycare centers in New York. National press coverage of these viewings gave the show glowing reviews and hyped the show's premiere.[53] Though the show was not a network product, ABC, CBS, and NBC promoted the show via interviews and the airing of free commercials. NBC even produced a one-hour Saturday-night special introducing it.[54]

Sesame Street premiered on November 10, 1969. From the outset, it was nothing short of a sensation.[55] Cooney said, "I could not believe the wild success.... When Big Bird hit the cover of *Time*, I knew we had something that would last forever."[56] By the end of the show's first season, *Sesame Street* was attracting an average audience of seven million preschoolers.[57] Television critic Les Brown said of the show, "If racial peace and harmony ever visit this country, [*Sesame Street*] may be one of the reasons why."[58] *Variety*, in its review, said, "The only thing wrong with *Sesame Street* is it took twenty years to get here."[59]

Though the show was not originally planned exclusively for public television stations, they have since become *Sesame Street*'s most regular home. In the early days, however, the show was seen on independent stations around the country, though under strict restrictions. Stations could not interrupt the show for commercials. Advertising was allowed only before the show began and after it ended. On their own, most stations would broadcast only public service announcements during the show's time periods.[60] Cooney has said,

"It is terribly wrong to be pitching products at the young. It's like shooting fish in a barrel. It is grotesquely unfair."[61]

Though the majority of television critics and childhood educators gave raves to the show, it was not without its critics. Many disapproved of its rapid pace. One "expert" feared that the show's quickness would give children epilepsy.[62] *Sesame Street* was also the subject of a five-page 1970 attack in *The New Republic*. That article criticized everything from the show's attempts at teaching ("unchallenging") to its cast's roles as teachers ("Grown-ups initiate everything").[63] Others wondered about the show's effectiveness in the long run: were children actually being *taught* by the repetition of concepts or only being *conditioned*?[64]

After some fine-tuning of the show, *Sesame Street* won over most of its critics. One of its first orders of business was to lessen its speedy pacing, which had originally been inspired by the rapid fire action of the comedy hit *Rowan & Martin's Laugh-In*.[65]

Gradually, *Sesame Street* began to have an overwhelming impact on children's lives and the educational community. *Sesame Street* has become the most researched television show in the history of the medium. Various studies have determined the effect it has had on teaching. Over the years *Sesame Street* has been praised for raising school reading scores and for developing proschool attitudes.[66] It has even gone international. Voice-dubbed editions or full foreign language productions are now being seen in such countries as Israel, Holland, Spain, Turkey, Germany, and several Arab nations.[67]

In April of 1970, with the success of *Street* now more than a flash in the pan, the Children's Television Workshop broke away from its parent, National Educational Television, and incorporated itself as a not-for-profit company. Installed as president of the Workshop was Joan Ganz Cooney.[68] She once said, "I've been boss, and I've been bossed. And believe me, being boss is better."[69]

From the beginning, funding for *Sesame Street* and the Children's Television Workshop was difficult to come by. Along with money pulled in from licensing agreements with toy manufacturers and clothing companies, the CTW also depended on large government grants, corporate donations, and public television underwriting. Even these various sources were not always enough. "The company is always potentially in financial trouble," Cooney once admitted.[70]

In 1978, when the US Office of Education withheld its two million dollar check until 4:30 P.M. on the last day of the CTW fiscal year, Cooney declared once and for all, enough was enough. She vowed to see the Workshop become totally self-sufficient. Licensing agreements were beefed up, and overseas distribution of the organization's programs were expanded to create greater cash flow. Some small funding still came from the government until 1981 when those sources dried up completely.[71] Today, *Sesame Street* receives no support from the US government, supporting itself instead on licensing arrangements, publishing, and international sales.[72] Cooney once said:

> I spend 90 percent of my time on survival issues. My largest function is to go out hat in hand.... [But] it's part of being boss. I was born to be an executive; I wasn't born to be a flunky.[73]

The second offspring of the Children's Television Workshop began in 1971. *The Electric Company* was a reading skills show aimed at children ages seven to ten. It starred such Oscar-nominated performers as Rita Moreno and Morgan Freeman.[74] Its purpose was to carry on the lessons started by *Sesame Street*; once children had learned their letters, they could now put them together and learn words. The show caught on nearly as quickly as *Sesame Street*, soon becoming the most used TV program in American schools.[75] That same year the CTW introduced an adult-oriented medical program titled *Feelin' Good* hosted by Dick Cavett. The show however lacked a clear direction and never found a large audience. It ended in 1974.[76]

Sesame Street has headed-off any such demise by keeping fresh and evolving over the years. "We started out thinking that it might teach simple things," Cooney has said. "We learned you could do so much more."[77] At first the show tried to teach only five to six topics; today it encompasses more than 200.[78] *Sesame Street* has also expanded beyond simple rote learning programs by discussing prominent life topics and social issues. Over the years *Sesame Street* has attempted to educate its preschool audience about racism, child abuse, death, and dying.[79]

The issue of racism has been gently introduced into young people's minds by Kermit the Frog's tender rendition of his signature song "It's Not Easy Being Green."[80] Big Bird was introduced for similar reasons. Big Bird could be seen making the occasional mistake and showing children that it is okay to do so without being insulting to, or being considered reflective of, any particular ethnic or racial group.[81]

In 1981 *Sesame Street* incorporated the death of show regular Will Lee, who played kindly shopkeeper Mr. Hooper, into the show, teaching children early lessons in life and death.[82] Though open to realistic issues, Cooney has been known to draw her lines: "I am not about to put a fifteen-year-old girl with a baby on *Sesame Street*."[83]

In 1975, with two successful shows on the air, Joan Ganz Cooney was suddenly hit by two personal blows. First, her eleven-year marriage to Timothy Cooney came to an end. As the couple's primary source of income over the length of the marriage, Joan (voluntarily) began to pay her ex-husband alimony—one of the first US women ever to do so.[84] She was still paying alimony as late as 1993.[85] A few months after the legal separation, Joan was diagnosed with breast cancer and underwent a radical mastectomy. Cooney said about her experience, "I've always believed that the cancer and the separation were connected—people who are under great stress do seem to have an unusual susceptibility to major diseases."[86] There have been no recurrences of the cancer since the surgery.

Over the years Cooney has acquired many important and influential seats on committees and corporate boards, including the National News Council, the Mayo Foundation, the Educational Broadcasting Corporation, the Chase Manhattan Bank, Johnson & Johnson, and Metropolitan Life Insurance.[87] In 1975 she was named the first woman director of the Xerox Corporation.[88] In 1986 *Working Woman* magazine named her as one of its first inductees into its "Working Woman's Hall of Fame." (Lucille Ball was also on the list.)[89] Cooney has said about her life in business:

> I like to feel I am a hardheaded business woman, but I suppose underneath it all I am still a crusader. I would like to bring about change for the better. CTW is not a democracy. It would be all over the lot if there were not a few of us with a vision who say no. I say no a lot.[90]

The Children's Television Workshop has diversified into many different areas over the years. The CTW now oversees an extensive line of products, a publishing empire, and programs for cable television. The CTW has 250 employees and annual revenues in the neighborhood of $55 million, much of which goes into future development.[91]

In 1980 Joan Ganz Cooney took a second walk down the aisle, marrying Peter Peterson, then Chairman of the Board of Lehman Brothers Kuhn Loeb, Inc. and former US Secretary of Commerce. With the marriage Cooney inherited five stepchildren.[92] That same year saw the start up of the CTW's newest show, *3-2-1 Contact*. It was aimed at children eight to twelve, and took on the task of teaching science-related topics.[93]

The next year, 1981, after government funding came to an end, the Children's Television Workshop encountered some difficult growing pains. *The Electric Company*—which had been running in reruns for several years—was abandoned by public television stations and *3-2-1 Contact*, because of low funding, was able to produce only thirty new shows that year.[94] While *Sesame Street* remained the organization's jewel in the crown, poor investments in video games, motion picture production, and other business ventures wounded the Workshop's pocketbook. By 1986, however, licensing revenues stabilized and the company was on an even keel again. It has remained steady ever since.[95] In 1987, after three years on the drawing board, the CTW premiered its math teaching show for children ages eight to twelve. *Square One TV* is meant to take the fear out of math through the use of sketches, songs, kid quiz shows, and a *Dragnet* parody called "Mathnet." The latter stars two crime-fighting mathematicians.[96] Later, in 1992, *Ghost Writer*, a mystery/reading show began.[97]

Sesame Street celebrated its twentieth birthday in 1989. Cooney continued her daily involvement in the show from her spacious office overlooking Lincoln Center and kept up-to-date on its content by watching the show as she got dressed each morning.[98] After twenty years, *Sesame Street* has been awarded more than thirty Emmy awards, and its creator has earned an Emmy for lifetime achievement.[99]

In 1990 Cooney stepped down as CEO and Chair of the CTW, turning control over to David Britt. At that time she assumed the role of Chair of the CTW Executive Committee, overseeing the Workshop's creative planning. An early concern of the Committee was adding more female puppets to the *Sesame Street* ensemble. Cooney said, "It remains a big cause with all of us who are women on the show.... Jim [Henson] never thought that way, and it was hard to get it right over the years."[100]

Also in 1990 Cooney was inducted into the Television Academy of Arts & Sciences' Hall of Fame, the first female nonperformer ever so honored.[101]

In mid-1995 the Children's Television Workshop, in an effort to "reorganize," announced layoffs of forty-seven staffers, about 12 percent of its employees.[102] Not long before, the CTW had announced it was entering into a partnership with the Sony Corporation to produce live-action feature films[103] and that it would soon begin development of a new show for cable's Cartoon Network.[104] There is also talk of the Workshop launching its own children's cable channel.[105]

Today Cooney, along with her continued work at the CTW, heads her own foundation devoted to supporting new, innovative children's programs. Said friend Diane Sawyer of Cooney, "[She] still believes you can and must change the world."[106]

Joan Ganz Cooney is so admired in the money-hungry, fast-buck world of American television that she is frequently referred to as the "Saint Joan of TV." One reporter said, "Even canonization is probably too small a reward."[107] Few women (or men for that matter) have had as positive an effect on television as Joan Ganz Cooney. She reinvented the world of children's television by making it more than a diversion, transforming it into an instrument to improve children's lives. Joan Ganz Cooney has created something that has taken the "vast" out of "vast wasteland." She molded together a vehicle that has taught children to relate to the world around them, to understand the people in that world, and to recognize their own place in it. Along the way her programs have even taught them to count to ten. And then to twenty. And then much higher. Her programs have taught them letters too, and then words—words like "reach," "hope," "future."

Joan Ganz Cooney

November 30, 1929   Born in Phoenix, Arizona.

May 1951   Graduated from the University of Arizona.

1953	Moved to New York City.
1954	Obtained job as copy writer for CBS's *US Steel Hour*.
1962	Departed *US Steel Hour*, hired by WNET, New York public television station.
February 22, 1964	Married Tim Cooney, New York City politician.
February 1966	Held dinner party in her home; Lloyd Morrisett, VP of the Carnegie Corporation, in attendance; began discussion of educational television.
May 13, 1966	Submitted short plan to Morrisett on use of television in educating elementary school children.
June 1966	Carnegie Corporation awarded funds for further study on education and television; Joan Ganz Cooney named as chief investigator; traveled across the United States conducting interviews and gathering information for final report study.
October 1966	Submitted final report, "The Potential Uses of Television in Preschool Education," to Morrisett.
May 1967	Officially broke ties with WNET to devote full energies to Carnegie project.
Spring 1968	Children's Television Workshop formed; Joan Ganz Cooney named president.
November 10, 1969	*Sesame Street* premiered.
April 1970	Children's Television Workshop incorporated as not-for-profit entity.
October 25, 1971	First episode of the CTW's *The Electric Company* aired.
November 20, 1974	*Feelin' Good*, health education show for adults produced by CTW, premiered.
January 1975	*Feelin' Good* aired last broadcast.
Spring 1975	Divorced from Tim Cooney. Joan Ganz Cooney named to board of directors of Xerox Corporation.
January 14, 1980	*3-2-1 Contact*, CTW science education series, premiered.
1980	Married Peter Peterson, former US Secretary of Commerce.
April 1981	New production on *3-2-1 Contact* ended due to funding shortage.
September 1981	Last episodes of *Electric Company* aired on PBS.
August 1985	CTW produced feature film, *Sesame Street Presents Follow That Bird*, opened in theaters.
January 1987	Math program from the Children's Television Workshop premiered, *Square One TV*.
October 1992	New reading show from CTW, *Ghost Writer*, premiered.
July 1990	Resigned position of CEO of Children's Television Workshop to take post of Chair of Executive Committee.

January 1990   Inducted into Academy of Television Arts & Sciences's
                      Television Hall of Fame; first female nonperformer so
                      honored.

NOTES

1. Les Brown, *The New York Times Encyclopedia of Television* (New York Times Books, 1977), p. 119.

2. *Current Biography* (1970), p. 97.

3. Gary Dreibelbis, "A Case Study of Joan Ganz Cooney and Her Involvement in the Development of the Children's Television Workshop," Ph.D. diss. Northern Illinois University (1982), p. 8.

4. Ibid., p. 9.

5. Michele Morris, "The St. Joan of Television," *Working Woman* (May 1986), p. 76.

6. Peter Hellman, "Street Smart," *New York* (23 November 1987), p. 51

7. *Current Biography*, p. 97.

8. Morris, p. 70.

9. Lynn Gilbert and Gaylen Moore, *Particular Passions* (New York: Crown, 1981), p. 295.

10. Ibid.

11. *Current Biography*, p. 97.

12. Hellman, p. 51.

13. Gilbert and Moore, p. 295.

14. "First Lady of 'Sesame Street,' Joan Ganz Cooney," *Broadcasting* (7 June 1991), p. 67.

15. Hellman, p. 51.

16. "First Lady of 'Sesame Street,' Joan Ganz Cooney," p. 67.

17. Hellman, p. 51.

18. "First Lady of 'Sesame Street,' Joan Ganz Cooney," p. 67.

19. Hellman, p. 51.

20. "Boss Is Better," *Forbes* (1 June 1975), p. 43.

21. Hellman, p. 51.

22. Morris, p. 76.

23. Hellman, p. 51.

24. Morris, p. 76.

25. Ibid.

26. Ibid.

27. "Boss Is Better," p. 43.

28. "From an Idea to an Institution," p. 3.

29. Hellman, p. 51.

30. Dreibelbis, p. 62.

31. Morris, p. 76.

32. Dreibelbis, p. 62.

33. "Forgotten 12 Million," *Time* (14 November 1969), p. 96.

34. Dreibelbis, p. 61.

35. Ibid., p. 69.

36. Ibid., p. 78.

37. Ibid., p. 69.

38. "Joan Ganz Cooney," Academy of Television Arts & Sciences (1989), p. 32.

39. Dreibelbis, p. 78.

40. Ibid., p. 86.

41. "Forgotten 12 Million," p. 96.

42. Hellman, p. 51.

43. Louise Sweeney, "Joan Cooney's Preschool TV Workshop," *Christian Science Monitor* (26 April 1968), p. 30.

44. Ibid.

45. Dreibelbis, p. 86.

46. Ibid., p. 96.

47. *Current Biography*, p. 98.

48. Dreibelbis, p. 124.

49. Hellman, p. 51.

50. Dreibelbis, p. 154.

51. Hellman, p. 52.

52. *Current Biography*, p. 98.

53. Dreibelbis, p. 144.

54. "Forgotten 12 Million," p. 96.

55. *Current Biography*, p. 98.

56. Cheryl Heuton, "TV Learns How to Teach," *Channels* (22 October 1990), p. 64.

57. Hellman, p. 50.

58. *Current Biography*, p. 99.

59. Ralph Tyler, "Cooney Cast Light on Vision," *Variety* (13 December 1989), p. 72.

60. "CTW's Big Act That No One's Followed," *Broadcasting* (20 November 1972), p. 50.

61. Cy Schneider, *Children's Television* (Chicago, IL: National Textbook Company, 1987), p. 174.

62. Hellman, p. 52.

63. Sedulus (pseud.), "Sesame Street," *New Republic* (6 June 1970), p. 23.

64. Erik Barnouw, *Tube of Plenty* (Oxford: Oxford Unversity Press, 1982), p. 437.

65. Hellman, p. 51.

66. Joseph Dominick, Barry Sherman, and Gary Copeland, *Broadcasting/Cable and Beyond* (New York: McGraw-Hill, 1990), p. 377.

67. "Bio Sketch: Joan Ganz Cooney," Children's Television Workshop News (1991), p. 1.

68. "TV's Switched-On School," *Newsweek* (1 June 1970), p. 71.

69. "Boss Is Better," p. 43.

70. Morris, p. 74.

71. Ibid., p. 76.

72. Joanmarie Kalter, "Survival Isn't Child's Play," *TV Guide* (25 July 1987), p. 38.

73. "Boss Is Better," p. 43.

74. Morris, p. 74.

75. Ibid.

76. Ibid.

77. Dan Moreau, "Change Agents," *Changing Times* (July 1989), p. 88.

78. Ibid.

79. Morris, p. 74.

80. "TV's Switched-On School," p. 71.

81. Dreibelbis, p. 125.

82. Hellman, p. 52.

83. Ibid.

84. Morris, p. 76.

85. Hilary Mills, "Pete and Joan," *Vanity Fair* (August 1993), p. 147.

86. Ray Robinson, "Big Bird's Mother Hen," *Fifty Plus* (December 1987), p. 27

87. "Bio Sketch: Joan Ganz Cooney," p. 1.

88. "Allied Fields," *Broadcasting* (17 February 1975), p. 62.

89. Kate Rand Lloyd, "America's Secret Weapon," *Working Woman* (November 1986), p. 158.

90. Gilbert and Moore, p. 297.

91. Morris, p. 70.

92. Ibid., p. 76.

93. "Bio Sketch: Joan Ganz Cooney," p. 1.

94. Kalter, p. 38.

95. Ibid.

96. Ibid., p. 39.

97. "Bio Sketch: Joan Ganz Cooney," p. 2.

98. Hellman, p. 53.

99. "Bio Sketch: Joan Ganz Cooney," p. 3.

100. Mills, p. 119.

101. "Joan Ganz Cooney," p. 34.

102. Lawrie Mifflin, "Maker of 'Sesame Street' Lays Off 12% of Its Staff," *New York Times* (7 June 1995), sec. B, p. 3.

103. "Sony Gets Many 'Sesame St.' Rights," *Publishers Weekly* (1 May 1995), p. 16.

104. Lawrie Mifflin, "Nonprofit Muppets Going to Commercial TV," *New York Times* (21 June 1995), sec. B, p. 2.

105. Mifflin, p. 3.

106. Ibid.

107. Michael Kramer, "A Presidential Message from Big Bird," *US News & World Report* (13 June 1988), p. 19.

Faye Emerson

In the very early days of television the airwaves were heavily populated not so much by actors, actresses, and clowns but by a type of "entertainer" previously unknown to the American public—something called the "television personality." "Personalities," their form and function, were detailed—as fully as possible—by Arthur Shulman and Roger Youman in their book *The Golden Age of Television*:

> Their unique talent [was] to succeed without benefit of a unique talent, at least in the traditional sense. In terms of television, however, they possess a formidable talent, desirable above all others. They can reach out and grab an audience. They establish rapport; they blend....
>
> Personalities are usually called hosts or hostesses, a most apt description. Like the hosts of a well-planned cocktail party, they contribute to the occasion by circulating quietly through the proceedings, never intruding unnecessarily, always attempting a smooth intermingling of their more volatile guests. They beam and greet their guests on arrival; they chat briefly and engagingly, perhaps including a mild jest or two; they have a smile and a handshake when the guests depart.[1]

Most of these early television personalities were women, the role of TV talk-show host/personality being one of the most wide open spaces for women in television at that time. The majority of them were former stage and film actresses. Some, like former film actress Wendy Barrie and fashion writer Ilka Chase, have faded from memory. Others continued with television, remaining active in the medium for years; those women include host and game show panelist Arlene Francis and host and author Virginia Graham.

But when talking about the dominant and most famous of the early television "chat show ladies," one name stands out from the rest—a woman so identified with early television that she is often referred to as its unofficial first lady, or as *People Today* coined her in the early 1950s, "Mrs. Television."[2] The original "hostess with the mostess" was Faye Emerson.

Faye Margaret Emerson was born July 8, 1917, in Elizabeth, Louisiana, the only child of Lawrence L. Emerson (a sometime rancher and court stenographer) and his wife Jean Emerson (later Young). Her parents left Louisiana in 1919 and moved extensively during her early childhood.[3] "The Emersons are rugged people," Emerson once said.[4] For a period of time, the Emersons

FAYE EMERSON

lived in Carlsbad, New Mexico, and then at different times Beaumont, Houston, and El Paso, Texas. Her parents divorced in 1920. In 1924 Faye (then known as Margaret) went to live with her father and new stepmother in Chicago. There she proved herself an extroverted tomboy who enjoyed the occasional fist fight and dangerous feat, like climbing telephone poles and having to have the fire department come get her down.[5]

Three and a half years later she left Chicago to go live with her mother in San Diego, California. Though a Baptist, young Faye was enrolled in convent school and remained there for two years.[6] There Emerson developed a flair for dramatics, putting aside her first dream of becoming a writer. At the convent Emerson often found herself cast in the school plays, though, to her disliking, usually in the roles of angels and not as sinners or as the devil as she had hoped.[7] After attending Point Loma High School and after a one-year stay at San Diego State College, she joined the St. James Repertory Theater in Carmel; she also, about this time, made an short, unsuccessful attempt at an acting career in New York. Later still, she joined up with the San Diego

Players where she earned a weekly salary of fifteen dollars.[8] In 1941 she took the first of three trips down the aisle and married San Diego auto salesman and former college classmate William Wallace Crawford, Jr. Her only child, William III, was born soon after. William III was soon nicknamed Scoop.[9]

Emerson was appearing in a production of the play *Here Today* at the San Diego Municipal Theater when a talent scout from Warner Brothers studios in Hollywood spotted her and offered her a screen test and a seven-year contract at $75 a week.[10] Though married (her husband was away serving in the US Navy at the time) and caring for a young son, she stifled worries that an acting career would strain her marriage when her husband returned and signed the contract. After her husband's return, Emerson drove daily from Hollywood to San Diego to spend time with him and their son. But her early fears proved correct; Emerson and Crawford divorced in 1942.[11]

Like many young actresses under contract to major studios, Emerson's film career was long on publicity photos and fan magazine interviews and short on actual screen time. Her film debut was a bit in Warner's 1941 film *The Nurse's Secret*.[12] This film was followed by a series of more than twenty similar grade "B" films, including 1941's *Bad Men of Missouri* in which she played a pioneer girl who died in a covered wagon. "I was determined to make it as pathetic as hell," she said, "and it was."[13] Usually, however, she played good girls gone bad in films like *Murder in the Big House* (1942), *Lady Gangster* (1942), and *Secret Enemies* (1943). Emerson's career took a slight upturn when actress friend Ann Sheridan convinced her to dye her brown hair blonde.[14] She was occasionally able to turn in an appearance or two in higher quality productions like *Destination Tokyo* (1944) and *The Mask of Dimitrios* (1944).[15] She told writer Pete Martin in 1951:

> In most of my pictures I had to paint bags under my eyes to look dissipated. When I took my small son, Scoop, to see one of them, he thought Peter Lorre was way ahead of me in attractiveness.[16]

While Emerson's film career might not have been going along as nicely as she would have hoped, her personal life was a completely different story. In 1944 Faye Emerson hitched her wagon to a Roosevelt, Franklin and Eleanor's second (and much-married) son, Elliott. She met him in 1943 after being personally invited by billionaire Howard Hughes to a party in Elliott's honor.[17] Elliott Roosevelt was then a handsome Air Force colonel, and he and Faye struck up a quick rapport. "We were both Democrats and got along fine," she said.[18] They were married in December 1944 on the lip of the Grand Canyon. The groom wore his military uniform, and the bride wore a "canyon blue" wedding suit with a mink coat and alligator shoes. The children of both parties attended the ceremony.[19]

Warner Brothers milked the Emerson-Roosevelt marriage for great publicity. Even so, Emerson's relationship with the studio, never very strong to begin with, became extremely strained: the company refused to loan her a mink coat to wear to the inaugural, and the movie scripts she was given grew even worse in terms of quality. Finally, one day in 1946, after reading "possibly the worst script ever written," Emerson walked off the set and out of films for good.[20] Warners agreed to cancel her contract.[21]

She quit with very few regrets:

> I never really liked pictures anyway; maybe that was the reason I wasn't a big success in them. And since I wasn't contributing anything to cultural America, I went east to be with Elliott. I've never missed the movies or the west coast. There were times when I felt they could give them back to the real estate promoters and the Chamber of Commerce.[22]

Besides having a knack for marrying well, and often, Faye Emerson also seemed to have an uncanny ability to get her name in the papers. Perhaps the young Roosevelts' most infamous caper involved their 150-pound pet dog, Blaze. Elliott Roosevelt purchased the mastiff in England and sent it to Washington, D.C., in a Flying Fortress. After its arrival in the capital, Anne Roosevelt Boettiger asked for the dog to be sent to Emerson in California in any extra room in an Air Transport Command.[23] An overzealous officer made Blaze A-1 priority, and by doing so, he displaced three servicemen from their flight, one of whom was on his way home to attend his father's funeral.[24] News of this was leaked to the press, who chastised Faye and Elliott. They were even topic for discussion on the floor of the Senate for a time before the controversy died down. "Blaze was ... blown up into the biggest thing since Benedict Arnold," Emerson said.[25]

Another of Emerson's attention-getting episodes took place at the 1945 Roosevelt inaugural when, seated next to "an ordinary looking little man" who wanted to talk to her, she ignored him and, in her own terms, gave him the brush off. The "little man's" name, she learned later, was Harry Truman. "Naturally, I had seen his pictures in the papers. Even so he still looked like anybody else to me," Emerson said afterward.[26]

Another headline-grabbing antic occurred when Elliott tried to corner the New York City Christmas tree market. He shipped thousands of trees from his Hyde Park estate to the city, trying to turn a profit. For a time Emerson was selling some of the evergreens herself at roadside stands in Hyde Park and in vacant lots in the city.[27]

This is not to say that Faye Emerson's entire time as a Presidential daughter-in-law was filled with scandal. She and Elliott made a very well-publicized, well-received, seven-week trip to the Soviet Union in 1946. The trip included an interview with Josef Stalin.[28] She was also a favorite of her in-laws. Franklin considered her a great listener and an even better talker, and Eleanor was a frequent baby sitter for Emerson's son Scoop.[29]

Emerson was back in the papers again, when, late one evening after a

Christmas dinner in 1948, she was hospitalized for thirty hours due to a slashed wrist. Newspapers reported that the wound was self-inflicted and followed a family argument. Though both Faye and Elliott denied any such reasoning, the office of the district attorney demanded an investigation anyway and ordered Elliott to appear for questioning.[30] The district attorney's office dropped the case a few days later.[31] "I had a headache and I went to the bathroom for an aspirin. I reached into the medicine chest and my wrist hit a razor blade," is how Emerson explained the whole incident in 1951.[32] All during this time, between her political globe-hoppings with her husband, Emerson was carving out a career for herself on radio. In 1949 she appeared regularly on the NBC program *My Silent Partner.*[33]

Emerson also kept busy doing occasional stage work. She made a much-ballyhooed debut on Broadway in May of 1948, in a production of *The Play's the Thing.* While critics couldn't deny her "likable charm,"[34] reviews of the play, and her performance, were definitely mixed, leaning toward negative.[35] Still, the show ran for six months.[36] Emerson continued to make theater appearances until the end of the 1950s, sometimes in New York, sometimes in Washington, and sometimes on tour.[37]

Faye Emerson seemed a natural for early television. Her combination of easy charm, blonde hair, Hollywood good looks, social connections, and practical "good sense" made her perfect for a medium that, in its early days, tried to bridge the gap between the cultural appeal of live drama and the mass popularity of roller derby and wrestling.

In 1948 Emerson made her debut on television (after an earlier one-time appearance that same year on *Tonight on Broadway*), and it was largely accidental and largely due to her husband. Elliott asked her to join him for one day on a TV quiz show he was taking part in, a show titled *Who Said That?* in which panelists tried to identify quotations by current newsmakers. By all accounts, Emerson was a sensation. She knew most of the answers to most of the questions and upstaged her husband so greatly she felt the need to apologize on air: "He's busy and I have plenty of time to read the papers."[38] Also, on NBC for one month in 1948, Emerson began the first of her regularly running programs, hosting *Paris Cavalcade of Fashions*, showing and narrating films about the latest French fashions.[39]

Faye Emerson's real television career, though, began in 1949 when actress Diana Barrymore became ill and the producers of an as-yet-to premiere, fifteen-minute, Monday night talk show on CBS asked Emerson the Thursday before to step in. She did. So was born on October 24, 1949, the local one-night a week (later three times a week) chat program, *The Faye Emerson Show.* By March the program was being broadcast nationally.[40] Though the show aired at eleven o'clock at night, and network executives doubted a higher rating than ten could ever be achieved, Emerson's show soon began delivering a twenty-two,[41] approximately one fifth of the close-to-midnight audience.[42]

One month later, Emerson began hosting another talk show, this time on NBC. It was called *Fifteen with Faye.* She thereby became the first individual ever to host two programs on two different networks at the same time.[43]

What made Faye Emerson so impressive on the small screen was a subject of frequent debate during the height of her TV fame. Many believed it had to do with her trademark, low-cut, revealing designer dresses. Emerson was always a sharp dresser. She was named to the International Best Dressed List in 1950, positioning herself between the likes of the Duchess of Windsor and Babe Paley, the wife of CBS czar Bill Paley.[44] When she came to television, she brought her off-the-shoulder evening gowns with her. Her décolletage—nothing by 1990s standards and really more suggestive than revealing by 1950s standards—caused a slight cause célèbre. One wit went so far as to say that Faye Emerson was the one who put the "V" in TV.[45] The topic became such good copy that *Life* magazine, in 1950, was compelled to do a photo rundown of television's other low-necked ladies, including, besides Emerson, Rebel Randall, Maggie McNellis and Arlene Francis.[46] Finally, talk of Faye Emerson and her dresses became so extensive that she brought the subject to an audience vote on her show. In the final counting, ballots ran ninety-five percent in Emerson's favor to keep her dresses as they were.[47] She explained her dress code this way:

> At eleven at night, I'd usually been to a party so I wore evening gowns.... When I'm going out, I dress up. When I'm not, I wear street clothes. You wear what is proper at the proper time.[48]

Mostly, though, as Val Adams in the *New York Times* reported in 1950, Emerson's real skill on TV came from something far less apparent:

> She just sits and oozes personality.... [She has a] female charm presented with careful, lady-like discretion.... She lays no claim to being a wit or a good storyteller, but conversationally she's in the upper brackets.[49]

Emerson's own theory dealt with how she addressed her audience: "I never talk up to them or down to them, but only as a friend."[50]

The video exposure generated by Emerson's two shows soon made her, at age 32, the most recognizable and busiest woman on television. Even today, the sight of Faye Emerson sitting behind a desk or table, her five-foot four-inch frame draped in a flowing evening dress, her hair gathered in a bun, "too wonderful" earrings dangling from her lobes, and a cigarette in hand is one of the most enduring images from early television. She was such a common sight that at one time TV critic John Crosby of the *New York Times* floated a theory that there must really be five of her.[51] Besides her own weekly shows, she was a frequent guest on others, either as herself or as an actress in live play productions. Emerson appeared so regularly on quiz shows that *Cue* magazine labeled her the "peripatetic panelist."[52] She was a frequent contributor to such early quiz shows as *Who Said That?* and *Leave It to the Girls.* She usually did more than just look pretty on all of them. In one day on two different quiz shows she answered questions dealing with such diverse topics as the Marshall Plan, the gold standard, and the reason for the high price of pork chops. On *Who Said That?* she held the highest average for accuracy, beating out the other panelists, including many newspapermen and radio commentators. Emerson said, "The thing with me is that I have a mind cluttered up with a lot of trivia that doesn't amount to a damn."[53]

Emerson was also a frequent guest host for the likes of Garry Moore, Dave Garroway on *Today,* and Edward R. Murrow on *Person to Person.*[54] She even found time to write a syndicated TV column three times a week for the United Press wire service, where, much as she did on the air, she chatted briefly about television happenings and figures. "I reserve the right to be peevish but not petty," she said in her kick-off article.[55] In her first article she lamented the high volume of real-life sob story game shows on the air, and in another she sang the praises of early television newswoman Pauline Frederick.[56]

At the height of all this, Emerson was taking home a regular salary of $60,000 a year.[57] One year that figure jumped to $200,000.[58] Still, Emerson's real fame came from her two weekly, late-night talk fests. Though each week's program varied a great deal from the one preceding it, the general scheme was to have two or three different guests from different areas of society and show business come and shoot the breeze with Faye for a few minutes. The show, though, began inevitably with Emerson talking about herself. She would tell her audience, a group she felt very close to, about her experiences over the past week—what parties she attended, who she had lunch with, where she planned to go this coming week. Then she'd bring on her first guest— perhaps an author with a new book, a film star with a new movie, or an actor appearing downtown.[59] Philip Hamburger, in his *New Yorker* review of Ms. Emerson's show, perhaps said it best, "Their [the guests's] sole object in appearing is to put in a plug for themselves."[60]

A later show garnered equally poor reviews. In this one, Emerson, with the help of guest star Zachary Scott, demonstrated to her viewers the proper way to ride in a New York taxi: know where you want to go, and enter the door nearest to you.[61] A later idea for a show was based on the idea "Wouldn't it be wonderful if all of the viewers knew how to make Swiss cheese?"[62]

In Emerson's view anything was fodder for discussion—from earrings to books to parties to people, anything "as long as it's not too heavy" and not too personal: "I don't rap people because I don't think I'm in a position to do so."[63]

Viewers frequently wrote to Emerson asking advice. She often answered these letters on the air. Once, she had on her show a group of high school journalism students who had requested an interview with her.[64]

Deb Myers's 1950 article in *Cosmopolitan* tried to sort out the average Faye

Emerson day: typically, Emerson would go to bed between three and four A.M. and would get up later that morning somewhere between ten and eleven. After a quick breakfast of toast and coffee, she read a few newspapers, dictated a few letters, talked on the phone, and went through her mail and lists of television requests, deciding which to accept and which to turn down. Lunch would be taken out, often at the Waldorf where she would hobnob and chat with whoever was there (bandleader Kay Kayser, Supreme Court Justice William O. Douglas). Then she'd go to the offices of Faye Emerson Enterprises and then to rehearsal where her own ideas and cries of "I don't like this!" affected production. She usually got her way. After dinner and changing into whatever ball gown suited her, Emerson would go to the studio where she would tape the show she was to do that night.[65] Tapes of her show were then shipped to forty-eight stations around the country.[66] After work, Emerson would most often top off the day by attending a party beginning at midnight or so.[67]

On January 17, 1950, in the midst of her TV fame, Faye Emerson was awarded a quickie Mexican divorce from Elliott Roosevelt. It was awarded on grounds of mental cruelty; charges that went unrebutted by Roosevelt.[68] The press had anticipated the divorce for some time. Emerson maintained that the couple's parting of the ways was "friendly."[69] Her divorce in Mexico was an event dutifully covered by *Life* magazine, which ran a full-page photo spread of Emerson attending a bullfight in Cuernavaca after the divorce decree was signed.[70] She said after the divorce, "Don't think it was easy giving up a mother-in-law like her."[71] By all accounts, Emerson didn't. Mrs. Roosevelt often said Emerson was her favorite daughter-in-law, and even after the divorce, Mrs. Roosevelt often invited Emerson and her son to visit her for extended periods, something that did not always sit well with Elliott and his new wife.[72]

In typical Emerson fashion, Mrs. Roosevelt's favorite ex-daughter-in-law wasted little time, announcing her engagement to musician and TV bandleader Lyle C. "Skitch" Henderson live on the air on November 8, 1950; she made the announcement so publicly, she told her audience, "because you are all my friends." It was believed she was the first to ever announce an engagement on television.[73]

In 1951 Emerson took on the hosting duties of what was at that time one of the most expensive shows ever produced, *Faye Emerson's Wonderful Town*. In this weekly live series, Emerson was flown around to different cities, which she profiled for the television cameras—interviewing important leaders, visiting famous sites. The show lasted for more than a year but found little critical favor. Robert Lewis Shayon in the *Saturday Review* gave the show a major thumbs down, calling it "the most unsatisfactory experience I have had in a long time."[74] Though he acknowledged that Faye Emerson possessed more "synthetic bounce to the ounce" than anyone else on television, he did not much care for her trip to Minneapolis or for the program's sponsor's tie-in, "Pepsi-Cola: cool and sparkling as a lake in Minnesota."[75]

Faye Emerson and husband, Skitch Henderson, had their own show for one year beginning in 1953, titled appropriately enough *Faye and Skitch*.[76] They divorced in 1958, ending the last of her three marriages.[77] In 1952 Emerson was the moderator for the series *Author Meets the Critics* and then for five years (1952–58) held court as a regular on *I've Got a Secret*. She was a panelist on the quiz show *Masquerade Party* from 1958 to 1960.[78] She continued to be a popular participant on panel shows and to work in weekly dramatic anthologies, including the *US Steel Hour*, until 1963.[79]

But by that time, Faye Emerson was rich and somewhat weary of show business.

In 1963 she sailed off for a year's vacation in Europe. Finding it to her liking, she seldom returned to the United States. She resided in Switzerland first and, later, from 1975, in Deya, Majorca, off the coast of Spain. It was there that she died of cancer at age sixty-five on March 9, 1993.[80]

Whatever it was that made Faye Emerson one of the first "personalities" created by the medium of television, it was special enough to make her a national household name, and a frequent household guest.

Today, few Emerson movies turn up on the late, late show or even on the all-night, all-movie classic cable channels. Even the concept of the television personality is little more than a distant memory. Except for a few individuals (often with very fleeting degrees of fame) Faye Emerson's kind does not exist anymore. But talk as a television staple still does, and, as in the early days of the medium, it remains largely in the control of women. Though their shows are very different from what Faye Emerson did, Oprah Winfrey, Sally Jessy Raphaël, Dinah Shore, and others have all followed in her footsteps to a certain extent. Emerson's closest counterparts today, though, would probably be the Joan Rivers or Kathie Lee Gifford types—sharply dressed, sharply witted TV talkers able to move effortlessly from fact to fluff, from serious to shtick. Nighttime talk has also become a TV norm. Emerson preceded them all, all the late-night, celebrity-filled talk feasts of Carson, Leno, and Letterman.

What survives of Faye Emerson's many hours of television is housed in libraries, many of those hours on fuzzy kinescopes. Her name is seldom heard today, and even if it is, it is usually only in regard to her semi-scandalous necklines. But in the beginning, as television was taking its first awkward steps and the public was becoming used to this new hearth in the corner of their living rooms, to thousands of Americans, television meant only one thing, one woman: fun, feisty, fabulous Faye.

Faye Emerson

| July 8, 1917 | Born in Elizabeth, Louisiana. |
| 1927 | Moved to California to mother's home from her father's home in Chicago. |

1941	Married William W. Crawford; gave birth to only child, William W. Crawford III, signed film contract with Warner Brothers studio; starred in first film, *The Nurse's Secret*.
1942	Divorced first husband William Crawford.
December 1944	Married Elliott Roosevelt.
March 1946	Left Warner Brothers and film acting.
Summer 1946	Staged successful good will trip to Russia with husband Elliott Roosevelt.
May 1948	Made first television appearance—guest spot on *Tonight on Broadway*.
November 11, 1948	NBC's *Cavalcade of Fashion* premiered. Faye Emerson served as hostess; first regular television assignment.
December 1948	*Cavalcade of Fashion* broadcasts ended.
October 24, 1949	*The Faye Emerson Show* premiered locally on CBS in New York.
January 17, 1950	Divorced Elliott Roosevelt.
March 15, 1950	*The Faye Emerson Show* aired nationally for first time on CBS.
April 15, 1950	NBC's *Fifteen with Faye* premiered. Emerson first person to star in two shows on two different networks at the same time.
August 1950	*Fifteen with Faye* aired last broadcast.
November 8, 1950	Announced engagement to Lyle C. ("Skitch") Henderson on weekly television series. Believed to be the first on-air announcement of its kind.
December 1950	Married Skitch Henderson.
June 15, 1951	CBS's *The Faye Emerson Show* rechristened *Faye Emerson's Wonderful Town*.
March 1952	Began acting as moderator for DuMont's *Author Meets the Critics*.
April 12, 1952	Final broadcast of *Wonderful Town* aired.
June 1952	Became regular panelist on *I've Got a Secret*; remained with show until 1958.
October 1952	Last appearance on *Author Meets the Critics* aired.
March 12, 1953	Acted as panelist on game show *Quick as a Flash*.
September 1953	Began writing nationally syndicated television newspaper column.
October 23, 1953	*Faye and Skitch* premiered.
February 25, 1954	Last episode of *Quick as a Flash* aired.
October 22, 1954	Final broadcast of *Faye and Skitch* aired.
Fall 1958	Served as regular panelist on *Masquerade Party*.
September 1960	Last episode of *Masquerade Party* aired.

September 1963 Made final television appearances.
Winter 1963 Left United States to live abroad.
March 9, 1993 Passed away in Deya, Majorca, Spain.

NOTES

1. Arthur Shulman and Roger Youman, *The Golden Age of Television* (New York: Bonaza, 1979), p. 51.
2. *Current Biography* (1951), p. 184.
3. Ibid.
4. Deb Myers, "Faye Emerson," *Cosmopolitan* (August 1950), p. 110.
5. Ibid., p. 25.
6. Ibid., p. 109.
7. Pete Martin, "The Blond Bombshell of TV," *Saturday Evening Post* (30 June 1951), p. 126.
8. Myers, p. 25.
9. Ibid., p. 111.
10. *Current Biography*, p. 184.
11. Martin, p. 126.
12. "Faye Emerson," *Variety* (16 March 1983).
13. Myers, p. 111.
14. Richard Lamparski, *Whatever Became Of...?* (New York: Crown, 1968), p. 30.
15. "Faye Emerson."
16. Martin, p. 126.
17. Myers, p. 111.
18. Ibid.
19. Julian Hartt, "Ceremony Performed in Ranger Station on Brink of Gorge," *Los Angeles Examiner* (4 September 1944), p. 1.
20. Martin, p. 126.
21. "Faye Emerson Quits Films to Be with Elliott," *Los Angeles Times* (4 March 1946).
22. Martin, p. 126.
23. Elliott Roosevelt and James Brough, *Mother R.* (New York: Putnam, 1977), p. 58.
24. Ibid.
25. Martin, p. 127.
26. Ibid., p. 24.
27. "Call Elliott in Faye's Wrist Slashing," *Daily News* (Los Angeles) (28 December 1948), p. 1.
28. John Kendall, "Faye Emerson, Actress, FDR Daughter-in-Law, Dies at 65," *Los Angeles Times* (11 March 1983), p. 3.
29. Lamparski, p. 30.
30. "Call Elliott in Faye's Wrist Slashing," p. 1.
31. "Roosevelt Case Dropped," *New York Times* (30 December 1948), p. 21.
32. Martin, p. 129.
33. *Current Biography*, p. 185.
34. "Faye and the Six Wise Men of Broadway," *Life* (24 May 1948), p. 85.
35. Martin, p. 129.
36. Val Adams, "Glamour Girl of the Television Screen," *New York Times* (19 February 1950), p. 11.
37. "Faye Emerson."
38. Joan King Flynn, "How Faye Emerson Got Into Television," *Los Angeles Examiner* (1 April 1951), p. 25.

39. Tim Brooks and Earle Marsh, *The Complete Directory to Prime Time Network TV Shows* (New York: Ballantine, 1981), p. 578.

40. Ibid., p. 247.

41. Martin, p. 129.

42. Flynn, p. 25.

43. Alex McNeil, *Total Television* (New York: Penguin Books, 1980), p. 240.

44. "Faye Joins List of Ten Best-Dressed," *Daily News* (Los Angeles) (1 January 1951).

45. "Transition," *Newsweek* (21 March 1983), p. 82.

46. "Faye's Décollete Makes TV Melee," *Life* (10 April 1950), p. 87.

47. Ibid.

48. Flynn, p. 25.

49. Adams, p. 11.

50. Flynn, p. 25.

51. Myers, p. 109.

52. *Current Biography*, p. 185.

53. Myers, p. 37.

54. Lamparski, p. 31.

55. John Crosby, "Faye Emerson's Now Columnist," *Daily News* (Los Angeles) (12 September 1953), p. 16.

56. *Current Biography* (1954) (Pauline Frederick), p. 293.

57. Myers, p. 34.

58. Flynn, p. 25.

59. Brooks and Marsh, p. 247.

60. Philip Hamburger, "Shall We Dance?," *New Yorker* (8 April 1950), p. 101.

61. Jack Gould, "Faye Emerson Officiates on New Video Program on CBS—Cab Driver, Bill Green, Guest," *New York Times* (29 September 1950), p. 54.

62. Martin, p. 129.

63. "Not Too Heavy," *Time* (24 April 1950), p. 57.

64. Flynn, p. 25.

65. Myers, p. 109.

66. Martin, p. 129.

67. Myers, p. 109.

68. "Divorce to Faye Emerson," *New York Times* (18 January 1959), p. 33.

69. Ibid.

70. "Faye Sheds a Husband, Sees a Fight," *Life* (23 January 1950), p.39.

71. Myers, p. 111.

72. Martin, p. 129.

73. "Faye Emerson Announces Betrothal on TV Show," *Los Angeles Times* (8 November 1950).

74. Robert Lewis Shayon, "Two Bravos and One Raspberry," *Saturday Review* (11 August 1951), p. 32.

75. Ibid.

76. McNeil, p. 240.

77. Kendall, p. 3.

78. Brooks and Marsh, p. 278.

79. "Faye Emerson."

80. Kendall, p. 3.

Pauline Frederick

The sight of a woman reporting on, or anchoring, a television newscast (or the sound of a woman's voice on the radio airwaves) is no longer considered unusual. Broadcast journalism, today, is full of female reporting superstars: Connie Chung, Andrea Mitchell, Jane Pauley, Diane Sawyer, Lesley Stahl, and others have all occupied places in front of the camera on the network nightly news. Their positions are thanks mostly to the United States Government and the Federal Communications Commission, which, in 1971, made affirmative action an important condition for broadcast station license renewal.[1] The women listed above have since continually referred to themselves as the "Class of 1972."

But to get to where they are they needed more than the US government. They needed the help of a group of earlier newswomen who pioneered the way. On the strength of their talent and toughness Marlene Sanders, Liz Trotta, Lisa Howard, Nancy Dickerson, Barbara Walters, and a few others all made it in the "man's world" of TV news before 1972, and one woman made it before all of them. She was Pauline Frederick, the first woman to work full-time in network television news.

Pauline Frederick was born on February 13, 1906 (some sources give 1908), in the coal mining town of Gallitzin, Pennsylvania. She was the second of three children born to Matthew P. and Susan Frederick. Her father was a postmaster and later an employee of the State Department of Labor.[2]

Though a self-described "ugly duckling" with allergies, buck teeth, and a height taller than most of the boys, she was, nevertheless, a good student and an avid reader.[3] While still in high school (after the family moved to Harrisburg) she put her love of writing to good use and worked as a reporter, detailing mostly society happenings for three local newspapers, the *Harrisburg Evening News*, *Patriot*, and *Telegraph*.[4] Covering such fluffy fare made her rethink journalism for a future career. Though neither of her parents were educated beyond the eighth grade, Frederick went off to the American University in Washington, D.C. — "when it was very new and very young" — at age seventeen. She was determined to get a law degree.[5] Frederick earned a bachelor's degree in political science and later, on a scholarship, a master's degree in international law. A history professor, however, advised her to "leave the law to others" and to go back to journalism. She did and later remembered that as the best decision she ever made.[6]

PAULINE FREDERICK

In 1931, lacking a few credentials but not chutzpa, Frederick struck on a plan to get news scoops and, hopefully, a job. Because few important men in politics at the time would be interviewed by a woman, she decided to interview the men's wives. She placed a call to the Czechoslovakian legation and asked to speak with the minister's wife. When the reporter-weary secretary asked where the piece would appear, Frederick responded, "That depends on the story I get."[7] She got the interview and later an interview with the wife of the ambassador of China.[8]

Frederick then sent the reports to the now defunct *Washington Star*. As the story goes, the editor of the paper thought that this Pauline Frederick was the silent film actress of the same name. Eager to gain publicity he hired her, only to find out later he had gotten the wrong Pauline. (The confusion about the two women with the same name plagued Pauline Frederick, the broadcaster, throughout her early career; often she received telegrams congratulating her on the ending of her retirement from public life.)[9]

Though not the Frederick he had wanted, the *Star*'s editor was so impressed by her writing that he bought both of the articles she offered and gave her a job churning out a weekly feature.[10] By the mid–1930s, Frederick was covering the State, War, and Navy Departments for the *United States News* (later renamed *US News & World Report*). Later, she worked for the North American Newspaper Alliance.[11] In 1938, with an eye on electronic communication, Frederick accepted a part-time job as an assistant to ABC radio commentator H.R. Baukhauge, helping him prepare his scripts. He gave her some advice she ignored: "Stay away from radio, it doesn't like women."[12]

Pauline Frederick's entrance into on-air broadcasting came in 1939, when NBC Radio's director of women's programs, Margaret Cuthhert, heard of Frederick's interviews with diplomats' wives and thought they would make a good radio feature.[13] She asked Frederick to record the interviews; the next week, the week after Hitler invaded Czechoslovakia, Frederick's talk with the wife of the Czechoslovakian minister was aired.[14] Pauline Frederick remained in Washington doing both newspaper and radio work for the next seven years.

Frederick's first big break as a broadcast reporter came in April 1945, when, again against the advice of employer Baukhauge, she set off as a war correspondent on a journalist's tour of North Africa, Asia, and China—nineteen countries in all.[15] She did her first overseas broadcast from Chungking, China, later that year. One of the events she covered was an all-male USO show—"The roughest thing I ever heard," she said in 1949.[16]

After the two-month tour, Frederick quit her job with Baukhauge to cover the Nuremburg trials. She freelanced for newspapers and ABC radio but was able to get on the air only once—when Hermann Goering took the stand and the first-string male reporter was busy doing something else.[17]

Despite Frederick's experience, and more than a few news coups, no network was then interested in hiring a woman reporter. NBC news and CBS news, the two giants in the field, both turned her down. In order to pay the bills, she went to work as a freelancer, covering women's stories for ABC.[18] One of Frederick's first, and most infamous, reporting jobs for ABC came when she was assigned to cover a special women's seminar titled "How to Get a Husband." She said later, "I don't think I learned anything from it, and I don't think the audience did either."[19] She was also asked to cover the shortage of nylon stockings and keep the female listening audience up-to-date on the ever fluctuating length of the Dior hemline.[20] She said of her experiences many years later:

> They just couldn't understand why I wasn't content to do women's news—fashion shows and that type of thing. I don't think they were trying to keep me down; they just felt the public wouldn't accept it at the time, and I'm not sure they weren't right.[21]

ABC also threw frequent travel junkets at Frederick, which the men—out covering "hard" news—were too busy to accept.[22] One of these junkets was in 1946, when she was the only woman—out of 135 male passengers—aboard a B-29 on a trip to Uruguay to cover the inauguration of that country's president. Not surprisingly, the Air Force did not much care for the presence of a woman reporter. Frederick responded to the Air Force's "no women" policy by informing them, "Relax, I'm not out to corrupt your men."[23] A second success story came that same year when she was sent to cover the last voyage of the Queen Mary as a troop ship. While on board Frederick was able to finagle an exclusive interview with General and Mrs. Eisenhower, who were along for the ride.[24]

Despite these successes at ABC, the network was not willing to hire Frederick full-time. Wanting to break into the broadcasting big leagues, she once again applied for work with the news divisions of NBC and CBS. She sent them copies of her interviews on "platters," 78 rpm records, the recording medium of the time.[25] She later obtained (and kept) a copy of the following memo from Edward R. Murrow, dated August 27, 1946:

> I have listened to the records submitted by Pauline Frederick. She reads well and her voice is pleasing, but I would not call her material or manner particularly distinguished. We have a long list of women applicants and, as you know, little opportunity to use them. I am afraid that Miss Frederick's name cannot be put very near the top of the list.[26]

Once again she was rejected by both networks.

Pauline Frederick's big break came when she was still freelancing for ABC in 1948. She was one of only two reporters in the ABC newsroom when two stories broke simultaneously: a trucking strike and the convening of the UN Council of Foreign Ministers. Since her editor feared violence at the strike, he sent Frederick off to the United Nations. Soon Frederick learned that if she uncovered exclusive stories at the United Nations, ABC would be forced to put her on the air.[27] She began to cultivate sources, sources that she would use for the rest of her career.

That same year Pauline Frederick made her television debut. "I got in that door because in those days the men didn't know any more about television than the women," she said.[28] A notice on a bulletin board at ABC informed reporters that the network would be televising the 1948 political conventions; anyone interested was asked to sign up.[29] By all accounts, Frederick was not interested. Her radio reporting career was just now taking off, and, additionally, she feared becoming known as a TV performer (and fueling continued confusion with the actress Pauline Frederick). Frederick thought herself a serious newswoman and saw no reason to change.[30] One of her bosses, Tom Vellotta, talked her out of it. He wanted someone to interview candidates' wives (and whatever female politician that could possibly be found) and considered her perfect for the job. Somewhat reluctantly, Frederick said okay.[31]

Frederick was promptly sent off to Elizabeth Arden to learn proper makeup techniques for television. Because no one at Arden knew for sure, they made her up for a still photography session and hoped for the best.[32] Frederick then went to Bonwit Teller to acquire clothes after management told her to avoid black, red, or white.[33] When she got to Philadelphia, where the convention was being held, she found that she was expected not only to apply her own makeup but also that of her interview guests, including California politician Helen Gahagan Douglas and Esther Stassen, wife of candidate Harold Stassen.[34]

The convention exposure gave a boost to Pauline Frederick's career. ABC agreed to hire her full-time, making her the first woman ever to work full-time for a US television network.[35] Soon she found herself reporting regularly on both ABC radio and ABC television. On average she appeared on six morning radio shows and on three weekly telecasts.[36] One of those telecasts included her own 15-minute television show, *Pauline Frederick's Feature Story.*[37]

In 1949 Frederick set off on a mind-boggling three-week trip covering the changes in Eastern Europe. *McCall's* magazine recounted her journey:

> She covered in New York the Jessup-Malik negotiations leading to the lifting of the Berlin blockade, took off the same day for Germany where she flew the airlift two ways, rode the first train into Berlin when the blockade was lifted, flew to Warsaw for a broadcast, from there to Southampton, on to Prague and then to Paris for the opening of the Council of Foreign Ministers meeting.[38]

In 1953 NBC hired Frederick away from ABC to continue her United Nations reporting. The UN was to remain her newsbeat at NBC for the next twenty-one years.[39] She became so identified with the United Nations that when UN Secretary-General Dag Hammarskjold died suddenly in an airplane crash, she received sympathy cards from concerned viewers.[40] In the 1960s the two most asked questions of UN tour guides were: "Where did Khrushchev bang his shoe?" and "Do you ever see Pauline Frederick?"[41] Many sightseers became disappointed when they found out she was not part of the planned tour.[42]

In 1956 Frederick was once again called on to cover the political conventions. According to reports, Frederick carried her reporting duties off well, yet some NBC executives did not believe she ad-libbed well enough to be assigned to cover future conventions.[43] She returned to her regular coverage of the United Nations, where future international conflicts and her handling of them proved her worth to the network. One of Frederick's first big scoops was her handling of the 1963 coup crisis in the African state of the Congo. She was on the air from the United Nations regularly from 8:30 P.M. to 3:30 A.M.[44] Then, after an hour of sleep, she was back on the air on the *Today* show at 5:45. She did a second newscast on NBC at 11 A.M. and then again at 4 P.M. That night she also took part in a taping of the news special *Emphasis.*[45]

Later events Frederick covered from the UN for NBC included the Korean War, the Mid-East turmoil, the Cuban missile crisis, and the Vietnam conflict.[46] Anchorman Chet Huntley summed up her work on the UN beat in 1963 this way: "[She is] our dependable right arm in sorting out the legalities, the propaganda, the nationalistic sensitivities and the international nuances which frequent the UN."[47]

Pauline Frederick was a tenacious, uncompromising reporter. Her regular work day began at 4:30 in the morning and usually ended around eight at night.[48] Once, while rushing to get a UN story involving the war between Pakistan and India on the air, she crashed into something and fell immediately to the ground. She picked herself up and hobbled into the studio where a nurse met her with an ice pack. She delivered the story with the pack pressed to her leg. Later at the hospital, she was told she had shattered the kneecap. She underwent surgery that evening.[49]

Once, to get a quote from a visiting Foreign Minister, Frederick bypassed barricades and police and knocked on his limousine window. "How does the United States look?" she asked after he lowered the glass and she pushed in her microphone. She got a quote to send back to the nightly news and nearly got her arm cut off when the window snapped shut.[50]

Pauline Frederick's first book, *Ten First Ladies of the World*, was published in 1967 by Meredith Press. In it, she profiled the lives of nine wives of world leaders, including Imelda Marcos and Lady Bird Johnson.[51]

In the late 1960s Pauline Frederick added yet another first to her life: she got married. There had never been enough time before. Frederick had approached her career with too much vigor and determination. She never let her personal life get in the way of her professional one: once she showed up in the newsroom in a formal black evening dress to update a story based on something she learned at a diplomatic dinner she had just attended.[52] Another time, she was hosting a dinner party in her home when the network called with some recent news about the Cold War. Needing a UN reaction, they phoned Frederick, who then phoned some of her sources and then broadcast her story over the phone while her dinner guests waited in the other room.[53] Additionally, Frederick had shied away from matrimony because of her inability to have children. She had undergone a hysterectomy while still a teenager.[54] On March 31, 1969, though, she walked down the aisle with Charles Robbins, managing editor of the *Wall Street Journal* and later the President of the Atomic Industrial Forum.[55] He died in August of 1989.[56]

Frederick was suppose to leave NBC in 1972 when she reached age sixty-five, NBC's mandatory retirement age, but she stayed. Frederick said in 1985:

> NBC decided to keep me on for another year or so because some of my friends over there thought there was no point in throwing me out on the ash heap, since I had been there for 21 years. [Plus] I was going on a very small salary, a pittance.[57]

NBC, however, finally retired Frederick in 1975, in a most unkind fashion. She was not contacted by the network but instead learned about her firing from reading the *New York Times*.[58] Ironically, the UN set aside that same year as the International Year of the Woman, yet for the first time in over twenty years, a woman was not among its on-air news correspondents.[59] Pauline Frederick, though, was not retired for long. She returned to the airwaves within the year, commenting on international affairs for National Public Radio. Radio had always been her first love; it was free of the glamour trappings of TV and allowed more time for background and analysis.[60] For a time on NPR Frederick hosted her own weekly, thirty-minute show on international affairs and foreign relations, *Pauline Frederick and Colleagues*.[61] In 1976 she moderated the televised presidential debate between President Gerald Ford and candidate Jimmy Carter in San Francisco—the first newswoman to ever perform that duty.[62]

Over the years her sure-footed, rational way of reporting acquired Frederick many awards and honors. She was a major hit on the public-speaking circuit where her fees, combined with her NBC salary, brought her an income of $60,000 a year.[63] She was the first newswoman to be named in the Gallup poll's list of most admired women, joining the likes of Jacqueline Kennedy, Eleanor Roosevelt, and Congresswoman Margaret Chase Smith.[64] She received the eleventh Alfred I. DuPont Award in 1953 for "meritorious service to the American people."[65] She received the George Foster Peabody Award (becoming the first newswoman to receive it) for her "outstanding work in the field of international understanding" in 1954.[66] In 1975 Pauline Frederick was named to the Hall of Fame of Sigma Delta Chi, the journalism professional society.[67] She also acquired during the course of her career honorary doctorate degrees in journalism, law, and the humanities from more than twenty colleges and universities.[68]

In 1980 Frederick received the Paul White Award for distinguished service to broadcast journalism from the Radio-Television News Directors Association, once again the first woman ever to be so honored. Previous winners of the award included Edward R. Murrow, Walter Cronkite, and Eric Sevareid.[69] She said in the course of her acceptance speech that "Ours [the job of broadcast journalists] is not to scare but to inform, not to speculate, but to analyze."[70] She was also the first woman to be elected president of the United Nations Correspondents Association.[71] She also won accolades from such diverse voices as Adlai Stevenson and poet Carl Sandburg, who valued her "rare solidus mind and spirit."[72]

Pauline Frederick left National Public Radio, and with it the field of broadcast journalism, in 1981, retiring to Sarasota, Florida. She was visiting relatives in Lake Forest, Illinois, on May 9, 1990, when she died of a heart attack. She was eighty-four.[73]

Though colleague and fellow news pioneer Marlene Sanders did not consider Frederick an "active feminist,"[74] Frederick was far too aware of the double standards of television news. Throughout her career she heard that women could not effectively report serious news because, as an ABC executive told her early in her career, "A woman's voice just doesn't carry authority." Frederick's response was, "I'll bet he never told that to his wife."[75]

Pauline Frederick often referred to the wall between female-dominated soft news and male-dominated hard news as "the iron curtain."[76] Her personal philosophy, though, drew no such lines:

> As I see it, news is news. It's about people and what they do. Taxes, war, peace affect women as much as men. There seems to be a feeling women can't understand or be interested in the more serious happenings, an assumption that news must be spoon-fed to women. I reject that idea because I reject that women are second-class citizens.[77]

In Frederick's early years, however, it was difficult to be the only woman in a world of men. She once referred to the sight of a woman reporter with a microphone and a camera crew as a "curiosity,"[78] as noticeable as "an elephant with a hat."[79]

She took on "looksism" in TV news as well: "If a man speaks on TV, people listen. But when a woman speaks, people look and if they like her looks, then they listen."[80] When reporting on the *Today* show she had to get up an hour earlier than her male counterparts to be made over by the make-up department.[81] She also kept her age a closely guarded secret so as never to be told she was "too old." She also put up with management's unending demands about her appearance. She said at one time:

> I got plenty of advice on how I should look. Management wanted me in navy colors with austere necklines; they insisted I lighten my dark brown hair.... They continually had my hair teased because they said I was too flat-headed.[82]

She waged one long battle (and lost) over the right to wear her eyeglasses on the air instead of the contact lenses the network insisted on.[83]

Pauline Frederick, though, did not let the mere matter of her gender stand in the way of an accomplished and respected career. She set the standard and the stage for generations of other newswomen. Soon after Frederick, women like Lisa Howard, Nancy Dickerson, and Barbara Walters were able to make a place for themselves in the world of broadcast journalism. Marlene Sanders, another early ground-breaker, said in 1988 that Pauline Frederick "was the only role model for people like me."[84] And a female network news executive said in 1976:

> The few women who were in television news proved to be outstanding and I think they really paved the way in a way that we really can't appreciate.... Pauline Frederick at NBC—they were knocking down those old barriers....[85]

A generation of women anchors and correspondents owe a part of their career to Pauline Frederick—the reporter and the pioneer—a woman who not only reported history but who made some herself.

Pauline Frederick

February 13, 1906	Born in Gallitzin, Pennsylvania.
1931	Landed first professional reporting job for *Washington Star*.
1939	Entered on-air broadcasting by reporting "women's features" for NBC radio.
1944	Ended affiliation with NBC radio.
1945	Made first overseas broadcast, from Chungking; covered Nuremberg trials.
April 1945	First "big break" in broadcasting; served as war correspondent on journalist's tour of Asia.
September 26, 1947	Adopted United Nations as regular news "beat."
1948	Began working as freelance reporter for ABC network.
June-July 1948	Covered political conventions for ABC television.
August 1948	ABC talk show *Pauline Frederick's Feature Story* premiered in New York.
Late 1949	Hired by ABC. First woman to work as a full-time reporter for a television network.
January 12, 1949	*Pauline Frederick's Feature Story* aired nationally for first time.
April 13, 1949	Last episode of *Feature Story* broadcast.
1950	Reported on Korean crisis from the United Nations.
October 1952	ABC premiered *All Star News*, news magazine, featuring Pauline Frederick.
June 1953	Left ABC for NBC.
August 1953	Covered national political conventions for NBC.
August 1956	Covered political conventions for NBC.
August 1963	Covered coup in Congo for network.
1967	Published book, *Ten First Ladies of the World*.
March 31, 1969	Married Charles Robbins, managing editor of the *Wall Street Journal*.
1975	Retired by NBC.
October 1976	Moderated presidential debates between President Ford and Governor Carter. First woman to ever perform that duty.
January 1977	Joined National Public Radio with own show *Pauline Frederick and Colleagues*.

1981	Left National Public Radio; retired from broadcast journalism.
August 1989	Suffered death of husband, Charles Robbins.
May 9, 1990	Passed away in Lake Forrest, Illinois.

NOTES

1. Barbara Matusow, *The Evening Stars* (New York: Ballantine, 1983), p. 181.
2. *Current Biography* (1954), p. 291.
3. Gay Talese, "Perils of Pauline," *Saturday Evening Post* (26 January 1963), p. 20.
4. Doris Willens, "Pauline Frederick: Only Woman Who...," *Editors & Publisher* (23 July 1949), p. 42.
5. Judith Gelfman, *Women in Television News* (New York: Columbia University Press, 1976), p. 31.
6. Gayle K. Yamada and David H. Hosley, "Pauline Frederick: Broadcast News Pioneer," *Communicator* (August 1990), p. 18.
7. "Spinster at the News Mike," *Newsweek* (27 October 1947), p. 66.
8. *Current Biography*, p. 291.
9. Willens, p. 42.
10. Ibid.
11. Eleanor Blau, "Pauline Frederick, 84, Network News Pioneer, Dies," *New York Times* (11 May 1990), sec. D, p. 18.
12. *Current Biography*, p. 291.
13. Yamada and Hosley, p. 18.
14. Ibid.
15. Ibid.
16. Willens, p. 42.
17. Yamada and Hosley, p. 18.
18. Marlene Sanders and Marcia Rock, *Waiting for Prime Time* (Chicago: University of Illinois Press, 1988), p. 8.
19. Blau, p. 18.
20. "She Scorns 'The Feminine Approach,'" *TV Guide* (4 May 1957), p. 21.
21. Yamada and Hosley, p. 19.
22. Sanders and Rock, p. 9.
23. Willens, p. 42.
24. Sanders and Rock, p. 9.
25. Ibid.
26. Yamada and Hosley, p. 18.
27. "She Scorns 'The Feminine Approach,'" p. 22
28. Myrna Oliver, "Pauline Frederick Dies at 84; Helped to Open Broadcast Journalism to Women," *Los Angeles Times* (11 May 1990), sec. A, p. 34.
29. Sanders and Rock, p. 9.
30. Ibid.
31. Ibid., p. 10.
32. Ibid.
33. Matusow, p. 79.
34. Gwenda Blair, *Almost Golden* (New York: Simon & Schuster, 1988), p. 79.
35. Sanders and Rock, p. 10.
36. Nancy MacLennan, "Only One of Her Kind," *New York Times* (5 December 1948), p. 15.
37. Willens, p. 42.

38. "Seven Women in Radio and TV Win the *McCall's* Mike," *McCall's* (May 1956), p. 75.

39. Oliver, p. 34.

40. Yamada and Hosley, p. 19.

41. Matusow, p. 181.

42. Talese, p. 21.

43. Yamada and Hosley, p. 19.

44. Talese, p. 22.

45. "Pauline Frederick Works Almost Non-Stop Covering UN Crises—With Little Time 'To Get Your Hair Washed for TV,'" NBC Biography (July 1960), p. 2.

46. Yamada and Hosley, p. 19.

47. Talese, p. 20.

48. Ibid., p. 22.

49. Mary-Ann Bendel, "Topic: Women on the Air," *USA Today* (14 January 1985), p. 9-A.

50. Talese, p. 21

51. Pauline Frederick, *Ten First Ladies of the World* (New York: Meredith Press, 1967).

52. "Pauline Frederick, 84; Veteran Broadcaster Helped Women in News," *Philadelphia Inquirer* (12 May 1990).

53. Talese, p. 20.

54. Yamada and Hosley, p. 19.

55. Gelfman, p. 135.

56. Blau, p. 18.

57. Bendel, p. 9-A.

58. Ibid.

59. Gelfman, p. 167.

60. Yamada and Hosley, p. 19.

61. "New from NPR," *Broadcasting* (17 January 1977), p. 41.

62. Oliver, p. 34.

63. Talese, p. 20.

64. Ibid.

65. *Current Biography*, p. 291.

66. "Seven Women in Radio and TV Win the *McCall's* Mike," p. 76.

67. Blau, p. 18.

68. Ibid.

69. "Highest Honor," *Broadcasting* (7 July 1980), p. 70.

70. Yamada and Hosley, p. 19.

71. Blau, p. D18.

72. Talese, p. 20.

73. Oliver, p. A34.

74. Marlene Sanders, letter to author (2 July 1991).

75. "Is the Lady Reporter 'For Women Only'?," *New York Mirror* (1 December 1960), p. 20.

76. "Seven Women in Radio and TV Win the *McCall's* Mike," p. 75.

77. "She Scorns 'The Feminine Approach,'" p. 23.

78. Gelfman, p. 32.

79. Matusow, p. 280.

80. Yamada and Hosley, p. 19.

81. Talese, p. 20.

82. Oliver, p. 34.

83. Gelfman, p. 50.

84. Sanders and Rock, p. 10.

85. Gelfman, p. 167.

Dorothy Fuldheim

While a handful of dynamic, intelligent women were making inroads into television with one of the three major networks, one woman was already cutting a wide path for herself in local television. While an even smaller handful of women were creating careers for themselves in the previously all-male world of broadcast journalism, one woman had already beaten most of her female (and male) counterparts to the news desk by seizing the top job of news anchor and news analyst. She was often affectionately called "Big Red" by friends—though never to her face—for her (dyed) mane of crimson colored hair and her mighty stature. She ruled Cleveland TV with her tart-tongued news commentaries, no-nonsense interviews, and her own brand of performance journalism for over thirty-five years, longer than any other individual in history, male or female. This woman, Cleveland's first lady of the airwaves, was Dorothy Fuldheim.

Dorothy Violet Snell was born on June 26, 1893, in Passaic, New Jersey. Her parents were of German and Russian ancestry. Their parents had been immigrants.[1] Though her father had a good job selling insurance, Dorothy remembered a childhood of extreme poverty. She remembered her mother making soup for the family out of apples and potatoes and wearing dresses made out of old curtains.[2] She remembered the death from strep throat of a baby brother who was buried by neighbors in an orange crate. There was no money to buy a coffin.[3]

Later, the family moved to Milwaukee in search of a better life but instead encountered more poverty. Years later, though, Dorothy Fuldheim held little bitterness: "Everyone ought to have been born poor. You have more respect for other people when you become successful."[4]

Despite the family's financial woes, the children were encouraged to indulge in artistic endeavors. An older sister became a dance prodigy, and a brother became a skilled musician, later working on MGM musicals.[5] Young Dorothy, a somewhat weak, sickly child, felt left out of the picture. Her father had a love for the English language and often took his daughter to courthouses to hear lawyers speak. On his suggestion, she attempted the writing of her first speech, which she later delivered to an all-male audience. "It was awful," she said: "those poor lodge members must have been bored to distraction."[6]

Dorothy Fuldheim got her first paying job at age twelve as a cash girl at the Boston Store in Milwaukee.[7] Saturdays alone she worked from 9 A.M. until 9 P.M. She earned $1.75 a week.[8] Though she dreamed of a career as an actress, Dorothy took her love of books and the English language and—like many young women at the time—studied to be a school teacher. Though money was tight, she was able to go to college and graduated from Milwaukee Normal College with an English degree in 1912.[9] She taught elementary school for three years before the lure of the stage became too great:

> I felt so confined. I had all this emotion within me and had to find a release for it. The stage seemed a natural outlet and, once I began acting, I was quite happy with my decision.[10]

Dorothy's first roles were at the Little Theater in Milwaukee.[11] Later she joined a touring repertory company and gradually rose from minor roles to leads in plays by Anatole France and Shakespeare. Once she even performed the role of Juliet in *Romeo and Juliet*. Though she forgot where she played the role, she later commented, "I must have made a lousy Juliet."[12] Dorothy even received a few film offers at the time:

> My stage training helped me considerably when I first appeared in front of the cameras. I never used a script or a teleprompter in my life. I learned my lines and I delivered them.[13]

In 1918 Dorothy was appearing in an antiwar play in Chicago titled *The State Forbids* when, after the performance, she was approached by social activist and reformer Jane Addams, who liked Dorothy's fiery temperament. Adams invited her to tea the next day at Hull House. Addams asked Dorothy to take part in a lecture she was organizing in Philadelphia. The lecture concerned the peace movement, and the guest speaker would be Hendrik Willen van Loon. "I told her I didn't know anything about speaking or what to say about peace. But she insisted I was just the speaker she needed," Dorothy remembered.[14] Though unsure about public speaking, Dorothy accepted the offer. Addams gave her one week to prepare. Dorothy said many years later:

> I don't think I added much fire to the proceedings, but I certainly added to the confusion. I really didn't know what I was doing. I wasn't dumb, but I was ignorant of many things that were taking place in the world at that time.[15]

Nevertheless, that speech launched Dorothy on a very busy and lucrative career as a lecturer.[16] In the beginning she charged $10 per speaking engagement.[17] Often she was flown around the midwest from engagement to engagement in open cockpit airplanes.[18] Eventually she began to travel nationally, giving speeches as far away as Texas.[19] Dorothy encountered many difficult audiences during her travels; men frequently groaned when they saw a woman take the podium.[20]

DOROTHY FULDHEIM

That same year, 1918, in Milwaukee, Dorothy married the first of her two husbands, Milton H. Fuldheim, a lawyer. She gave birth to her first and only child, also named Dorothy, in 1920. Not long after, the Fuldheims settled in Cleveland, a frequent performing spot for Mrs. Fuldheim.[21]

Fuldheim's lecturing continued to gather attention. She shocked early audiences with her fiery temperament, her views in favor of women's rights and birth control, and, her fulminations against public utilities.[22] Soon she was commanding audiences of 2,000 or more.[23] "I have a dramatic sense. I can dramatize any story. I'm honest. I'm exactly as I sound. I'm a person, and people can identify with that," Fuldheim said.[24] During her twenty-year career as a speaker, Fuldheim delivered more than 3,500 addresses.[25] In 1927 she accepted an offer from the Liberal Women of Wisconsin to become their mouthpiece at the Wisconsin legislature. For the next year Fuldheim spoke at labor institutes and Wisconsin universities, stressing the fact that arbitration was the next step in evolution.[26]

To ferret out topics for her lectures, Fuldheim often traveled the globe. In Europe, in 1932, she obtained one of the news scoops of the century. She interviewed Adolf Hitler in Munich just before he came to power. "I spoke German and he didn't know I was Jewish," Fuldheim said. "I just walked up to him and began asking questions."[27] One of those questions concerned why Germany lost World War I. Unfortunately, Fuldheim did not possess a recorder and his answer was lost to history.[28] After the interview and further travels in Germany, Fuldheim sent back a report to the States saying that this young politician would reduce Europe to ruin: "I said he was the Samson of Europe, pulling it down by its bootstraps,"[29] Fuldheim remembered, "The US newspapers said I was a hysterical woman."[30] When Fuldheim returned to the states, she lectured often about the rise of Hitler and the evil she thought he represented. News of her views somehow got back to Germany, which immediately canceled her visa, preventing her return.[31] Fuldheim had a similar experience with Italy after she interviewed Mussolini.[32]

In 1934 Fuldheim was able to arrange an interview with Englebert Dollfuss, the Austrian Chancellor. "He predicted at that meeting he would never be assassinated," Fuldheim said. "We had tea and ate in the room where he was later murdered." He was killed by the Nazis the day after the interview.[33]

Dorothy Fuldheim began her career in broadcasting in 1944 as a news commentator for WJW radio in Cleveland.[34] The radio job guaranteed more money and less travel than her public speaking work, so Fuldheim jumped at the chance. In 1947 the Brotherhood of Railroad Trainmen enlisted her to do a weekly ABC network radio show as a news commentator.[35] Fuldheim flew to New York City once a week to broadcast a radio show sponsored by the Brotherhood after the airing of the Metropolitan Opera. Sometimes, "when the opera ran late, when Wagner played," they did not make the air at all.[36]

In 1947 WEWS, Scripps-Howard Broadcasting Company's first TV property and the first television station between Chicago and New York, was about to hit the airwaves. Based on her local notoriety, WEWS hired Dorothy Fuldheim two months before they went on the air to be their nightly newscaster.[37] This assignment made Dorothy Fuldheim television's first female news anchor and, possibly, TV's first news commentator, male or female.[38] Fuldheim was offered the job after she was spotted one day by the station manager sashaying along in a large hat and carrying a parasol. "He thought I was innovative," Fuldheim said later.[39]

WEWS began broadcasting on December 17, 1947, with Dorothy Fuldheim doing straight news and commentaries mixed in with the occasional interview.[40] "I charged $5,000 for the year and they questioned me as though I was out of my mind," Fuldheim said, "They expected me to ask for $25,000."[41] Part of Fuldheim's TV job also included hosting one of the first live variety series, *The One O'Clock Club*. The show was sponsored by a local brewery, the

Duquesne Beer Company, and although she did not drink, Fuldheim signed off with "Have a Duke" every night for over fifteen years.[42] It is the longest single sponsorship of a show in television history.[43]

When Dorothy Fuldheim began her television career with WEWS, she was already 54 years old. Though she was at an age when many would start thinking about retiring, Dorothy Fuldheim was just beginning.

During her early days on TV Fuldheim staged the first television event of its kind when she invited labor and management from a transit dispute to settle their disagreements on her show.[44] The broadcast averted a strike. "There had been no precedent for a broadcaster to take such an action, and I was considered a freak. I didn't know how closed [television] was, I just did it," Fuldheim related later.[45]

Fuldheim anchored the news show alone for ten years before being promoted to doing only news commentary and interviews.[46] Fuldheim's interviews read like a who's who of the twentieth century. Besides interviewing every president from FDR to Ronald Reagan,[47] she also sat down for talks with Pope Pius XII, Albert Einstein, Dr. Benjamin Spock, Edward R. Murrow, Dr. Martin Luther King, Madam Chaing Kai-shek, Charles Laughton, Cecil B. DeMille, Helen Hayes, Margaret Chase Smith, union leader Jimmy Hoffa, Jane Fonda, Senator Hubert Humphrey, and others. Hers was one of only two American interviews ever granted by the Duke of Windsor. Fuldheim remembered that interview:

> The Duke was very pleased with the outcome. He said to me, "Do you do this often?" And I said, "Well, yes, everyday." He wanted to know why. [I said,] "To pay the rent, sir."[48]

Fuldheim's favorite subject, however, was Helen Keller:

> She never saw any sunshine, never saw a smile, never heard the ripple of water, the sound of music, and yet this woman understood everything. It was a moment of emancipation from the senses that left me awed.[49]

Fuldheim was also famous for her in-depth book reviews, a Fuldheim favorite and specialty. Fuldheim more or less acted out the characters of the book she was critiquing; friend and frequent on-air coworker Bill Gordon has said, "There are book reviews and there are book reviews, but a Dorothy Fuldheim book review was a show."[50] On average she delivered three book reviews a week. "I can read a book in one night," she said, "I read diagonally."[51]

Many of her commentaries drew such response over the years that WEWS began to make reprints available to the public. Her most popular was titled "An Ode to the House I Live In on My Eighty-Sixth Birthday." It was a metaphor for the human body as a structure surviving rain, snow, anguish, and pain.[52] After Fuldheim delivered it, the station received more than 25,000 requests for copies.[53]

Fuldheim's workday usually began around 6:30 A.M. when she would have breakfast (consisting only of gingersnaps) and would select one of her 175 dresses. She read until 9:30, when a chauffeur-driven car (paid for by her) came to pick her up and deliver her to WEWS studios. For an hour Fuldheim would look over wire copy and newspapers and then greet her guests for that day's program. Her show was usually taped between 10:45 and 11:15. Each Wednesday at noon she turned her attentions to the lovelorn, taking phone calls from viewers and answering their questions live on the air.[54]

After the taping Fuldheim usually lunched on chocolates or a sandwich from a neighborhood restaurant. Afternoons were filled with dictation and correspondence. She answered fan mail and prepared the two commentaries she was to do that day. At 6 P.M., Fuldheim was back in the studio to deliver her first commentary of the day. The second would be taped to air on the news at 11.[55] On average she did ten such news commentaries a week. Fuldheim said, "I average four good ones and six lousy ones. I know how they rate once they go on the air."[56] By the end of her career Dorothy Fuldheim had written and broadcast more than 13,000 commentaries,[57] most of them steering clear of crime issues—a topic she considered sensational.[58] Fuldheim said, "My greatest trouble is finding two different subjects a day. It exhausts my intellectual resources."[59]

Over the years Fuldheim also found time to author four books: a full autobiography, *I Laughed, I Cried, I Loved* in 1966; a collection of remembrances, *A Thousand Friends* in 1974; a meditation of the Middle East, *Where Were the Arabs?* in 1967;[60] and in 1976, *Three and a Half Husbands*, a biographical novel about her Auntie Mame–like Aunt Molly who, over the course of her prefeminist life, buried three different mates all within the first year of marriage, leaving her, in the process, with nine stepsons to raise.[61]

Throughout Dorothy Fuldheim's workday, her office phone rang nearly none stop. She employed no secretary to screen her calls, and every call received the same hello: "This is Dorothy Fuldheim, how may I help you?"[62] Sometimes the callers were viewers offering compliments. More often than not, though, they were viewers nearing the end of their rope and feeling they had no one to turn to but Dorothy. Her lengthy career in the city gave her a vast working knowledge of available social programs and resources with which she could help people.[63] For many years her name and home phone number were even listed in the Cleveland area phone directory.[64]

Fuldheim usually left the studio around 7:30 P.M., just in time to be driven to that night's speaking engagement.[65]

Along with her commentary work Dorothy Fuldheim frequently traveled the world, reporting on important stories and meeting with world leaders. Her biggest news coup—and the one that attracted the most national interest—occurred in 1955, when she traveled to Hong Kong to interview two brainwashed American hostages just released by Red China. When Fuldheim heard the two Americans had taken up residence at the YMCA, she rushed to the scene. On arriving she found dozens of newspapermen already there, but of all of them only Fuldheim had brought a tape recorder. She got the interview (and a recording of it) and the world scoop.[66] The recently released men (neither of whom had ever been employed by the US government) denounced the United States, praised the qualities of Communism, and "confessed" to being spies for the United States. Fuldheim remembered, "I asked them whether they were Communists. 'Oh, no,' they told me. 'We are not good enough to be.'"[67] The tape of that interview now resides in the Library of Congress. Fuldheim received the National Overseas Press Club award that year for her work.[68]

Though she was considered Cleveland's First Lady and their undisputed "Queen of TV," not everyone was a fan. Maurice Condon, in a *TV Guide* article in 1966, called her the woman Clevelanders most loved to hate. One newspaper critic had previously summed up her effect on TV viewers this way:

> Not all viewers like her and many seldom agree with her. They watch the show in fixed fascination, much the same as a holdup victim keeps his eye on the muzzle of the gun.[69]

Concurring with her reputation for being both loved and loathed, Fuldheim recalled the following story for that interview:

> I left the station late one evening, [and] a woman attacked me with a hammer. Fortunately, some of the station personnel came to my aid. As they took her away, poor woman, she was shrilling that God had ordered her to destroy Dorothy Fuldheim and Arthur Godfrey. It was rather flattering, really, to get top billing over Mr. Godfrey.[70]

High on the list of persons who disliked Dorothy Fuldheim would have to be 1960s radical and alumnus of the Chicago Seven, Jerry Rubin. Fuldheim had one of her most famous "interviews" with him in 1970. The interview was barely two minutes old when Rubin began speaking about the social pluses of revolution and free sex and referring to the police as "pigs." After he asked Fuldheim if she had ever tried "pot" and attempted to show a nude photo on the air, Dorothy Fuldheim lost her usual cool. She slammed the book he had written down on the counter in front of her and ordered him to leave. "Out!" she yelled, "The interview is over. Get off my show, just get out."[71] The show proceeded with Queen Farida of Egypt. After the interview ran, Fuldheim received letters and flowers of support. She told Nancy Gray for *Ms.* in 1976, "I was sick of the subculture that was living off those who took care of the lighting and sewage."[72]

Fuldheim gained more attention—and caused greater controversy—that same year, 1970, after she condemned the killing of four students at Kent State by US National Guardsmen. During her speech on WEWS she broke down in tears. Fuldheim said after the incident:

I frequently am indignant over what people have to suffer, I show that indignation. When I returned from Kent I wept ... wept because part of the soul
of America was sullied by such useless killing.[73]

Letters of protest over Fuldheim's outburst came pouring into the station; 70
percent of them denounced her sympathy for those slain.[74] WEWS received
one letter stating that more students should have been killed.[75] Said Fuldheim:

I took so many calls—ninety-five percent against the students—that I became
jittery and stopped taking calls, but the letters came pouring in and I groaned
as bag after bag was delivered.[76]

Dorothy Fuldheim, herself, received several death threats, many of them serious enough to eventually warrant police protection.[77]

When the controversy peaked, Fuldheim offered her resignation to the
station. They refused to accept it.[78] Fuldheim reflected on the incident many
years later in a criticism of the robotic, stiff delivery of many newscasters:
"They report a murder in the same way they talk about applesauce."[79]

Dorothy Fuldheim never forgot the loyalty and support WEWS showed
her, and she regularly paid the station back by turning down offers from other
stations and national networks at much higher salaries. Fuldheim remembered, "[WEWS] took me when the thought of a woman in television news
was absurd, and the management has stood by me regardless of what stand
I've taken on issues."[80]

Her calm veneer broke once again after an incident took place at the
Solon Citizens League in 1980. Fuldheim was giving a speech when she was
hit in the face by a Reddi-Whip pie thrown by two members of the Revolutionary May Day Brigade who considered Fuldheim the "John Wayne of
Cleveland."[81] Said Fuldheim shortly afterward, "I thought everyone loved
me."[82] On a broadcast on the subject later, Fuldheim stopped just short of
asking for blood in retaliation for the attack. She later testified against the
two women charged in the incident, stating she sustained cuts from the pie
plate and an inflamed eye. The defendants were found guilty, and each
received $500 fines and sixty-day jail sentences.[83] A bodyguard hired by
WEWS accompanied Fuldheim on her speaking engagements for some time
after the incident.[84]

Dorothy Fuldheim's greatest personal blow occurred that same year when
her daughter, Dorothy Fuldheim II, died at age sixty.[85] The younger Dorothy
had enjoyed a brief career as an actress and TV personality but spent the
majority of her life teaching courses in Slavic languages at Case Western
Reserve University.[86] Dorothy Fuldheim I had also outlived her first husband, who died in 1952, as well as her second, William L. Ulmer, a Cleveland metals company executive, to whom she was married from 1953 to 1971.[87]

Dorothy II gave her mother one granddaughter, Halla, who became physically and mentally handicapped while still an infant.[88] The senior Fuldheim set up large trust funds to provide for her granddaughter's care long after both mother and grandmother died.[89]

Fuldheim never completely recovered from the loss of her daughter. In her usual way, though, she shared her grief with her viewers. Her commentary on her daughter's death delivered on December 1, 1980, was one of the most moving of her career:

> Her death has not only saddened me, but I will never be whole again.
>
> I told her daughter, Halla, my granddaughter, that we all have an appointment with God. My daughter received her summons last Monday. I told Halla that her mother was in heaven, and was free of all pain, and that someday she and I would join her.
>
> She said, "Will you be there?" I nodded. "And will God make you young again? ... Will my mother be without pain? ... And when I go to meet her, will I walk without braces and crutches?"[90]

To recover from the loss Fuldheim threw herself back into her work. In 1981, at age 88, she traveled to London to cover the royal wedding of Charles and Diana, to Egypt for the funeral of Anwar Sadat, and then to Ireland to interview the mother of IRA hunger-striker Bobby Sands.[91] Back in the states she quizzed Casper Weinberger on nuclear armaments.[92]

Just before her ninetieth birthday, Dorothy Fuldheim made national news when she signed a three-year contract with Channel 5 in 1983. Along with carrying her into her ninety-third year, the renewed contract also carried with it a "substantial" raise in salary.[93] She was never a pushover on contract renewal: "She drives a hard bargain," WEWS general manager Edward Cervenak once said.[94]

The attention from the deal gained such press around the country that Fuldheim was soon asked to appear on *Nightline* and *Donahue*. She was a five-time guest with Johnny Carson on the *Tonight Show*.[95] Later, Fuldheim signed a contract that would have kept her on the air until age 115.[96] Even at this time, very late in her life, Dorothy Fuldheim was still highly active, not only in the news department of WEWS but also in all the technical aspects of the station.[97] She also kept busy playing mother hen to TV crew and staff, in the words of one reporter, "fussing and clucking at them to guard their health."[98]

Dorothy Fuldheim conducted her last interview in 1984, with Ronald Reagan via satellite from Washington. She had earlier interviewed him when he was governor of California. She had said about him in 1982, "I thought he was phoney then and I think he is now."[99]

Fuldheim was never known for mincing words. Once during a commentary on an Arab oil embargo, Fuldheim asked: "Just who do those 'Sah-oo-dis' think they are?"[100] Such straightforward outspokenness won the hearts of Dorothy Fuldheim's Cleveland audience. Her broadcast viewership often tipped the quarter million mark.[101] In writing about Fuldheim's on-camera attitude reporter Barbara Kingsley noted:

> The dramatic gestures, the voice that trembles with indignation at the world's injustices, seems more suited for Shakespeare than the mundane business of daily television commentary.[102]

Yet that disposition is what kept audiences watching for over thirty years. She was, in the words of another reporter, "Flamboyant, witty and accessible."[103] Reporter Bill Barrett said of her in 1974, "[She's] full of passion and the itch for raising hell."[104] And a fan once said of her, "She has what many of her peers lack, courage and good taste."[105]

Fuldheim devoted herself tirelessly to charitable causes: heart disease, pro-Israel fundraisers, social welfare. Frequently, Fuldheim used her commentaries to come to the aid of her fellow citizens; she once campaigned for a wage raise for Cleveland postal workers.[106]

In mid–1984, shortly after presenting a commentary on WEWS, Dorothy Fuldheim suffered a stroke. Though she would go on to regain most of her mental and physical abilities, she retired soon after. She had been with WEWS for thirty-seven years.

She suffered a second stroke in 1985 and died of a third on November 3, 1989, at age ninety-six.[107]

Dorothy Fuldheim logged more on-camera television hours than almost anyone in history, locally or nationally, outlasting even Ed Sullivan.[108] Cleveland considered her its official first lady, its own homegrown natural wonder, and its greatest living monument.[109] By the time she hit her mid-eighties, Cleveland citizens and reporters could not say enough about her. One article said in part:

> Dorothy Fuldheim is Cleveland. She's the beautiful gardens, ... the executive officer, the man on the street. And whether you consider her a flaming liberal or one of the smartest women of our time, there's one fact that no one disputes. Dorothy Fuldheim is held dear to the hearts of Clevelanders.[110]

The Cleveland Press called her in 1980 "a remarkable and indomitable woman."[111] A rose, a scholarship fund, and a Cleveland theater all bear Dorothy Fuldheim's name.[112] In 1973 the Jewish National Fund Council of Cleveland established the Dorothy Fuldheim Forest in Israel.[113]

Barbara Walters noted in 1989 that Dorothy Fuldheim "was probably the first woman to be taken seriously doing the news." She added:

> She had verve, courage and personality. She showed that age need not be a factor when you have the expertise and the energy. Dorothy Fuldheim ... made us proud.[114]

A former colleague of Fuldheim's concurs:

> Of course she was a pioneer for women in television. But she did commentary when no male or female in the country was doing commentary. She had a capacity for interviewing people and a command of the language that doesn't exist any more.[115]

A record and a life like hers will not be soon repeated. Dorothy Fuldheim smashed the gender barrier, the women/news barrier, and the age barrier by simply being herself. She was a thinker and a dedicated journalist in tune with the times. Yet, somehow she was also ahead of her time, broadcasting out to a single city and embracing the world.

Dorothy Fuldheim

June 26, 1893	Born in Passaic, New Jersey.
1905	Obtained first job, as a cash girl at the Boston Store in Milwaukee.
1912	Graduated from Milwaukee Normal College with degree in teaching.
1915	Launched career as stage actress.
1918	Delivered speech at Hull House at request of Jane Addams; married Milton H. Fuldheim, lawyer.
1920	Had daughter, only child, also named Dorothy.
November 1927	Named spokesperson for Liberal Women of Wisconsin for one year.
1932	Interviewed Adolf Hitler in Germany.
1944	Obtained first job in broadcasting, as radio commentator for WJW in Cleveland.
December 17, 1947	WEWS, Cleveland television station, signed on the air; Dorothy Fuldheim hired as nightly newscaster.
1952	Suffered death of first husband, Milton Fuldheim.
1953	Married William L. Ulmer, Cleveland businessman.
February 1955	Interviewed recently released American POWs in Hong Kong; received National Oversees Press Club Award for interview.
June 1966	Published autobiography, *I Laughed, I Cried, I Loved.*
May 1970	Broadcast editorial denouncing student killings at Kent State.
January 1971	Suffered death of second husband, William L. Ulmer.
December 17, 1972	Celebrated twenty-five years on the air for WEWS.
November 1980	Suffered death of only child, Dorothy.

March 1983	Renewed contract with WEWS for three more years with substantial pay increase.
July 27, 1984	Suffered stroke; retired from WEWS and broadcast journalism.
May 1985	Suffered second stroke.
November 3, 1989	Passed away in Cleveland, Ohio.

NOTES

1. "The Non-Retiring Ways of a Nonagenarian Newswoman," *Broadcasting* (4 July 1983), p. 103.

2. Alan Seifullah and Mary Strassmeyer, "Dorothy Fuldheim, News Legend, Dies," *Cleveland Plain Dealer* (4 November 1989), sec. A, p. 2.

3. Maurice Condon, "She Keeps the Citizenry Seething," *TV Guide* (22 October 1966), p. 43.

4. Mary Strassmeyer, "A Monument Named Dorothy," *Sunday Cleveland Plain Dealer Magazine* (9 May 1976), p. 11.

5. Dorothy Fuldheim, *I Laughed, I Cried, I Loved* (Cleveland, OH: Cleveland World Press, 1966), p. 8.

6. Ibid., p. 10.

7. Ibid., p. 2.

8. Strassmeyer, p. 11.

9. "Dorothy Fuldheim," *Scripps-Howard News* (7 November 1983), p. 8.

10. William Hickey, "The Redhead Sets a Record," *Cleveland Plain Dealer* (1 October 1972), sec. F, p. 6.

11. "Lecturer Finds Dictatorships Equally Cruel," *Cleveland Plain Dealer* (5 October 1936).

12. Barbara Kingsley, "Bash to Honor Fuldheim," *Cleveland Plain Dealer* (21 June 1983).

13. Hickey, p. 6.

14. Nancy K. Gray, "Before Barbara Walters There Was Dorothy Fuldheim," *Ms.* (December, 1976), p. 43.

15. Hickey, p. 6.

16. Clintie Winfrey, "She Startled Clubwomen," *Cleveland Plain Dealer* (23 June 1939), p. 3.

17. Strassmeyer, p. 11.

18. Hickey, p. 6.

19. "The Non-Retiring Ways of a Nonagenarian Newswoman," p. 103.

20. Ibid.

21. Nancy Gallagher, "Here's Dorothy Fuldheim!," *Cleveland Press* (8 August 1959).

22. "The Non-Retiring Ways of a Nonagenarian Newswoman," p. 103.

23. Gray, p. 43.

24. Kingsley.

25. Seifullah and Strassmeyer, p. 2.

26. "Dorothy Fuldheim Was Forever Asking 'Why?,'" *Cleveland Plain Dealer* (27 November 1929), p. 9.

27. Strassmeyer, p. 11.

28. "The Non-Retiring Ways of a Nonagenarian Newswoman," p. 103.

29. Suzanne Larronde, "At 89, She's Still a TV News Queen," *Modern Maturity* (December 1982–January 1983), p. 58.

30. Harry F. Waters, "The First Lady of TV News," *Newsweek* (11 June 1979), p. 91.
31. Condon, p. 43.
32. Gallagher.
33. Charlotte Taubman, "Mike Maids," *Cleveland Press* (20 February 1954).
34. Russell Cook, "Dorothy Fuldheim's Activist Journalism and the Kent State Shootings," unpublished paper, E.W. Scripps School of Journalism, Athens, Ohio (1992), p. 7.
35. Gray, p. 43.
36. Ibid.
37. Hickey, p. 6.
38. Bob Seltzer, "Heart in Her Work," *Cleveland Press* (21 February 1975).
39. Waters, p. 91.
40. Gray, p. 43.
41. Ibid.
42. Ibid., p. 44.
43. WEWS News Release (25 January 1962), p. 1.
44. Gray, p. 43.
45. Ibid.
46. Cook, p. 1.
47. "The Non-Retiring Ways of a Nonagenarian Newswoman," p. 103.
48. Larronde, p. 58.
49. "The Non-Retiring Ways of a Nonagenarian Newswoman," p. 103.
50. Bill Gordon, "Dorothy," *Cleveland Magazine* (February 1990), p. 23.
51. Gallagher.
52. "The 'House' Dorothy Lives In—An Encore," *Cleveland Press* (26 June 1979), sec. A, p. 13.
53. "Dorothy Fuldheim," p. 10.
54. Gray, p. 45.
55. "Dorothy Fuldheim," p. 9.
56. Ibid.
57. WEWS News Release (11 March 1985), p. 1.
58. WEWS News Release (25 January 1962), p. 1.
59. Gray, p. 45.
60. "The Non-Retiring Ways of a Nonagenarian Newswoman," p. 103.
61. Cook, p. 6.
62. "Dorothy Fuldheim," p. 7.
63. Ibid., p. 9.
64. Robert Dolgon, "City's Grande Dame Going Strong at 81," *Cleveland Plain Dealer* (12 January 1975).
65. Strassmeyer, p. 9.
66. Gray, p. 44.
67. "Miss Fuldheim Returns Home," *Cleveland Plain Dealer* (6 March 1955).
68. "Congratulations," *Cleveland Plain Dealer* (2 March 1956).
69. Condon, p. 42.
70. Ibid., p. 43.
71. Gray, p. 45.
72. Ibid.
73. Strassmeyer, p. 6.
74. Dorothy Fuldheim, "Dorothy's First 25 Years Were the Hardest," *Cleveland Press* (13 July 1973), p. 25.
75. Waters, p. 91.
76. Cook, p. 13.
77. Ibid.
78. Seifullah and Strassmeyer, p. 2.
79. Strassmeyer, p. 7.

80. "Dorothy Fuldheim,"p. 8.

81. Jerry Kvet, "Fuldheim Pie Throwers Get 60 Days, $500 Fine," *Cleveland Press* (20 June 1980), sec. B, p. 5.

82. Cook, p. 2.

83. Kvet, p. 5.

84. Cook, p. 2.

85. Larronde, p. 58.

86. Strassmeyer, p. 9.

87. Seifullah and Strassmeyer, p. 2.

88. Gallagher.

89. Seifullah and Strassmeyer, p. 2.

90. Dorothy Fuldheim, "I would like to thank ...," WEWS Commentary (1 December 1980), p. 1.

91. "Dorothy Fuldheim," p. 7.

92. Larronde, p. 58.

93. William Hickey, "Dorothy Fuldheim Gets 3-Year Contract," *Cleveland Plain Dealer* (30 March 1983).

94. "Dorothy Fuldheim," p. 9.

95. Seifullah and Strassmeyer, p. 1.

96. "Dorothy Fuldheim," p. 9.

97. Bill Sammon, "Dorothy Fuldheim: The Woman Behind the Famous Face," *This Week* (Cleveland, OH) (3 September 1982), p. 6.

98. John J. Minch, "Decisive Dorothy Salts City TV," *Cleveland Plain Dealer* (15 July 1965).

99. Sammon, p. 30.

100. Mary Anne Sharkey, "The End of the Fuldheim Era," *Cleveland Plain Dealer* (4 November 1989), p. 6-B.

101. Larronde, p. 58.

102. Kingsley.

103. "Dorothy Fuldheim,"p. 7.

104. Ibid.

105. Cook, p. 2.

106. Julius Kerekes, letter to author (19 July 1991).

107. Seifullah and Strassmeyer, p. 1.

108. Waters, p. 91.

109. Strassmeyer, p. 5.

110. Sammon, p. 30.

111. "The 'House' Dorothy Lives In—An Encore," p. 13.

112. "Dorothy Fuldheim," p. 7.

113. Cook, p. 3.

114. Seifullah and Strassmeyer, p. 1.

115. Ibid., p. 2.

Betty Furness

If she had been just a pretty face with a certain way with refrigerators she would not be remembered today. But her unique brand of informative, soft sell (in the high-energy, hard-sell days of early television) made her a beloved, believable commercial spokeswoman, a national presence, a '50s media darling. Later, the same finesse and forthrightness that made her television's very first commercial spokesperson superstar would later take her to the upper echelons of government power, then back to television where she would pioneer an entire field of broadcast journalism. Over the years she encountered many critics and eventually silenced them all. She earned praise in every job she ever held (in advertising, politics, and journalism) and during her long, varied career was described, at one time or another, with such words as capable, reliable, direct, common-sensical, candid.

Her career was played out in front of the public and, except for an extended intermission in politics, always on television, where her mind-boggling longevity in a medium known for its short career spans made her one of its true originals. Her first regular television appearances were in 1945. Her last were in 1992. The life and career that book-ended the twentieth century's most influential medium belonged to Betty Furness.

Betty Furness was born Elizabeth Mary Furness on January 3, 1916, in New York City. Her father, George C. Furness, was a media pioneer himself, having created and produced radio's *The Everready Hour*. He also served as an executive for the Union Carbon and Carbide Corporation.[1] Her mother, Florence, was an ex-newspaper sketch artist and later an interior decorator.[2] Betty Furness had a very upper-class upbringing, living on Park Avenue and attending the Brearley School and Bennett Junior College in Middlebrook, New York (she never graduated).[3]

She was fourteen in 1930 when she landed her first job in front of a camera. Furness remembered, "Dad thought I should go out and get a job for the summer, so I summoned all the courage I could muster, and stormed the citadel of the great John Robert Powers—the head of Powers Models ... and to my surprise he hired me."[4] She worked two summers for Powers, posing for pictures, and earned a total of eighty dollars.[5]

Pert and pretty at five foot, five and a half inches tall and 105 pounds, well-educated and very well spoken, Powers picked Furness out of all of his girls to screen test for RKO movie studios in 1932. Though her only acting training had come in school productions, Furness, accompanied by her mother, flew to California that same year to test for the movies.[6] She was quickly signed by the studio. She appeared in her first film in 1932—a run-of-the-mill western titled *Renegades of the West*—while taking her senior year of high school on the studio lot.[7] Later, Furness would be put under contract to MGM.[8]

Author John Springer has described Furness's acting style—indeed, her persona—as too "brisk and efficient" for the froth she usually found herself cast in.[9] Of the more than thirty-five films she made in her five years in Hollywood, only two have really endured: the first production of *Magnificent Obsession* (1935) and *Swing Time* (1936), where Furness was one-third of a love triangle with Fred Astaire and Ginger Rogers. (By closing credits, not surprisingly, Furness was the odd girl out.) Years later Furness assessed the bulk of her screen work with straightforward disdain; "minor disasters" she called them.[10]

Dissatisfied with the work being offered her in motion pictures, Furness took to the stage. Her first stage role was in 1937 in a west coast production of *Golden Boy,* directed by Stella Adler. She got fine notices in the play and would continue doing stage and stock work for the next several years. She would go on to tour in versions of *My Sister Eileen* and *The Doughgirls*.[11]

At twenty-one, Furness entered the first of her three marriages. Johnny Green was a conductor and composer, the writer of "Body and Soul"; he and Betty were married on November 26, 1937.[12] Furness's only child, Barbara (nicknamed Babbie), was born in 1940. Furness stayed out of acting for a short time after Barbara's birth, but, she said of her marriage later, "It was always understood I would work."[13]

She and Green divorced in 1943.[14] (Furness would later marry radio announcer Hugh Ernst in 1945. He died, leaving Furness a widow, in 1950).[15]

Acting roles on stage and screen were not easy to find after her divorce from Green. For a time she went to work in designer and friend Don Loper's new LA couture shop. She protested at first that she didn't know anything about selling. He replied, "You're an actress, aren't you? Well, play a saleslady."[16] Still, that role was short-lived. To "get back to work," Furness and daughter left for New York in the mid-1940s, where Furness intended to try her hand at the Broadway stage.[17] But after being out of the public eye for a while, and out of New York for several years, Furness found getting work an uphill climb. "Nobody cared," she said in 1953. "My name was completely dead."[18]

Furness stated in a Westinghouse bio in 1957, "It was far from easy; I started what was probably the most unceasing campaign for jobs ever conducted by an actress. I bombarded every producer in town with postcards and telephone calls, and it finally began to pay off."[19]

BETTY FURNESS

Television, at that time, was in its infancy, and as a self-described "out of work actress," Furness found herself able to get in on the ground floor. Furness said in 1979: "I was in television before there *was* television."[20]

After a few "isolated" shows at CBS,[21] Furness's first regular New York job (and her first television assignment) came in the spring of 1945 on the now defunct DuMont television network's *Fashions, Coming and Becoming*. For fifteen minutes, once a week, and for a reported salary of about $25 a show, Betty Furness guided viewers through the latest couture collections from Paris and New York. The program was produced by Worthington Miner.[22] Furness remembered those early days of TV this way:

> The studio was in an office building on Madison Avenue.... We had to dress like firemen for rehearsal, heads covered, dark glasses. The heat [from the studio lights] was unendurable. The temperature was 130 in five minutes. I wore combs in my hair at the time and burned my hand touching one. The program went off the air in the summer because of the outdoor heat![23]

She added later: "But I was fascinated by television. It combined movie and stage experience. You have to keep talking. And the camera never frightened me."[24]

A few years later, in 1948, Miner was producing the CBS dramatic anthology *Studio One*, which had just acquired Westinghouse as a sponsor. Always a fan of Betty's, Miner called her and cast her in what Furness would remember as an "infinitesimal bit."[25] That week's episode was titled, ironically, "Let Me Do the Talking."[26]

In those days TV programs were aired live. So were their commercials, which usually took place in the same studio on a set just a few feet from where the show was being performed. Everything, program and ads, had to end on time. There was no leeway for goofs or gaffes.

Betty Furness, while rehearsing her part on *Studio One*, became appalled at the lack of professionalism demonstrated by the commercial performers. The majority of actors in commercials, at that time, had come from radio. While they were good with their lines they didn't handle props very well and often failed to make eye contact with the camera.[27] Furness volunteered to try her hand at it, and before even she knew it, the ad agency was offering her the job. Since it paid $150, she took it.[28] The next week Betty Furness was again a regular part of *Studio One*, delivering one three-minute-long commercial and two one-and-one half-minute commercials.[29] Said Furness of her new role:

> Everything had to come out on time ... the drama and the commercials. The teleprompter hadn't been invented and I wasn't comfortable using cue cards; I wanted to look into the eye of the camera, therefore the eye of the viewer. So I memorized.... Once I opened my mouth, there was no way out. I *had* to know [the words] and say them correctly and promptly. It was quite stimulating.[30]

After a few months of work for Westinghouse, Furness was finally put under full contract by the company as their one and only on-air representative.[31] This deal started Betty Furness, at age 33, on an entirely new career path. It also made her TV's very first female commercial spokesperson and, suddenly, an extremely famous and familiar face.

While Furness made no bones about her real-life lack of domestic prowess—she never did her own laundry and wasn't much of a cook—it did not matter in the eyes of Westinghouse and the audience.[32] She *looked* like she knew what she was doing: she had the image of the All-American wife in the All-American kitchen.

Nevertheless, Furness's success did not prevent company chiefs from trying to tamper with her style. There was talk of having her wear a wedding ring to look more "wifey" and to have her wear an apron and adopt a stage name so she would become something of a company mascot. "We want you to be more like Betty Crocker," the agency told her.

"But I'm not," she protested, "I'm Betty Furness."[33]

Sticking to her guns Furness got to do the ads her way and became an invaluable company asset. Nobody seemed to have the knack for moving the merchandise like Betty Furness. Dealers in Dallas, for example, reported being sold out of refrigerators (at $400 a pop) two days after Furness demonstrated one of them on TV.[34]

Later she had similar luck with Westinghouse floor fans. Big and bulky, the fans cost a pricey $69.50 and had always been slow sellers in Chicago. After Furness pitched them at the end of a *Studio One* episode, however, Chicago stores sold $70,000 worth of them in four days.[35]

In addition Furness received, on average, over one thousand pieces of fan mail a week.[36]

So valuable was saleslady Furness to the company, Westinghouse—then the twelfth largest corporation in the nation—that Westinghouse was paying Furness over $75,000 a year to be its "Westinghouse girl."[37] Additional income also came her way as lead actress in the short-run, live series *Byline* and as hostess of *Penthouse Party*, among other shows.[38]

In a bold move, Westinghouse purchased in 1952 sole sponsorship of the first televised coverage of the two national political conventions. As their on-air representative, Furness packed enough clothes for three changes a day and began memorizing her copy for the twenty-five different ads she would do, live, every day for the duration of the conventions.[39]

For two weeks convention business and news analysis came to a halt when CBS anchor Walter Cronkite turned to the camera and instructed home viewers to pause "for a word from Betty Furness and Westinghouse."[40]

By the end of the two conventions, Betty Furness appeared on the air a total of 160 times. In doing so she logged more screen time than any speaker of either party and became as well known as almost any person in the nation. Her commercial closing line, "You can be *sure*, if it's a Westinghouse," became a national catch-phrase. And one of the best known political cartoons of the era summed up her media omnipresence when a young boy was pictured asking his convention-watching, bleary-eyed father, "Who's ahead now, Pop—Ike, Taft, or Betty Furness?"[41]

Barbara Matusow wrote in her 1983 book *The Evening Stars* that only three stars emerged from the '52 conventions: Eisenhower, Cronkite, and Betty Furness.[42]

Furness's appearances for Westinghouse at the conventions of 1956 and 1960 would follow. So high-profile was Furness's presence during the conventions that there was a wide-spread (though tongue-in-cheek) movement on the floor to nominate her for Vice President. Some even professed plans to start a write-in campaign for her for the nation's top job. Said Furness about the fuss, "I'm not ready to be President. Yet."[43]

Furness said many years later, "The best part of all [the conventions] was that I could run into the newsroom and ask Walter Cronkite what was happening, and he could tell me."[44] The conventions solidified her role and value to the company, and Betty Furness's salary shot to over six figures. Said Gil Baird, a Westinghouse executive at the time, "When Betty Furness walks down the street, everyone thinks Westinghouse."[45] Said Furness in 1953, "I *am* the kitchen."[46]

Said Furness of her role and work:

> It may seem an easy job to talk for about six minutes each week before the TV cameras about appliances and products I've been studying for years ... but it really isn't that simple. I put in a full eight-hour day, six days a week. First, on Saturday, I lock myself in the study of my apartment, and spend about four hours memorizing the lines, letter-perfect. Then, on Monday, I'm off to the studio at noon for camera rehearsals and then the show at ten o'clock.[47]

Extra time (what there was of it) went to starring in various Westinghouse special films, taking part in an out-of-town sales convention, delivering a speech, or making an in-store appearance. "I travel about fifteen to twenty thousand miles a year and spend abut thirty to forty days 'on the road.' I love the chance to get out of New York and see what people in other parts of the country have on their minds," Furness said in 1957.[48]

Contrary to television folklore, Furness never struggled with opening a refrigerator door—at least not on the air. While that event did take place in a Westinghouse commercial it happened to actress June Graham who was filling in for Miss Furness for a few weeks.[49] Furness did, however, once struggle with a not-so-easy-to-remove "Easy to Remove" vacuum cleaner hose during a *Studio One* break. Unable to shake it loose, she ad-libbed, "You take it out ... if you can get it out," finally gave up and continued with the commercial.[50] Afterward, she and Westinghouse executives were devastated and worried, but Furness fans did not let anybody down. Over the next few weeks the company began to get letters: "What happened could have happened to anybody, and I don't want you to lose your job on account of it" and "I went and bought [a vacuum] anyhow. I know you wouldn't recommend anything that wasn't really good."[51]

In January 1953, Westinghouse packaged Furness into her own daily talk show. *Meet Betty Furness* was the type of daily, fifteen minute, (hopefully) female-friendly talkfest typical of the 1950s. It intermixed celebrity chatter with practical, easy-to-do household hints (making your own slipcovers, etc.). Furness carried it all off with the same easy grace she had in her commercials—moving smoothly from one segment to the next, pausing briefly between each to step over to the kitchen set and sing the praises of Westinghouse waffle irons and other small appliances.[52] The program ran until July.[53]

Furness continued with her work as Westinghouse's on-air spokesperson and added to her resume by becoming a regular panelist on the game shows *What's My Line?* and *I've Got a Secret.* She occasionally turned thespian again for roles on *Climax* and *The Colgate Comedy Hour.*[54]

In 1954 she became a regular part of the Westinghouse-sponsored program *The Best of Broadway.* For the first time, her ads were produced in color.[55]

Furness's tenure with Westinghouse came to an end in November of 1960, more or less by mutual agreement. For Furness, the advent of the teleprompter and increasing use of tape took the challenge (and the fun) out of doing commercials.[56] In addition, Westinghouse, Inc., had a new president who wanted a new company image—one without Betty Furness. (Insiders also hinted he did not care for her, since he had not invented her.)[57]

Whichever was the case, Betty Furness, after eleven and a half years pitching products, was now a free agent.

Though out of work at Westinghouse, Furness was never one to sit idle. She kept her fingers busy doing needlepoint (a life-long passion and one which often saw her work exhibited in shows) and her mind busy as the President of the New York branch of the National Academy of Television Arts & Sciences. She was elected to the two-year post in 1961.[58] Later, in October 1964, as chair of the NATAS awards committee, she shook up the organization by announcing a revamping of the bestowal of the Emmys.[59]

Inspired by her first-hand knowledge of both the political process and broadcast journalism, Furness sought employment in network news in the early 1960s. She said, "I'd like to do something like Dave Garroway does. There is room for women in that field."[60] She applied for interviewer jobs at each of the networks only to be turned down; "The networks don't want women," Furness lamented at the time.[61]

Nevertheless, WNTA-TV in New York *was* interested. Her assignment: act as host of *At Your Beck and Call*, a live, phone-in talk show that aired two hours daily. Said the *New York Times* of Furness's performance, "her alertness, brevity, and slightly edged barbs reflect mental tidiness ... very much preferred to distaff gushiness."[62] *Beck and Call* ran until December of 1961.[63]

By February of the next year, Furness was back on the air as host of CBS radio's "A Woman's World," part of their series *Dimensions.* Soon after, her second CBS radio series *Ask Betty Furness* also began.[64] In 1964, when she returned to the conventions, this time it was as a reporter for her own radio show and not as Westinghouse's window dressing. "I want women to get more involved in what's going on in the world," she said.[65]

Furness returned to television as host of WABC's daily talk program *Answering Service* in 1962 and held that post until the show's demise in April 1963.[66]

Her ongoing radio work did not earn her enough money or take up all her energy, so she began to pursue her Democratic party political interests.

She began traveling and campaigning for Democratic candidates in 1962 and would labor away for LBJ and Humphrey in 1964.[67] That same year she toured the country promoting such federal programs as Head Start and VISTA.[68]

After these posts came to an end, Furness returned to New York in need of work. She tried to break into broadcasting again but was (at age 51) considered too old and (as a result of her Westinghouse affiliation) too "visible" to be easily hired.[69]

During a particularly low low-point, she accepted a dinner party invitation from her old friends Walter and Betsy Cronkite. Also on the guest list that night was CBS news producer Leslie Midgley. As Cronkite remembers, "... magic. None of the rest of us ever had a chance to talk to either of them.... [T]hey went out of that house arm in arm, never to let go."[70] Betty and Les were married August 15, 1967.[71]

As they were busy planning their wedding and refurbishing their dream home in Hartsdale, New York, a phone call from the White House came and launched Betty Furness—TV spokeswoman, actress, and sometime reporter— onto a brand new career.

President Johnson was seeking a replacement for Esther Peterson as his Special Assistant for Consumer Affairs. (Peterson, who ruled with a heavy hand in the position, was returning to her other duties as Assistant Secretary of Labor).[72] Based on his knowledge of Betty as a Democratic Party public relations dynamo and fundraiser, he chose her. In keeping with her motto never to turn down a job, Furness accepted the $26,000 a year position.[73]

At their first meeting Johnson told her, "Betty I want you to go out and tell the consumer her country cares about her, and I want you to come back and tell me what's on her mind."[74] She was to be, in her own words, his reporter, his "liaison."[75]

Because Furness was still thought of by many as the "Westinghouse woman," consumer groups and the press cried foul at news of her appointment. They seized on such revelations as Furness not knowing the prices of eggs and the fact that her housekeeper did much of the household shopping.[76] Ever candid, when Furness was asked what her qualifications for the job were, she replied, "that I was asked."[77] Said Furness about her new assignment, "You don't refuse a President."[78]

Furness remembered:

> There was hostility, especially at first when I used to speak before business groups. It bothered me, because as a performer I had always worked to applause. But then I came to the conclusion that their reaction meant that I was doing something right. So the hostility became a compliment.[79]

Furness threw herself into her new job. She said once, "Through several careers I have had nothing but on-the-job training."[80] She quickly put her

TV image behind her. She proved herself a knowledgeable and unflappable witness before congressional committees, delivered sixty major addresses before consumer and trade groups, got the voices of consumer groups heard in the White House, and, during her first year in office, made over 151 trips around the nation to bring consumer information to many audiences who had never heard it.[81]

Her early critics soon became her strongest supporters. Ralph Nader turned from cynic to lifelong fan.[82] *Consumer Reports* magazine went from quietly dismissing her in 1967[83] to naming her to its board in 1969.[84]

During her time in office—an office that overlooked the White House rose garden—Furness worked to pass laws regarding truth in lending and flame-resistant fabrics for children.[85] Before leaving the post she would add regulations regarding meat inspection and credit rates to her list of accomplishments.[86] Said Furness in 1968, "I don't take easy jobs."[87]

Peter Benchley, then a White House speech writer, said of her: "They thought they were getting this little lady who opened refrigerator doors. They didn't know they were getting Attila the Hun."[88]

When Johnson left the White House in 1969, Furness followed. She landed a job quickly, however, chairing the New York State Consumer Protection Board.[89] But she resigned the position in 1971, stating, "The legislators are not serious about protecting consumers."[90] Of the one dozen pieces of legislation she had proposed, the congress had acted on only three. After they slashed her budget "ludicrously low," Furness called it quits, saying, "I think there is a great deal to be said for the Ralph Nader approach, [to] stand outside and holler at everybody."[91]

But by 1973 she had rethought her stand enough to take the job of New York City Consumer Affairs Commissioner under New York Mayor Lindsey. She succeeded former Miss America and TV personality Bess Myerson in the role.[92] Furness held the position for one year.[93]

In 1974 Betty Furness reentered broadcasting.

WNBC-TV in New York was looking for someone to report, exclusively, on consumer news. With her background in both TV and consumerism, no one fit the bill like Betty Furness.

By taking the WNBC job, Furness became the first consumer reporter (male or female) to contribute regularly to a nightly news program.[94] "Miss Furness essentially created a place for consumer advocacy on local television," the *New York Times* wrote in 1994.[95] When she took the job Furness said, "I think the boundaries have been broken in news regarding consumer and medical issues. This is news and it is important."[96]

In writing on Furness's new role in 1974, the *New York Times* reported that Furness's Channel 4 reports were "stirring up a lot of dust."[97] She got on the air and was unafraid to name names or to take her cameras right into the businesses where customers were being bilked. Soon Furness and her office were being flooded with upwards of 400 letters a week from viewers with consumer complaints. "Nothing in the world has the impact of TV," Furness said of her on-air advocacy.[98]

During her tenure with WNBC, Furness and her staff took on a variety of cheats, frauds, and ripoffs: Sears, Lane Bryant, Kaufman Carpets, BankAmericard, and Alamac Drugs were all topics of reports.[99]

In 1976, in the right place at the right time, Furness became the sole fill-in anchor on the *Today* show when Barbara Walters left for ABC. Besides her cohosting duties, Furness began to contribute consumer news pieces to the morning program. Though she returned to WNBC when Jane Pauley was hired, Furness continued to produce weekly segments for the show.[100] For *Today*, Furness addressed such topics as the numerical discrepancies between the quantities of hot dogs and hot dog buns in a package and the problem of ill-fitting fitted bed sheets.

Everyday from 6 A.M. to 6 P.M., Betty Furness played the role of broadcast journalist as consumer watchdog. The late 1970s and the 1980s presented a host of business abuses, and Furness and her staff had the task of staying on top of all of them. Together they were the first to report on the unexpected acceleration of Audi automobiles, the first to report on the Cabbage Patch Kid phenomenon, and on everything from faulty Bic Lighters to faulty heart valves.[101]

As the *New York Times* reported in 1994, Betty Furness, as reporter, didn't pull any punches and didn't play favorites: "She reported on a hamburger that was too fat, on warranties that were too lean, and on business ethics that she saw as seriously flawed. She even scolded Macy's."[102]

Along with her nightly news reports and *Today* show activities, Furness also hosted her own weekly, local consumer news show *Buyline: Betty Furness*; the program won a Peabody in 1977.[103]

Furness told *Vogue* magazine in 1979, "One thing I've learned in the last few years is that work is *it*. Work is what life is about."[104]

But in 1992, after eighteen years with NBC, Betty Furness's professional, on-air life came to an abrupt halt. Called into the chief offices of WNBC, she was told the station was taking a new direction in consumer news, a direction that did not include her.[105] Since battling stomach cancer in 1990, Furness had abbreviated her work week to four days. "Since I was sick ... that's all the steam I have," she said.[106] The station used that excuse and its desire for harder hitting reporting to oust her. Furness said about the switch, "I'm not capable of doing it. I'm not good at kicking in a door and saying, 'I want to talk to you.' It's harder getting all the information to the public on how to avoid them in the first place."[107]

She added, "They [the stations] will gather some of the material from my life and give me a hearty handshake, but I'm off the air."[108] On March 18, *Today* and WNBC both aired tributes to her, with her present on the set, and sent her off with good-bye bouquets.

Her dismissal was reported, among other places, in the *New York Post* and *People*. She told the latter, "I don't know what's next because, frankly, I don't know what's out there. I do not [though] intend to retire at this time."[109]

Soon after NBC retired her, Furness sat down with author David Halberstam to be interviewed for his landmark, award winning book *The Fifties*. And she finished up some large-scale needlepoint pieces. But a reoccurrence of her cancer kept her from reentering the work she loved. She would battle the disease for two years before passing away at Memorial Sloan-Kettering Cancer Center at age seventy-eight on April 2, 1994.[110]

The death of Betty Furness ended one of the most distinguished, fascinating, and diverse careers in public service and American broadcasting.

There are traces of both romantic, popular-novel protagonist and fairytale heroine in the life of Betty Furness: the pretty girl who made it first in the movies, then as an early TV media darling before finding her greatest fulfillment, not in soft sell, but in hard news. And by doing so, she created a new and vital type of television reporting. She was a real-life (working) woman, progressing along with the twentieth century: moving from the world of (movie) make believe to the All-American kitchen and then to the White House and the TV anchor desk.

But no pseudo-Cinderella ever worked this hard or did this much. And none ever left such a decided mark on a medium. Friend and admirer Ralph Nader said of her, "She pioneered consumer TV news reporting and she pursued it with intelligence, inquisitiveness, and irrepressibility."[111]

In her movement from political insider to television communicator she laid out the footsteps that have been followed by the likes of Diane Sawyer and most recently Mary Matalin. Newswoman and *Today* show successor Jane Pauley has said of her, "She was my role model. There isn't anybody in television that I admired more."[112]

But Betty Furness was always her best when speaking herself. She said of her transition from spokeswoman to political appointee and then to newswoman:

> I always played parts. I was playing a part for Westinghouse. I was playing the part of a saleslady. And I wanted to somehow express myself. I didn't know what I meant by that, it was an urge. So, being intrigued with the news world and the real world, I thought, if I could get on television talking about the real world, I'd have it made.... I guess the most wonderful thing that's happened in my life has been to be able to be me, and to have it accepted; for it to be okay for me to be me.[113]

And asked late in her life and career by friend and WNBC producer Rita Satz how she wanted people to think of her, Betty Furness replied, "That I'm a pro."[114]

Betty Furness

January 3, 1916	Born in New York City.
June 1930	Landed first job, as model, for John Robert Powers agency.
June 1932	Signed to movie contract by RKO studios; first film, *Renegades of the West*, released that year.
November 26, 1937	Married musician Johnny Green.
1940	Daughter Barbara born.
August 1943	Divorced Johnny Green.
January 3, 1945	Married radio performer Hugh Ernst.
Spring 1945	Made first regular television appearances on *Fashions, Coming and Becoming* for DuMont network.
Fall 1948	Acted in episode of *Studio One* and did show's commercials for Westinghouse for first time.
May 1949	Formally named on-air spokeswoman for Westinghouse.
April 1950	Suffered death of husband Ernst.
September 15, 1950	*Penthouse Party*, with Betty Furness as hostess, sponsored by Westinghouse, premiered.
June 8, 1951	Last *Penthouse Party* aired.
November 11, 1951	Worked as lead actress in live series *Byline*.
December 16, 1951	Last *Byline* aired.
July 7, 1952	Performed commercials for Westinghouse during Republican Convention.
July 11, 1952	Convention ended.
July 21, 1952	Performed commercials for Westinghouse during Democratic Convention.
July 24, 1952	Convention ended.
January 2, 1953	Daytime talk show *Meet Betty Furness* aired for first time.
July 1953	Last installment of *Meet Betty Furness* aired.
September 15, 1954	First episode of *The Best of Broadway* aired; Furness ads for Westinghouse broadcast in color for first time.
May 4, 1955	Last episode of *The Best of Broadway* aired.
October 13, 1958	Westinghouse-sponsored *Desilu Playhouse* premiered with Betty Furness as commercial spokesperson.
June 10, 1960	Last *Desilu Playhouse* aired.
November 1960	Ended affiliation with Westinghouse.
February 1961	*At Your Beck and Call*, hosted by Betty Furness, began on WNTA-TV in New York.
June 1961	Elected to two-year term as president of the National Academy of Television Arts & Sciences.

December 1961	*At Your Beck and Call* canceled.
October 1962	First episode of WABC's *Answering Service* broadcast.
April 1963	Last episode of *Answering Service* broadcast.
Spring 1964	Began working actively for Democratic candidates and programs.
October 1964	Elected to two-year term as president of National Academy of Television Arts & Sciences.
March 1967	Approached by Johnson Administration to be Special Assistant for Consumer Affairs.
August 15, 1967	Married Leslie Midgley, CBS news producer.
January 1969	Left White House position.
August 11, 1970	Joined New York State Consumer Board as chair.
July 1971	Resigned from Consumer Board.
March 1973	Named New York City Consumer Affairs Commissioner.
March 1974	Resigned post as Consumer Affairs Commissioner.
April 1974	Hired by WNBC. First television consumer advocate.
June 1976	Named temporary cohost of the NBC *Today* show.
March 1992	Retired by WNBC, New York and the *Today* show.
April 2, 1994	Passed away at Memorial Sloan-Kettering Cancer Center in New York City.

NOTES

1. *Current Biography* (1968), p. 134.
2. Lynn Gilbert and Gaylen Moore, *Particular Passions* (New York: Crown, 1981), p. 143.
3. Ibid.
4. "Betty Furness Bio," Westinghouse, Inc. (1957), p. 2.
5. Anne Chamberlin, "And Now, For the Consumer, Miss Betty Furness!," *Saturday Evening Post* (18 June 1967), p. 26.
6. Albert Morehead, "America's Top Saleswoman: Betty Furness," *Cosmopolitan* (February 1953), p. 136.
7. Ephraim Katz, *The Film Encyclopedia* (New York: Perigee, 1979), p. 458.
8. Herbert Dalmas, "Betty Furness: No. 1 Saleswoman," *Coronet* (October 1953), p. 38.
9. John Springer, *They Had Faces Then: Superstars, Stars and Starlets of the 1930s* (Secaucus, NJ: Citadel, 1974), p. 110.
10. James Brown, "Summer Job for Betty Furness," *Los Angeles Times* (7 June 1976), p. 14.
11. Myrna Oliver, "Betty Furness; Ad Star, Consumer Advocate," *New York Times* (4 April 1994), p. 26.
12. *Current Biography*, p. 134.
13. Chamberlin, p. 26.
14. Morehead, p. 136.
15. *Current Biography*, p. 136.
16. Chamberlin, p. 28.

17. Ibid.

18. "Kitchen Riches," *Newsweek* (12 January 1953), p. 70.

19. "Betty Furness Bio," p. 3.

20. Amy Gross, "Betty Furness: Consumer Reporter/Advocate, Breaking the Age Barrier—With Wit, Wisdom and Style," *Vogue* (October 1979), p. 380.

21. Robert L. Hilliard and Michael C. Keith, *The Broadcast Century* (Boston: Focal Press, 1992), p. 143.

22. "Betty Furness Bio," p. 3.

23. Hilliard and Keith, p. 143.

24. Chamberlin, p. 26.

25. "Kitchen Riches," p. 70.

26. "Betty Furness Bio," p. 3.

27. David Halberstam, *The Fifties* (New York: Villard, 1993), p. 498.

28. Ibid.

29. Ibid.

30. Hilliard and Keith, p. 143.

31. Dalmas, p. 38.

32. Morehead, p. 136.

33. Halberstam, p. 498.

34. Dalmas, p. 37.

35. Ibid.

36. Ibid, p. 39.

37. Morehead, p. 135.

38. "Betty Furness Bio," p. 4.

39. Halberstam, p. 498.

40. Ibid.

41. Morehead, p. 137.

42. Barbara Matusow, *The Evening Stars* (Boston: Houghton Mifflin, 1983), p. 65

43. Betty Jo Ramsey, "Betty Furness: Quick-Change Artist," *Good Housekeeping* (June 1960), p. 30.

44. Chamberlin, p. 27.

45. Halberstam, p. 500.

46. "Kitchen Riches," p. 70.

47. "Betty Furness Bio," p. 1.

48. Ibid., p. 2.

49. Charles A. Ruch, Westinghouse historian, letter to author (14 October 1994).

50. Dalmas, p. 36.

51. Ibid., p. 37.

52. Episodes of *Meet Betty Furness* can be viewed at the Museum of Broadcast Communications, Chicago, Illinois.

53. Alex McNeil, *Total Television* (New York: Penguin, 1980), p. 420.

54. "Betty Furness Bio," p. 4.

55. Tim Brooks and Earle Marsh, *The Complete Directory to Prime Time Network TV Shows* (New York: Ballantine, 1992), p. 74.

56. "Star In Consumer Role," *New York Times* (6 March 1967), p. 37.

57. Halberstam, p. 500.

58. Steven H. Shever, *Who's Who in Television and Cable* (New York: Facts on File, 1983), p. 171.

59. *Current Biography*, p. 135.

60. Val Adams, "Betty Furness Quitting? You Can Be Sure," *Los Angeles Times* (11 November 1960), p. 15.

61. Sue Carswell, "Gritty Woman," *People* (14 April 1994), p. 74.

62. *Current Biography*, p. 135.

63. Ibid.

64. Shever, p. 171.

65. Hal Humphrey, "Betty Furness All Burned Up," *Los Angeles Times* (22 July 1964).

66. Shever, p. 171.

67. Oliver, p. 26.

68. Brown, p. 14.

69. Interview with Leslie Midgley (25 October 1994). All other information and quotes from Mr. Midgley in this chapter were taken from this interview.

70. Memorial Service for Betty Furness, Studio 8-H, NBC, New York, NY (18 April 1994), p. 12.

71. Midgley interview.

72. "New 'Shopper' for LBJ," *US News & World Report* (20 March 1967), p. 21.

73. "Star in Consumer Role," p. 37.

74. Meg Whitcomb, "You Can Be Sure If It's Betty Furness," *Fifty Plus* (August 1980), p. 49.

75. "Star in Consumer Role," p. 37.

76. Ibid.

77. "The 100 Days of Betty Furness," *New Republic* (5 August 1967), p. 10.

78. Ibid.

79. Brown, p. 14.

80. Gilbert and Moore, p. 144.

81. Elizabeth Shelton, "Betty Furness: One Year on the Job," *Washington Post* (5 May 1968), p. 17.

82. Midgley interview.

83. "Can Betty Furness Help the Consumer?," *Consumer Reports* (May 1967), p. 258.

84. "Betty Furness, Broadcaster and Longstanding Member of CU's Board, Dies," *Consumer Reports* (June 1994), p. 370.

85. "Betty Furness, Broadcaster," p. 370.

86. Oliver, p. 26.

87. Shelton, p. 17.

88. Carswell, p. 74.

89. Shever, p. 171.

90. "Betty Furness," *Newsweek* (26 July 1971), p. 11.

91. Ibid.

92. "Miss Furness Named to N.Y. Consumer Post," *Los Angeles Times* (31 March 1973), p. 10.

93. Shever, p. 171.

94. Carswell, p. 74.

95. "Betty Furness, Broadcaster," p. 370.

96. Brown, p. 14.

97. Judy Klemesrud, "Can She Be a Ralph Nader on TV?," *New York Times* (21 July 1974), p. 15.

98. Ibid.

99. Ibid.

100. Jill Brooke, "NBC Pulls the Plug on Betty Furness," *New York Post* (9 March 1992), p. 20.

101. Interview with Rita Satz, WNBC news producer (1 November 1994). All other information and quotes from Ms. Satz in this chapter were taken from this interview unless otherwise noted.

102. "Betty Furness, Broadcaster," p. 370.

103. Shever, p. 171.

104. Gross, p. 380.

105. Brooke, p. 20.

106. Ibid.

107. Ibid.

108. Ibid.

109. Lisa Russell, "Passages," *People* (23 March 1992), p. 70.

110. Raymond Hernandez, "Betty Furness, 78, TV Reporter and Consumer Advocate, Dies," *New York Times* (3 April 1994), p. 27.

111. Oliver, p. 26.

112. Carswell, p. 74.

113. Memorial Service for Betty Furness, p. 24.

114. Carswell, p. 74.

Frieda Hennock

From its earliest days, the industry of television has reached far beyond the plush, New York offices of the major networks and the large, cold television studios where TV programs are produced. One of the most notable places of power and influence in the field of television is Washington, D.C., where major decisions regarding the television industry's business, financial, legal, and technical aspects are debated and decided by the Federal Communications Commission. The FCC is a government regulatory agency established by Congress in 1934 to oversee all legal issues pertaining to most forms of mass communication. In 1948 the Federal Communications Commission welcomed Frieda Hennock, its first female member. During her seven-year term, Hennock made an assortment of policy decisions that continue to affect television to this day. Almost single-handedly, she waged an exhausting campaign to create educational television and, by doing so, helped redefine television, creating out of it a more responsible and socially uplifting medium.

Frieda Barkin Hennock was born in Kovel, Poland, on September 27, 1904, the youngest of eight children (five girls and three boys) of Boris and Sarah Hennock.[1] When Hennock was six her parents moved to America, where her father found work in real estate and banking. Frieda Hennock became a citizen of the United States in 1910 upon the naturalization of her father.[2] The family settled in New York City and Frieda attended New York public schools, graduating from Morris High in the Bronx.[3]

Though her early career plans revolved around being an actress on the stage or becoming a pianist, at age 18 Hennock stunned her parents by saying she was intent on becoming a lawyer.[4] Neither her mother nor father approved of careers for women. They told her, "If you are determined to be a lawyer, we will not stop you. But we will not help you either."[5]

In 1922 Hennock enrolled in Brooklyn Law School, taking night courses in order to be able to work and pay her tuition. She gained legal experience by working days at the law firm of Thomas and Friedman.[6] She obtained her LL.B. in 1924 at the age of nineteen. Codes of the New York Bar Association, however, would not allow Hennock to join for two years, until 1926, when she turned twenty-one.[7]

In 1926, with $56 of capital and the assistance of a friend who offered her office space in exchange for legal work, Frieda Hennock opened up shop

FRIEDA HENNOCK

as a lawyer. Her first earnings as a practicing attorney were $3,000.[8] Hennock put the money to good use that same year when the city appointed her as counsel for "Red" McKenna, a man accused of committing murder during a payroll robbery. She immediately ordered sketches of the architecture of the crime scene and studies in ballistics. "It was my first big case; I was determined to win it," Hennock said.[9] In a dramatic turn, though, her client escaped from prison and committed suicide just before the case was scheduled to begin.[10] Hennock's efforts on McKenna's behalf however garnered her attention as a savvy criminal lawyer.[11]

During her early years of practice Hennock also helped several bootleggers get off with easy fines.[12] Later, she would go on to defend several accused murderers and win seven acquittals.[13] Hennock also found a niche, though not much money, as a divorce lawyer: an attractive single woman still in her twenties, however, did not always sit well with the wives, estranged or not, of male clients. "The wives of clients who don't understand women have cost me a fortune," she said.[14] For fifteen years Hennock regularly turned down fees in divorce cases and usually sought reconciliation. "Any lawyer who really tries," she said, "can show a couple that it's better to rebuild their marriage than to go through the bitterness and misery of divorce."[15]

In 1927 Hennock formed a partnership with another lawyer, Julius Silver, believing she would gain more clients if she were practicing in association with a man.[16] The partnership lasted until 1934 when it was dissolved because of disagreements between the two. Hennock later took Silver to court and won $9,000 and court costs over a partnership share in a new invention by Edwin H. Land: the Polaroid camera.[17] She returned to solo practice where she would remain until 1941.

Gradually, Hennock began to phase out her work as a criminal attorney after the experiences began to affect her health.[18] Hennock said, "I'd feel myself growing older, waiting for a verdict knowing my work was mixed up with a person's liberty."[19] She said later, "I'm glad I was a criminal lawyer when I was young. Knowing these people gave me an adult sense of values."[20] As a replacement for criminal law, Hennock began to specialize in corporate law, earning a fee of $55,000 in 1927 to arrange a company merger.[21]

Hennock also began to dabble in government and politics. From 1935 until 1939 she was assistant counsel to the New York State Mortgage Commission in its study of low-cost housing.[22] She served on the Executive Committee of the National Health Assembly for a few years as well. Its job, as sponsored by the Federal Security Administration, was to create a ten-year national health program.[23]

For a year, in 1937, Hennock returned to her alma mater, Brooklyn Law School, and taught courses in law and economics.[24] In 1941 she joined the 141-year-old previously all-male, all-Republican New York Law firm of Choate, Mitchell, and Ely. She said at the time, "They don't discriminate against women or Democrats" (of which she was both).[25]

Until 1948, when she left to join the FCC, Frieda Hennock worked out of the Choate, Mitchell, and Ely century-and-a-half old offices—"One hundred and forty years without so much as a remodeling," Hennock lamented.[26] She also observed the firm's English tradition of tea and crumpets every day at four.[27]

During this time Hennock was a frequent visitor to Washington, D.C., to see to business matters of two of the firm's clients, DuPont and J. P. Morgan.[28] Her work for the firm was netting her an annual pay of $40,000 and allowed her to own both a New York Park Avenue apartment and a seaside weekend home.[29]

Hennock's involvement with city and Democratic politics continued to deepen. She was a tireless campaigner and fundraiser for William O'Dwyer in his run for New York mayor.[30] She was a strong supporter of India Edwards, director of the Women's Division of the Democratic National Committee, a group which had greatly pressured the Truman administration to put more women into top government jobs.[31]

On May 24, 1948, President Truman nominated Hennock to the Federal Communications Commission after Clifford J. Durr declined his reappointment.

Many historians, today, believe the nomination was a calculated political move. A refusal to confirm Hennock, a Jewish woman, would run senators the risk of being labeled antifeminist and/or anti-Semitic.[32] Others felt Hennock's nomination was a reward for her hard work and strong support of Democratic causes.[33] For whatever reason, most noted that her confirmation would maintain the relative political balance of the seven-member commission—three Republicans, three Democrats, and one independent.[34]

Broadcasting magazine opposed Hennock's nomination because of her lack of communications credentials.[35] In a 1948 article it listed four other possible female choices, all with longer broadcasting resumes than hers.[36]

From the outset of the confirmation hearings, Hennock showed no signs of selling out her strong political leanings or selling out herself. She was amazingly frank in her answers to questions. She told the all-male, all-Republican panel at the opening of the hearings:

> I'm against you and I always have been. I have done my best to collect money for Roosevelt and have probably taken a lot of good Republican money away from what you wanted to collect.[37]

When a Republican Senator attempted to get to the matters at hand and asked Hennock, "Do you know anything about radio?" She shot back, "Only that I've raised a lot of money for radio programs for Roosevelt."[38]

Frieda Hennock's unanimous confirmation by the Senate was its last official act before the end of the 1948 session. Hennock became the 24th commissioner in the FCC's fourteen years of existence.[39] Not only was Hennock the first woman to serve on the Commission, but she was also the first woman to serve on any federal regulatory agency.[40] She became the second highest ranking woman in the Truman Administration, after Labor Secretary Frances Perkins.[41] Hennock was 43 years old at the time she accepted the $10,000-a-year position—a considerable drop in pay from her days as a New York attorney. She said of her new role:

> I got bored telling my clients how to make a lot of money. I wanted to render a service to my country in a position where I could be of some use. I think that next to atomic energy, communications is the most important thing we have to regulate. Radio can be the mechanism of true democracy.[42]

Hennock said after her appointment to the FCC, "It seems fundamental that in this field—so peculiarly affecting women—the viewpoint of their sex should be presented."[43] She added, "My zeal will not be feminine zeal. It is one which I shall expect to find in all of my colleagues."[44]

Hennock quickly learned as much as she could about the industry and the technology of mass communication. She readily admitted to lacking knowledge about her new field, but made no excuses for it, saying, "Senator

Brewster [part of the committee which approved her nomination] wanted an unbiased, fresh viewpoint, away from the industry."[45] Later she commented:

> I have wide experience in business and law. All of these were useful and essential qualifications for my new job. No one has ever suggested that all seven members of the FCC should be engineers, any more than it would be wise for them all to be lawyers or members of any other particular profession.[46]

One of Hennock's earliest requests after joining the FCC was that Commission witnesses simplify their technical jargon to something more understandable to the mass populace.[47]

The FCC, with Frieda Hennock now present, found that it also had to change a few other business-as-usual practices. She said:

> The men around here couldn't be more helpful or co-operative, but they don't quite know what to make of me. It's the first time they've had to worry about opening doors and making way for a woman in these rooms.[48]

Hennock was also not above calling attention to whatever position she held by exploiting her good looks or her designer wardrobe and, on occasion, shedding a few tears.[49] She frequently startled colleagues and journalists by kicking off her shoes while working at her desk or granting an interview. Once she invited a flat-footed reporter to take his shoes off too.[50]

When Hennock joined the FCC, she did so at a difficult and unpopular phase of its history. Because of the popularity explosion of broadcasting, huge numbers of radio and television stations started up operations in a very short time, so many in fact that their broadcast signals began to interfere with one another. Additionally, the rapid demand for new television licenses left too little space in the VHF band to accommodate all of them. There were also new concerns about the coming trend of color broadcasting. To gain time to study and decide on these problems, the FCC imposed a sweeping "freeze" on all further broadcasting growth until conflicts and standards could be worked out by the commission. The freeze took effect in 1948 and lasted until 1952; during that time no new television stations were allowed to join the airwaves.[51]

Though during the freeze, the FCC did not have to handle requests for new television licenses, the settling of the old problems from before the freeze took an extraordinary amount of time. Commissioner Hennock's average day began at 8:30 in the morning, conferencing with her secretary about the day's work. At ten she would ride (via station wagon) with the other commissioners to the site of the that day's hearings. Hearings usually ran to as late as five or six at night. After a quick dinner Hennock would return to her office and work with two stenographers. She would also start answering the phone, which did not usually become active until the evening, when parties knew that Hennock could be reached.[52] Citizens consulted her about issues on a wide variety of topics, from lawyers looking for advice to station managers putting in a good word for their stations or individuals wondering about walkie talkies and radios for taxi services. "One boy [called and] wanted to use his amateur station to advertise a diaper pick-up service," Hennock related.[53]

Frequently, Hennock worked on Saturdays catching up, familiarizing herself with decisions and the upcoming week's agenda.[54] Saturday nights were reserved for dancing and Sundays for golf.[55]

As during the confirmation process, Hennock showed no signs of remaining in the shadows of her male counterparts or supporting their views if they clashed with hers. She said later, "I try to stir up everybody I can on a subject."[56] She made a habit of giving preferential treatment to weaker signal UHF stations and to battling broadcast editorials and the concept of multiple ownership.[57] Additionally, Hennock believed that stations that broadcast excessive violence and brutality and billed it as children's programming deserved to lose their licenses.[58]

Hennock was a frequent dissenter from the majority opinion of the Commission as well. Though she stood on record opposing radio lotteries, she dissented in October 1949 when the FCC voted to create an all-out ban on the radio giveaways. She did not believe that an administrative agency should interpret a criminal statute more broadly than the courts.[59]

When the FCC selected a national standard for color television broadcasting in October 1950, Hennock was one of only two dissenters (along with George E. Sterling) in rejecting the proposed CBS color system supported by five other Commissioners.[60] Hennock believed that a decision in favor of CBS would benefit the already rich and influential network while placing eight million consumers at a disadvantage, forcing them to buy adapters for their current televisions in order to enjoy the wonders of color.[61]

In February 1953 Frieda Hennock again bucked the system when she voted against a proposed merger of ABC and United Paramount Theaters. While other commissioners believed the association would help the then struggling ABC network by gaining it much-needed new resources, Hennock feared a conflict of interest and a possible monopoly in the near future. By recognizing the competitive nature between television and the film industry, Hennock held that the larger of the two companies would dominate and absorb the other one. In this case Paramount Theaters could use the ABC airwaves and resources to greater advantage than the television network could exploit the resources of the theater chain. Thus ABC, in the long run, would be left at a marked disadvantage.[62]

Parade magazine once estimated that Hennock as commissioner made an average of sixty regulatory decisions a day, ranging from technical requirements to guidelines concerning broadcast editorials.[63]

Hennock's most important cause, however, and her greatest claim to fame while at the FCC, involved the hot topic of educational television. Some FM radio frequencies for educational use had already been reserved, but setting aside television channels for those same purposes was more controversial.[64]

Early in Hennock's term she adopted the issue of not-for-profit educational television channels and frequencies as a personal cause:[65]

> Television has failed to live up to its promise.... American television by winning public confidence also inherited a public obligation. The airwaves are in the public domain. A television station operates in the public interest ... [making] the broadcaster in effect a trustee of a valuable public property.[66]

To further her new cause, that of 25 percent (or about 500 channels) of all color television channels being set aside for educational use, Hennock staged a multimedia attack. She wrote dozens of articles on the subject for such publications as the *Saturday Review of Literature*, *Variety*, and *Women Lawyers Journal*. She also took part in numerous radio broadcasts and she took to the road on weekend, whistle stop–like tours of cities across the country promoting the idea of television for education, for the people.[67]

In 1950 Frieda Hennock achieved a small victory when several organizations met to form the Joint Committee on Educational Television; the issue of educational TV would now have an organization and a voice all its own. These groups included the National Association of Educational Broadcasters and the American Council on Education.[68] They, as Hennock was doing on the FCC, began to push for the allocation of channels for educational use and to drum up interest from the educational community for such channels.[69] Soon the idea of educational facilities holding rights to broadcast frequencies began to catch on. Michigan State University, Ohio State, Cornell, and Iowa State all filed for broadcast licenses.[70] Of the commissioners, only Hennock emerged as the committee's champion. Commissioner Paul C. Walker added some support; others were only vaguely interested or not interested at all. The movement was not much more popular in the industry. *Broadcasting* magazine called the attempt to reserve channels "illogical, if not illegal."[71]

In fighting for education TV Frieda Hennock was fighting an uphill battle; she was threatening to take growth potential and profits away from industry leaders. She believed that if certain frequencies were not specially set aside by the commission, they would be quickly bought up by large networks and corporations and fall forever out of the reach of educational organizations and institutions.[72] While others believed that all frequencies should be granted on a first-come, first-served basis, Hennock knew that educators would not be able to compete financially with businesses and media corporations in buying available licenses. She sought to reserve some space on the spectrum for the day when educators could afford them. Even if no educators were interested in the channels at first, they would remain there, reserved until they were needed or desired.[73] Hennock said, "A school has to get its money from its trustees or its state legislature; it can't possibly get its plans in shape as fast as a businessman can."[74]

In 1952 Hennock drew up the blueprints for the programming for first educational television station, envisioning at the time "an electronic black-board."[75] Throughout her campaign she envisioned many uses for educational television. One of them was the idea of "in-school viewing" where overworked teachers could take a break, turn on a television in the classroom, and have a lesson taught to their students from across town or from thousands of miles away.[76]

Hennock also saw educational TV as a powerful social force in educating adults denied educational advantages over the years. Even in 1951 thirty percent of the US population was without a grade-school education; many of these people were functionally illiterate. Hennock believed that through the use of TV as teacher a more competent and informed nation could emerge.[77]

Additionally, Hennock foresaw a medium for higher education courses, skill training, and even household tips. Educational television, in her mind, could teach members of the viewing audience how to speak French, take and develop photographs, or pick the right melon at the supermarket.[78] She also put in a plug for cultural programming, believing television to be the perfect medium for the works of Shakespeare and presentations of such plays as Robert E. Sherwood's *Abe Lincoln in Illinois*.[79] Literally, Frieda Hennock wanted to create a classroom in the living room.

Thanks to public support of Hennock's crusade and a desire on the Commission's part to remain within the country's good graces, the concept of educational television on prereserved channels throughout the country began to gain momentum both inside and outside of the commission's offices.[80]

Nineteen fifty-two saw the lifting of the long-standing broadcasting "freeze" when the FCC issued the momentous document "The Sixth Report and Order." It attempted to clear up many of the complex and confusing issues that had existed in broadcasting before the freeze in 1948. Among its many statutes, including those regarding color broadcasting and the addition of more UHF channels, the report forever set aside 242 station assignments for educational use. Some years later that number was increased.[81]

It was a hard-won victory for Hennock and her supporters. In 1953 she was guest speaker on the first day of broadcasting for KUHT-TV in Houston, Texas, the country's first educational television station. She wrote later of the event:

> They said I would not get a channel, that I would not get an application and that a station would never get on the air. Well, it was a pretty good feeling to be there in Houston and see educational television become a reality.[82]

Near the end of her term with the FCC, President Truman nominated Hennock for a federal judgeship. Though she received the support of her FCC colleagues, she incurred controversy because of a friendship with a married federal judge. The matter of her gender was also an issue. Seeing the handwriting on the wall, Hennock withdrew her name from consideration.[83]

In 1955 Dwight Eisenhower failed to reappoint Hennock to the FCC. Thereafter, she assumed a less hectic, if not less public life. She continued to dabble in national and city politics and became a regular feature of Washington society life, where she became known for her collection of clothes and spectacular hats.[84]

Just after her exit from the FCC, Frieda Hennock saw to a new piece of business in her life: her marriage. She became Mrs. William H. Simons on March 31, 1956. Simons was a real estate developer, and after the wedding Hennock was formally known as Frieda Hennock Simons.[85]

Frieda Hennock Simons returned to practicing corporate law, practicing from 1955 until 1956 with the Washington law firm of Davies, Richberg, Tydings, Beebe, and Landa.[86] In 1956 Hennock went once again into solo practice, setting up a private practice in Washington and sharing office space with her husband.[87]

Hennock would remain active in her legal work, as well as in Washington, D.C.'s political and social circles, until her death at age fifty-five of a brain tumor on June 21, 1960.[88]

Though her career in television, as part of the FCC, was relatively short, Hennock's influence is unending. Every major media history book cites her as the "mother" of noncommercial, educational television. By championing the educational TV cause, Hennock sent a message to broadcasters and audiences, one which decreed television for the common good, a responsible instrument and not just a money-making tool. At that time in television's history, and the time of Hennock's term on the FCC, only she and a few others dared to take that unpopular stand—the stand against the profit-motives of big business and in favor of public utilization of the airwaves.

Educational Television (ETV), Hennock's dream, continues today. It has, however, had its name changed by the Public Broadcasting Act of 1967. Public television and PBS were born out of that legislation.[89] Today the Public Broadcasting System encompasses more than 300 stations across the United States, showcasing outstanding documentaries, instructional series, children's shows, play and opera productions.[90]

Though Frieda Hennock was the first of her sex on the commission, she was not the last. Since Hennock, a handful of other notable women have brought their voices to the broadcasting world's most influential group. They include Charlotte Reid, Anne Jones, and Sherrie Marshall. Hennock's gender, though, compared to what she achieved while on the FCC, seems today to be just a footnote, a bit of trivia. She was thirty years ahead of her time, foreseeing television as a learning device, part of the educational mix of computers and interactive video.

Still, while other women were making space for themselves in front of or behind the TV camera, Frieda Hennock was making a "woman's place" on the Commission.

Frieda Hennock

September 27, 1904	Born in Kovel, Poland.
1910	Came to America.
1916	Became United States citizen upon naturalization of father.
1922	Entered Brooklyn Law School.
1924	Graduated from law school.
September 1926	Became member of New York Bar association; youngest woman ever admitted; opened first law office in New York City.
1927	Formed legal partnership with Julius Silver; began to ease out of work on criminal cases.
1934	Dissolved partnership; returned to solo practice.
1935	Entered politics for first time as assistant counsel for New York State Mortgage Commission.
1937	Taught for one year at Brooklyn Law School.
1941	Joined New York law firm of Choate, Mitchell, and Ely.
May 24, 1948	Nominated by Harry S Truman to Federal Communications Commission.
June 20, 1948	Nomination confirmed by US Senate.
July 6, 1948	Sworn in as FCC commissioner. First female to hold rank of commissioner.
October 1948	FCC halted issuing licenses for new stations; action became known as "freeze."
September 26, 1949	FCC hearings began on possible allocation of television frequencies for educational use.
October 1949	Dissented from majority commission opinion on possible ban of radio lotteries.*
October 30, 1949	Published first article, "FCC Planning TV Future," promoting educational television; piece appeared in *New York Post*.
1950	Joint Committee on Educational Television formed.
October 1950	Dissented from majority commission opinion on adoption of CBS color system as universal standard.
1952	First guidelines for educational television station created by Hennock.
April 14, 1952	"Sixth Report and Order" issued by FCC; allowed for lifting of "freeze."
July 1952	"Freeze" lifted.

February 1953	Dissented from commission on proposed ABC network/Paramount theater merger.
June 1953	First educational station, KUHT-TV, Houston, signed on air.
June 30, 1955	Departed FCC after failing to be reappointed by President Eisenhower.
1955	Joined law firm of Davies, Richberg, Tydings, Beebe, and Landa.
1956	Left Davies, et al.; reentered solo practice in Washington, D.C.
March 31, 1956	Married William H. Simon, real estate developer.
June 21, 1960	Passed away in Washington, D.C.

*Only the most historically significant decisions are listed among those made by Frieda Hennock while on the Federal Communications Commission.

NOTES

1. *Current Biography* (1948), p. 278.
2. Ibid.
3. Ibid.
4. Laurence C. Eklund, "Portia on the FCC," *Milwaukee Journal* (2 September 1948).
5. John MacLeod, "Woes and Triumphs of a Lady Advocate," *American Weekly*, (5 September 1948).
6. Ibid.
7. *Current Biography*, p. 278.
8. Eklund.
9. MacLeod.
10. Ibid.
11. *Current Biography*, p. 278.
12. Eklund.
13. *Current Biography*, p. 278.
14. MacLeod.
15. Ibid.
16. Barbara Sicherman and Carol Hurd Green, *Notable American Women: The Modern Period* (Cambridge: Belknap, 1980), p. 332.
17. Ibid.
18. "Our Respects to—Madame Commissioner," *Broadcasting* (31 May 1948), p. 44.
19. *Current Biography*, p. 278.
20. Ibid.
21. Ibid.
22. "Commissioner Frieda B. Hennock," Federal Communications Commission (6 July 1948), p. 1.
23. Ibid.
24. *Current Biography*, p. 279.
25. "First Woman Member of FCC Makes Impression on Senators with Frankness," *Washington Post* (6 July 1948), p. 2.
26. Martha Millspaugh, "Miss Commissioner Hennock," *Hamilton Sun* (8 August 1948), p. 5.

27. Ibid.

28. "Our Respects to—Madame Commissioner," p. 44.

29. Eklund.

30. "Woman Nominated as Member of FCC," *New York Times* (25 May 1948), p. 6.

31. Sicherman and Green, p. 332.

32. Erik Barnouw, *The Golden Web* (New York: Oxford University, 1968), p. 293.

33. *Current Biography*, p. 279.

34. Ibid.

35. "Our Respects to—Madame Commissioner," p. 43.

36. Ibid.

37. "First Woman Member of FCC Makes Impression on Senators with Frankness," *Washington Post* (6 July 1948), p. 2.

38. Ibid.

39. "Wanted Woman," *Time* (19 July 1948), p. 56.

40. Erwin Krasnow, Lawrence D. Longley, and Herbert A. Terry, *The Politics of Broadcast Regulation* (New York: St. Martin's Press, 1982), p. 41.

41. Eklund.

42. Ibid.

43. "Wanted Woman," p. 56.

44. "Woman in a Man's World," *Talks* (January 1949), p. 37.

45. "Wanted Woman," p. 56.

46. "Woman in a Man's World," p. 37.

47. "Miss Hennock's Warpath," *Pathfinder* (12 July 1950).

48. Millspaugh, p. 5.

49. Sicherman and Green, p. 333.

50. Eklund.

51. Lynne Schafer Gross, *Telecommunications* (Dubuque, IA: William C. Brown, 1986), p. 81.

52. Millspaugh, p. 5.

53. Ibid.

54. Ibid.

55. Ibid.

56. "Miss Hennock's Warpath," *Pathfinder* (12 July 1950).

57. Sicherman and Green, p. 332.

58. Ibid.

59. "Never Underestimate...," *Fortune* (October, 1949), p. 22.

60. "TV Color's Future: 7 Who Rule," *US News & World Report* (27 October 1950), p. 34.

61. Ibid.

62. "The First Fifty Years of Broadcasting," *Broadcasting* (23 May 1981), p. 101.

63. Mary Van Resselaer Thayer, "Washington's Most Influential Women," *Parade* (*Washington Post*) (31 July 1949), p. 6.

64. Interview with Max Paglin (26 October 1991).

65. Ibid.

66. Frieda B. Hennock, "The 3 R's on TV," *Variety* (3 January 1951).

67. Sicherman and Green, p. 332.

68. Erik Barnouw, *The Golden Web* (New York: Oxford University, 1968), p. 293.

69. Christopher H. Sterling and John M. Kittross, *Stay Tuned* (Belmont, CA: Wadsworth, 1990), p. 268.

70. Mary Scott Welch, "Donna Quixote," *Look* (17 July 1951), p. 76.

71. Erik Barnouw, *Tube of Plenty* (London: Oxford University Press, 1982), p. 142.

72. Frieda B. Hennock, "TV—Problem Child or Teacher's Pet?," *New York State Education* (March 1951), p. 400.

73. Welch, p. 76.

74. Ibid.

75. "Flunked," *Broadcasting* (5 February 1973), p. 74.

76. Welch,, p. 76.

77. Hennock, "TV—Problem Child or Teacher's Pet?," p. 399.

78. Welch, p. 76.

79. Hennock, "TV—Problem Child or Teacher's Pet?," p. 398.

80. Barnouw, *Golden Web*, p. 294.

81. Barnouw, *Tube of Plenty*, p. 142.

82. Sicherman and Green, p. 332.

83. Ibid., p. 333.

84. Ibid.

85. "Frieda Hennock Simons Dead; Lawyer, 55, Had Been on FCC," *New York Times* (21 June 1960), p. 2.

86. Sicherman and Green, p. 333.

87. "Frieda Hennock Simons," p. 2.

88. Ibid.

89. Les Brown, *The New York Times Encylopedia of Television* (New York: Times Books, 1977), p. 136.

90. Ibid., p. 345.

Lucy Jarvis

Networks and their news departments, hard-pressed by declining revenue and declining audiences, now do little in the way of producing documentary films for television. The days of the major networks devoting an hour, or several hours, of prime time to place important issues beneath the magnifying glass of the television camera has past. The production of investigative, hard-hitting documentaries like Murrow's *Harvest of Shame* now seem as foreign as a black-and-white variety show. Similarly, television documentaries which took American audiences to far off countries and cultures, many never before seen by those audiences, have today been replaced by quickly and cheaply made magazine-type specials on tabloid topics. The TV documentary is a form largely forgotten, something for history books or retrospectives.

Before its demise, however, the television documentary enjoyed a great many remarkable moments, bringing into American homes such exotic places as the Kremlin in Russia and the Louvre in France. These films were produced by the first female producer in prime time network television. She set a standard of excellence, unparalleled by anyone in the field before or since. Her hallmark, as veteran newsman and sometime collaborator Edwin Newman once said, "[was to] take her cameras where cameras have never gone before."[1] This producer is Lucy Jarvis.

Lucy Howard was born to Herman M. and Sophie Howard in New York City.[2] Jarvis remembers:

> I grew up in a family in which aunts and uncles and cousins and grandparents were all within a mile of each other. We fed into each other. There was an enormous amount of goodwill and guidance.[3]

Lucy Jarvis's mother, who had formally been a pattern artist for *McCall's* magazine, was a gifted seamstress. "[She] could sew anything in the world, sew, crochet, create, whatever," Jarvis once said.[4] Once, on a family dare, Lucy's mother sewed her own umbrella. According to Jarvis, her mother was also something of a feminist: "My mother was a very advanced woman, really, but she was born thirty years too soon," Jarvis has said, "She had an enormous drive that I have inherited."[5]

149

LUCY JARVIS

After high school, Lucy began study at Cornell University. "I went away to school, which was rare for women. I was one of the few of my set who did."[6] At Cornell she learned how true that was: the ratio of men to women was ten to one. An older brother was already at Cornell studying for a master's (and later a Ph.D.) in engineering. The cost of two children in college took a toll on the family finances. Lucy said:

> The fact that I went into home economics was a great help because it was a scholarship class.... I spent all my extra time in the dramatic club and as the advertising manager of my college humor magazine.... Communications was my bent then as well.[7]

She graduated with a bachelor's degree in 1938 and promptly found employment as a dietitian in the New York Hospital-Cornell Medical Center.[8] Though the job gave her the opportunity to engage in research, Lucy found it all a bit of a bore. The next year, after leaving her prior position, Lucy became director and chief copywriter for a promotional campaign initiated by Beechnut Foods.[9]

The year after that, in 1940, Lucy Howard got married. Her husband, Serge Jarvis, was a specialist in corporate and international law and was fluent in eight languages. They subsequently had two children, Barbara and Peter.[10]

Also in 1940 Jarvis moved to *McCall's* magazine to take a position as the magazine's associate foods editor.[11] Later she was named full editor. That job gave Jarvis her first taste of television. She frequently traveled the country for *McCall's*, giving speeches and appearing on talk shows:

> I was fascinated by the whole medium. I realized that no matter how successful I might be in the written media, I could still only reach a handful of people. If I really wanted to make an impact ... then, television, was, and is, the way.[12]

McCall's financed Jarvis's graduate work at Columbia Teachers College, where she earned her master's degree in 1941.[13] Later, in 1942, Jarvis took additional classes at the New School for Social Research, also in New York. That same year, she found time to author her first book, *The Pocket Book Cook-Book*.[14]

While still with the magazine, Jarvis dreamed up the idea for a magazine-type television show for women. But family came first. Lucy and her husband were expecting their first child and decided to move to Connecticut so the children could grow up in the country. She left *McCall's* and did not return to the work force until both her children were teenagers.[15] She said:

> Those years that I spent at home with my children were very fulfilling. They were years I enjoyed enormously.... I would say to any woman today that I would have [spent those years] exactly the same way.[16]

Between housewife duties, Jarvis immersed herself in charity work and in being active in a cultural organization that granted scholarships to gifted artists. One of their beneficiaries included violinist Itzhak Perlman.[17] To raise money for the scholarship fund Jarvis once arranged a dinner at the Waldorf-Astoria. She planned the menu, the decor, and the publicity. She even found the entertainment—a young Mike Nichols and Elaine May, then just starting in show business. They were paid $75 for their appearance. Jarvis said, "It was then that I knew I'd be a producer."[18]

Lucy Jarvis began her broadcasting career in the early 1950s by joining the staffs of various radio and TV productions. From 1955 until 1956, she held a position with talk-show host David Suskind's company, Talent Associates.[19]

After that, she was named women's TV editor for the Pathé news service. Jarvis held that position for one year. In 1957 Lucy's husband introduced her to former NBC news producer Martha Rountree, the woman who had originated *Meet the Press*. Together Jarvis and Rountree put together a show titled *Capitol Close-Up*, with Jarvis serving as the program's coproducer. That program consisted of profiles of such notable political newsmakers as Dwight D. Eisenhower, John F. Kennedy, and J. Edgar Hoover. The show aired on the WOR-Mutual Broadcasting System.[20]

In 1959, as part of news producer Irving Gitlin's staff, Jarvis moved to NBC and became associate producer (and, later, in 1961, producer) of a Saturday-night debate program, *The Nation's Future*.[21] Jarvis would stay with the NBC network for sixteen years. One of Jarvis's early duties on *Nation's Future* was to make sure that the studio audiences for each program were equally divided between both sides of the issue. The show debated topics from birth control to US policy in Cuba. Jarvis remembers the latter show: "We had fist-fights in the hallway, but the most difficult chore was finding enough pro–Castro people."[22]

Another program had US astronaut John Glenn discussing space exploration with cosmonaut Gherman Titov.[23] That show was an unheard-of international coup for Lucy Jarvis; with the assistance of the White House and the Kremlin, Jarvis, working mostly in secret, was able to organize and produce the debate. In an unprecedented move, all three major networks carried the program when it aired.[24] During *The Nation's Future's* brief (1960–61) run, however, the most heated debate took place over the issue of fluoride in public drinking water. Jarvis recalled that episode: "I still don't understand it.... Extra police had to be called out, and everyone was still arguing when we went off the air."[25]

In 1962 Jarvis started on her next major, and to that time largest, undertaking. After two years of unsuccessful attempts to gain access to the Kremlin, the "inner sanctum" of the Soviet government, Jarvis was able finally to gain Russian approval to produce a film there. It was by far the most challenging duty Jarvis had yet taken on. In preparation she brushed up on her conversational Russian by taking a three-month refresher course.[26] She also devised a plan to get into the "sanctum" by getting the okay of Russia's top man, Khrushchev. Lucy Jarvis said, "I wanted to meet Khrushchev personally in order to explain to him why I wanted to do a film on the Kremlin."[27] With the help of President Kennedy and his press secretary Pierre Salinger, Jarvis arranged to tag along on a Presidential trip to Vienna, where she knew she would be able to get close to Khrushchev. NBC had already filled its quota of reporters, so it took something of a Presidential act to enable Jarvis to go. John Kennedy sent the following letter to the NBC network: "I would like to give Lucy Jarvis permission to accompany us on the trip to Paris, Vienna and London as a guest of the White House."[28]

Once in Vienna, Jarvis met Khrushchev and told him of her desire to make a film of the Kremlin—something even the Soviets themselves had never allowed. After that initial conversation, though, nothing much happened. Jarvis returned home with no firm commitments. Then, one year later, she received word that Khrushchev was expecting her and her crew in Moscow on June 23 (which happened to be Lucy's birthday). She flew to Moscow to begin preproduction.[29]

Life during the Cold War in pre-Glastnost Russia was not easy. Jarvis found herself under a windfall of red tape and dead ends. She said in 1963, "Never again will I complain about Washington bureaucracy. The Russians try to emulate us in every way; they have surpassed us in this art."[30] Jarvis also encountered other problems:

> I never overcame the Russian telephone! Russia was, and may still be, a country of unlisted telephone numbers. You couldn't call anyone ... the minister of culture, or even the ministry. Every time I wanted to make an appointment with someone, I'd have to go there.[31]

Finally Jarvis devised a way to get around the problem. Every time she was in an official's office, she made a habit of going to his telephone and taking down his number. Gradually she developed one of the most comprehensive Russian phone books in history.[32]

Still things moved slowly. Jarvis cooled her heels and continued her study of the Russian language for two months while trying to gain access to the Kremlin or to Khrushchev. Finally she invited herself to a party at the Austrian Embassy where she knew she would run into Khrushchev again. In broken Russian sentences, Jarvis asked the Premier once again to allow her to make a film of the Kremlin. "I asked him why I had to wait so long—and he corrected my grammar—and suddenly he said, 'You and your crew can come in next Monday; bring your director.'"[33] Later the Premier added:

> My dear, there is a man from CBS who has been trying to get in the Kremlin for two years. He would have kissed my hands if I let him do that TV program, and you think two months is a lot of time![34]

Later that week, Lucy Jarvis flew out of Russia to Paris to pick up her technical director, John Peters, but once again nothing went smoothly. She told Edwin Newman in the interview introduction to the Kremlin film:

> When I went to the Russian embassy in Paris for our visas back into Moscow, they said they'd never heard of us. But I wasn't giving up. Johnny and I got on an AirFrance plane without visas—he kicking and screaming—and [we] flew to Moscow.... When we arrived the [guards] gave us a hard time. But it was Sunday, they couldn't reach their superiors and they didn't know what to make of this American woman who was dropping all these names and phone numbers [belonging to] their top leaders.

> So they put us in a building—a holding center really—over night and in the morning Johnny and I were bailed out by Andre Gromyko.[35]

Further problems occurred before any production began. Jarvis insisted that her film crew be housed within one or two hotels, rather than scattered all over Moscow. The arranging of these accommodations alone took two weeks.[36] Gaining access to every nook and cranny of the Kremlin was not easy either. Most of Jarvis's negotiations took place with Igor Mayorov, the Soviet official given the duty of overseeing the project. Jarvis remembered, "We started off battling and ended ... in tears at the airport."[37] Along the battle front, she slowly gained permission to film inside the private quarters of Ivan the Terrible and Peter the Great, but only on the condition that those areas remain closed to the public and even Kremlin personnel.[38]

Determined to present more than just a tour of the building's architecture, Jarvis and crew presented a colorful retelling of 700 years of Russian history. Brilliantly using original settings, music, sound effects, and priceless artifacts, Lucy Jarvis and company created an actorless "drama" based on historical facts: doors opened and slammed shut again, long swords crossed each other in pretend fights, and paintings of the leaders on the Kremlin walls seemed to come to life.[39] To simulate the invasion of the Napoleonic forces in 1812 and the burning of a part of the Kremlin, Jarvis and crew staged a mock fire complete with smoke and imitation flames. The blaze appeared so realistic that Soviet fire fighters were called out, only to be put to a halt by producer Lucy. Speaking now in more understandable Russian, she told the fire officials that her crew had permission to start the fake blaze and that the smoke could be put out only after the filming had been completed.[40]

Lucy Jarvis's command of the many situations at hand got her dubbed the "Field Marshal" by her Russian hosts.[41] To keep many of her new Russian friends happy, Jarvis acquired stashes of American cigarettes and baked batches of homemade brownies during occasional trips back to the US. After returning to Russia she gave them to Soviet technicians and soldiers.[42]

It took three months of filming inside the Kremlin, and a second crew two months on the outside of it, to complete principal photography for the documentary.[43] Outdoor shoots included views of the building by river boat and helicopter.[44]

Though the outdoor requirements were sometimes difficult to arrange, filming inside the Kremlin caused greater difficulties:

> Normally we worked all night, after the Russians went home; one night they didn't leave and I was very annoyed. And the next day our American ambassador, without revealing the whole story, simply said, "President Kennedy and Khrushchev were having an argument."[45]

Jarvis was not amused. She immediately cabled then Presidential Press

Secretary Pierre Salinger to tell the President of the United States that he was causing production delays; could he please wait until the film was completed to hold his little argument with the Russian government?[46]

After Jarvis returned to the States, she learned that the "little argument" was the Cuban missile crisis. At a dinner some time later at the White House, she began to apologize to the President for her message. Kennedy cut her off in the middle of her explanation. He said, "Didn't you know, Lucy, I told Khrushchev that if he got the missiles out of Cuba, … I'd get Lucy Jarvis out of the Kremlin?"[47]

Jarvis said in 1981, "I was the only producer allowed into the Kremlin with cameras, and since then, I understand nobody has been allowed back."[48] Said Jarvis recently, "The Russians have honored the exclusive contract I negotiated with them."[49]

The film *The Kremlin* aired on NBC-TV on May 21, 1963. It would go on to win an Emmy and *McCall's* Golden Mike Award.[50] It was also distributed worldwide by the NBC network. In the Soviet Union, the film was shown to Russian "special audiences" as a reward for "good activities."[51]

On her return from Russia, Lucy Jarvis took on a new challenge: producing the first television special using a communications satellite.[52] Titled *Museum Without Walls*, the special, which aired on NBC on November 17, 1963, was concerned with both the Louvre in France and the National Gallery in Washington, D.C. A dual tour of the two buildings and their vast holdings made up the program.[53]

With contact with the Louvre curators and French government officials already established, Jarvis decided to embark on a long-held dream: to film a documentary on the history and contents of the Louvre museum. However, piercing the Louvre's golden veneer proved as difficult as breaking through the Iron Curtain. Jarvis found that "The museum curators didn't like the public coming into their museum, much less an American film crew."[54] Also working against them was an incident of ten years earlier when some paintings were allowed to be still-photographed. The intense lighting needed for the cameras caused several thousand dollars worth of damage to a number of Rembrandts.[55] To bypass this particular problem, Jarvis made careful plans to see that no hot lights would be used near any of the art objects: the lighting crew employed type 10K lamps to assure the art's safety.[56]

Even with these assurances, Louvre curators were still unsure of this American woman and her camera crew. Finally, she was forced to play her trump card; she asked the foreign ministers flat out, "If Khrushchev trusted me, why can't you?"[57] On the strength of that question—and the quality of the film *The Kremlin*—Jarvis became the first producer, French or otherwise, to be allowed inside the museum.[58] French actor Charles Boyer was hired as narrator.[59]

Jarvis arrived in France in June of 1963. As with *The Kremlin* shoot, filming frequently took place after the museum closed, and again, as with *The*

Kremlin shoot, filming did not always proceed as planned. One incident presented an especially perplexing problem. The documentary's opening scene—a lengthy, withdrawing crane shot of the museum's sculpted masterpiece *Winged Victory*—was proving impossible to get. Holding the camera by hand proved too shaky and even using a dolly to track the shot was not working out. While Jarvis and crew were trying to figure out a way to get the shot, a French film grip came up to Jarvis and uttered something. Though she did not know exactly what he said, she was desperate and was willing to try just about anything. A few moments later, the man returned driving a small French automobile into the museum's foyer. The television camera was mounted on top of it. The film crew got the shot they wanted. Jarvis learned later that what the man had said, in colloquial French, was the expression for "two horses," as in two horsepowers, the size of his little car.[60] All was going quite well with the after-hours *Winged Victory* shot until the Minister of Culture walked into the museum with a group of guests and found the film crew gathered around an automobile in the middle of his Louvre. He was stunned and Jarvis was red-faced, but both proceeded with their business.[61]

After-hours filming, when the crew had the museum to themselves, presented a few unique problems. One night, after finishing filming for the evening, Jarvis and her crew were dismayed to learn that they had been locked inside the building. Nevertheless, that negative was turned to a positive. The idea of being trapped for a night alone with the greatest works of art in history proved too great a fantasy to ignore. The final documentary contains a short segment based on this art-lover's dream.[62]

The film *The Louvre* detailed the building's complicated construction history. The Louvre has been built, rebuilt, and added to many times over the centuries. To help viewers keep track of the structure's many different incarnations over the years, the film's production designer ordered a small wooden model of the Louvre that was seen throughout the documentary being pieced together and taken apart much like a child's erector set.[63]

Of course, the film also contained ample footage of the museum's many treasures, all filmed using 35 mm. color film stock instead of the usual 16 mm. in order to gain greater detail from each of the art works.[64]

The Louvre: A Golden Prison, directed by John Sughrue and written by Sidney Carroll, aired for the first time on November 17, 1964.[65] It was a critical and commercial smash. NBC received more than 100,000 complimentary letters, and the network found the film so popular that it aired it three more times within the year.[66] The film, shown worldwide, would garner a Peabody Award, a Radio-TV Critics Award, and six Emmys.[67] It remains the definitive film on the museum.

Though Lucy Jarvis was gaining fame as a prominent producer of the "theme" documentary, historically showcasing extraordinary events and places around the world, she shifted gears in 1965 to take on a hard-hitting topic involving life, death, and the medical community. *Who Shall Live?* dealt with the topic of kidney dialysis and asked why thousands of patients in need of the procedure were being denied it.[68] Jarvis, her film crew, and a team of experts in the field studied the medical, economic, and moral reasons for this situation for two months. When the program aired on November 28, 1965, public outcry against the US government's failure to meet the demand for dialysis machines was so great the government immediately granted an additional six million dollars to fund kidney machine centers across the nation.[69] The program was awarded the American Medical Association's Journalism Award, and a spokesperson for the National Dialysis Committee said, "Each new patient treated ... on the artificial kidney will owe some portion of his life to the camera and cutting shears of Lucy Jarvis."[70] Other Lucy Jarvis–produced health documentaries followed: *Pain! Where Does It Hurt Most?* and *What Price Health?*[71]

In 1966 Jarvis made one of her first trips to the Far East when she accompanied actress Mary Martin and her stage production of *Hello, Dolly!* on a tour of Japan and South Vietnam. Jarvis and her film crew documented Martin and cast performing on stage and interacting with the people of the East and with American military troops. *Mary Martin*: Hello, Dolly! *'Round the World'* aired on February 7, 1966.[72]

Next, Jarvis returned to the area of new technology to coordinate a stirring television tribute to the life and work of Pablo Picasso, *Bravo Picasso!* Using the Early Bird Satellite, Jarvis showcased the largest collection of Picasso's work ever seen by combining two different exhibitions, one in Paris and one in Dallas, Texas.[73] The life of the artist was detailed through viewings of his paintings and sculptures and through narration by actor Yves Montand.[74] The artist himself took part in the program by donating a painting for sale in order to raise money for an Italian art restoration project. To have the sale take place during the live program, Jarvis organized a global auction by overseeing four different film units, one in Paris, one in Texas, one in London, and one in New York. The show aired on February 5, 1967.[75] The success of this special, combined with her earlier achievement with *The Louvre*, caused the French government to knight Lucy Jarvis in the Order of Arts and Letters—making her one of only twelve Americans ever to be so honored.[76]

Lucy Jarvis filled the next few years at NBC with equally well-received work. She tackled such topics on film as *Dr. Barnard's Heart Transplant Operations* (1968), *Vietnam and After* (1969), and an examination of mental illness among teenagers in *Cry Help!* (1970).[77] Also in 1970, Jarvis and her cameras were the first to bring national attention to the plague of drug abuse among America's young people. Her film *Trip to Nowhere* focused on the existing drug problems and available recovery programs in a middle-class section of Phoenix, Arizona.[78]

Returning in 1971 to the form in which she obtained her greatest fame, Jarvis achieved the third of her big coups (after the Kremlin and the Louvre) by gaining the cooperation of Scotland Yard in the making of a film on its crime-solving expertise. Typical for Lucy Jarvis, she was the first producer ever allowed in with television cameras.[79] Actor David Niven was hired as the film's narrator. Said Jarvis of her choice, "He's bilingual.... [He is] equally at home in the English language and the American language." *Scotland Yard* aired on March 30, 1971.[80]

In 1973 Jarvis added yet another unprecedented achievement to her career: the right to film the Forbidden City in the People's Republic of China. Lucy Jarvis had been in negotiations with the Chinese government for more than ten years.[81] To gain final approval, she "camped on the doorstep" of the Chinese Embassy in Ottawa, Canada.[82]

Just as plans were getting underway for Jarvis and her crew of eight to head to China, she received a confidential telephone call from Henry Kissinger concerning the planned—but as yet unannounced—Nixon presidential trip to the Far East. Kissinger, worried that the NBC film crew would steal some of the President's thunder, asked Jarvis if she would mind waiting to make her film after the Presidential visit was completed. Jarvis recalls: "I did mind." Nevertheless, she put the film on hold for one year.[83]

Lucy Jarvis finally arrived in China to begin filming in August of 1972.[84] Along with looking at the history of the many Oriental dynasties, her film looked at the changing lives of contemporary Chinese citizens.[85]

At one time during the production, while filming in the Ming Tombs located seven stories underground, Jarvis spotted a telephone used by the caretakers of the monument. She picked it up and called NBC in New York—collect.[86] Edwin Newman said of the incident, "Leave it to Lucy; she'll find a telephone any-where."[87] That 1973 film was not only a success in this country but was such a success in the People's Republic that RCA, the then parent company of NBC, received the rights to build the first satellite ground station in that country.[88]

After her latest adventure abroad, Jarvis returned to films with social implications. One of her most notable examined the issue of hand guns. *A Shooting Gallery Called America* caused a storm of controversy even before it was aired:

> People knew we were doing it, and we began to get lots of mail. Probably they were alerted by a national organization.... There was such an emotional reaction, I didn't want the program to go until I was doubly sure that everything was checked out.[89]

To that end, the original air date for the program was set back by Jarvis on two separate occasions. The program finally aired on April 27, 1975.[90]

In 1976, as network interest in television documentaries lessened, Lucy Jarvis, after sixteen years with NBC, decided it was time to strike out on her own:

Documentaries were splintering into more commercially geared magazine shows. I had the rights to the Mexican Anthropological Museum and I got into a big hassle about it. NBC didn't want to put any time, money or priorities into that kind of programming.[91]

Though Jarvis found it invigorating to be out from under the network, she quickly learned that life on her own was not always going to be easy:

> I was going to be the first woman to get out there and start her own production company and go around hustling and selling. That's a lot different. I mean, I couldn't just sign a voucher for my telephone bills and throw it into the out box anymore.[92]

By founding her own business, Creative Projects, Inc., in 1976, Jarvis became the first woman in America to head her own independent production company.[93]

One of Jarvis's first projects was producing Barbara Walters's first prime-time interview special; guests included Barbra Streisand and President and Mrs. Carter.[94] A second major project was Jarvis's first entirely fictional film. A miniseries for the NBC network, *Family Reunion*, aired on April 11th and 12th of 1981. It starred the legendary Bette Davis.[95]

In more recent years Jarvis has returned to cross-cultural productions and projects. In 1988 she produced the first joint American-Soviet production of a Broadway musical. *Sophisticated Ladies*, based on the music of Duke Ellington, was staged by a combination American/Soviet crew and opened in Moscow on October 1, 1988. Later the show traveled to Leningrad and Tbilisi. In April of 1989, the show began a six-month tour of the United States, premiering at the Kennedy Center for the Performing Arts.[96] Jarvis remembers that during the planning stages of the production, "They [Soviet officials] said, 'We don't think that's possible.' I said, 'Watch me.'"[97]

In 1990 Jarvis arranged for the importation of the Russian rock opera *Junon and Avos: The Hope* to the United States. Jarvis had become a fan of the play while in the USSR and decided to bring the show to this country with the backing of another of the show's fans, couturier Pierre Cardin. The two-million-dollar production opened in New York City on January 7, 1990.[98]

Once again Lucy Jarvis's work had transcended the boundaries of political difference. She has said:

> I believe in what I'm doing and I guess I make other people feel that belief in it…. I do believe that everything we do can contribute to better understanding and peace. Since my milieu is communication I think I should use it any way I can to make that happen. It makes a difference when you are engaged in a project that involves more than meets the eye.[99]

Today Lucy Jarvis heads two production companies, Jarvis Theatre & Film and Creative Projects, Inc. She has several projects in development, including a series of television specials in association with the New York City Mayor's Office and a theatrical film based on Philip Hallie's book *Lest Innocent Blood Be Shed.*

Jarvis's work, by bringing together national issues and international cultures, has aided the cause of national and international understanding. No other filmmaker in television or motion pictures, male or female, can parallel her list of credits. She has created a staggering body of work. Films like *The Kremlin, The Louvre, Who Shall Live?* and *Trip to Nowhere* have stood the test of time, remaining in every case the definitive film record on their respective subjects.

Lucy Jarvis's international and prosocial successes aside, though, her real success, perhaps, has come not by choosing to turn her television cameras on important issues, individuals, and places, but, through the medium of television, turning them on ourselves. Her work reevaluates and expands the standards by which and with which we define our times, in the process adding to the progress of cultural transmission and the perpetuation of the human myth.

Lucy Jarvis

1938	Graduated from Cornell University.
July 18, 1940	Married Serge Jarvis, international and corporate law specialist.
1940	Joined *McCall's* magazine as foods editor.
1941	Earned master's degree from Columbia College.
1942	Wrote and published *The Pocket Book Cook-Book.*
1955	Joined David Susskind's Talent Associates organization; first job in television.
1956	Left Susskind to be women's editor for Pathé news.
1957	Joined NBC; cocreated talk show *Capitol Close-Up.*
1959	Promoted to associate producer by NBC network.
November 12, 1960	First broadcast of *Nation's Future,* series produced by Lucy Jarvis.
September 16, 1961	Final broadcast of *Nation's Future.*
1961	Named full producer by NBC network.
June 1962	Arrived in Russia for preproduction on *The Kremlin.*
May 21, 1963	*The Kremlin* aired.
June 1963	Arrived in France for preproduction on *The Lourve.*
November 17, 1963	*Museum Without Walls* aired.
November 17, 1964	*The Louvre* aired.
November 28, 1965	*Who Shall Live?* aired.
February 7, 1966	*Mary Martin*: Hello, Dolly! *'Round the World'* aired.
February 5, 1967	*Bravo Picasso!* aired.

July 11, 1967	*Khrushchev in Exile: His Opinions and Revelations* aired.
1968	*Dr. Barnard's Heart Transplant Operations* aired.
1969	*Vietnam and After, Christopher Discovers America*, musical drama, aired.
April 26, 1970	*Cry Help!* aired.
August 24, 1970	*Trip to Nowhere* aired.
December 19, 1970	*What Price Health?* aired.
March 30, 1971	*Scotland Yard* aired.
March 12, 1972	*The Peking Ballet: First Spectacular from China* aired.
March 28, 1972	*Pain! Where Does It Hurt Most?* aired.
August 1972	Arrives in China for preproduction on *China and the Forbidden City*.
1973	*China and the Forbidden City* aired.
1974	*The Pursuit of Youth* and *The Russian Connection* aired.
April 27, 1975	*A Shooting Gallery Called America* aired.
1976	Departed from NBC; formed Creative Projects, Inc. First American woman to head own production company.
September 1976	Named to produce ABC television specials for Barbara Walters.
December 14, 1976	First *Barbara Walters Special* aired; produced by Lucy Jarvis; guests included President and Mrs. Jimmy Carter.
April 11-12, 1981	*Family Reunion* aired. Lucy Jarvis's first all fictional television film.
April 1988	Signed agreement in Russia to produce musical *Sophisticated Ladies* in Soviet Union.
October 1, 1988	*Sophisticated Ladies* opens in Russia.
April 1989	*Sophisticated Ladies* imported into America.
January 7, 1990	*Junon and Avos: The Hope* debuted in America.

NOTES

1. *The Kremlin* (motion picture) (National Broadcasting Company, 1963).
2. *Current Biography* (1972), p. 241.
3. Lynn Gilbert and Gaylen Moore, *Particular Passions* (New York: Crown, 1981), p. 307.
4. Ibid., p. 308.
5. Ibid.
6. Ibid., p. 303.
7. Ibid.
8. *Current Biography*, p. 241.
9. Ibid.
10. Ibid., p. 243.

11. "Lucy Jarvis," National Broadcasting Company (April 1981), p. 1.
12. Gilbert and Moore, p. 303.
13. *Current Biography*, p. 241.
14. "Lucy Jarvis,"p. 2.
15. Gilbert and Moore, p. 304.
16. Ibid.
17. Ibid.
18. Ibid.
19. *Current Biography*, p. 241.
20. Ibid.
21. Ibid.
22. Hal Humphrey, "TV's Other Lucy," *Los Angeles Mirror* (22 December 1961),
p. 17.
23. *Current Biography*, p. 241.
24. Lucy Jarvis, letter to author (16 July 1992).
25. Humphrey, p. 17.
26. John P. Shanley, "Woman Producer Conquers Kremlin," *New York Times* (19 May
1963), p. 17.
27. Gilbert and Moore, p. 301.
28. Ibid.
29. *The Kremlin.*
30. Shanley, p. 17.
31. Gilbert and Moore, p. 302.
32. Ibid.
33. *The Kremlin.*
34. Gilbert and Moore, p. 302.
35. *The Kremlin.*
36. Shanley, p. 17.
37. Ibid.
38. Ibid.
39. *The Kremlin.*
40. Shanley, p. 17.
41. *Current Biography*, p. 241.
42. Ibid., p. 242.
43. Gilbert and Moore, p. 303.
44. Shanley, p. 17.
45. *The Kremlin.*
46. Jeff DeBell, "Sophisticated Lady," *Roanoke Times & World News* (12 April 1989),
p. 2.
47. *The Kremlin.*
48. Gilbert and Moore, p. 301.
49. Jarvis letter.
50. *Current Biography*, p. 242.
51. *The Kremlin.*
52. "Lucy Jarvis,"p. 2.
53. *Current Biography*, p. 242.
54. *The Louvre* (motion picture) (National Broadcasting Company, 1964).
55. Henry Giniger, "Art for TV's Sake," *New York Times* (27 October 1963), p. 13.
56. Jarvis.
57. "Mission: Impossible," *Time* (12 January 1968), p. 52.
58. Giniger, p. 13.
59. *The Louvre.*
60. Ibid.
61. Ibid.

62. Ibid.

63. Ibid.

64. Giniger, p. 13.

65. *Current Biography*, p. 242.

66. *The Louvre.*

67. "Lucy Jarvis," p. 2.

68. Ibid.

69. Ibid., p. 3.

70. *Current Biography*, p. 242.

71. Ibid.

72. "Lucy Jarvis," p. 3.

73. *Current Biography*, p. 242.

74. "Lucy Jarvis," p. 2.

75. *Current Biography*, p. 242.

76. "Lucy Jarvis—Jarvis Theatre and Film Productions Bio," Jarvis Theatre & Film Production (1992), p. 1.

77. *Current Biography*, p. 242.

78. "Lucy Jarvis," p. 3.

79. Ibid.

80. *Current Biography*, p. 243.

81. Robert Campbell, *The Golden Years of Broadcasting* (New York: Rutledge, 1976), p. 135.

82. *China and the Forbidden City* (motion picture) (National Broadcasting Company, 1973).

83. Ibid.

84. "Inside China with NBC," *Broadcasting* (21 August 1972), p. 35.

85. Ibid.

86. *China and the Forbidden City.*

87. Ibid.

88. "Lucy Jarvis—Jarvis Theatre & Film Productions Bio," p. 1.

89. Charles Montgomery Hammond Jr., *The Image Decade: Television Documentary 1965–1975* (New York: Hastings House, 1981), p. 87.

90. Ibid.

91. Gilbert and Moore, p. 305.

92. Ibid.

93. "Lucy Jarvis—Jarvis Theatre & Film Productions Bio," p. 1.

94. Ibid.

95. Jeffrey Robinson, *Bette Davis ... Her Film and Stage Career* (London: Proteus, 1982), p. 126.

96. DeBell, p. 3.

97. Ibid.

98. Timothy W. Ryback, "East Woos West in a Romantic Soviet Rock Opera," *New York Times* (7 January 1990), p. 25.

99. DeBell, p. 2.

Ida Lupino

Few women have had the talent and skill to break the stereotype that television directing is a "man's job." Those women directors who (like their male counterparts) take an idea from script to screen—controlling the actors, the lighting, the sets, and the all-seeing eye of the camera—must excel not only in ability but in stamina as well. One woman to defy the "men only" notion was a former film star and film director sometimes known affectionately as "Loops," "Loop," or "Lupie." Those closest to her—her actors, crew members, technicians, and stagehands—even called her "Mother."[1] She was also regarded as one of the most skillful, inventive, and professional directors in the history of television—male *or* female. She was Ida Lupino.

Ida Lupino was born in London, England, on February 4, 1918. Her birth took place under a dining room table during a World War I Zeppelin raid.[2] Her parents were Stanley and Connie Emerald Lupino, both well-known, active stage performers.[3] Lupino's father's family could trace its theatrical roots back to Grimaldi, the Italian Renaissance clown. From that early beginning more than 500 years ago, the Lupino family tree hung heavy with writers, singers, acrobats, and jugglers. Ida Lupino has said about her choice of career, "I became an actress just to show my father I wouldn't let him—or the other Lupinos—down."[4] That desire began early. At age seven, she wrote and produced a play titled *Mademoiselle* for school friends.[5] At age ten, she talked her father into constructing a "miniature" theater for her and her sister Rita in the family's backyard. The finished structure consisted of lights, orchestra pit, and seating for one hundred. At twelve, she was in a children's parody ensemble.[6]

In 1931 young Ida began planning for her professional acting career by attending the Royal Academy of Dramatic Arts. She lied about her age to get in, saying she was fifteen.[7] Between school and touring in a few traveling productions, Ida began moonlighting as an occasional film extra.[8] Lupino's first major film role came in 1933, playing a pretty, blond ingenue in Allan Dwan's film *Her First Affair*. The director had originally auditioned Lupino's mother but was struck instead by her "provocative" eighteen-year-old daughter.[9] For her part in that film, Ida dyed her hair blond and thinned out her eyebrows. She was soon labeled "The English Jean Harlow."[10]

From that beginning Lupino became a mildly popular English screen starlet. Often she played characters older than her real age, and seldom did she play anything nice. Lupino remembers: "My Father once said to me, 'You're born to be bad.' And it was true. I made eight films in England before I came to America, and I played a tramp or a slut in all of them."[11] That badness paid off, sort of, in 1933.

Ida Lupino and her mother came to Hollywood in August of 1933, when Ida was fifteen. Executives at Paramount Studios had seen one of Lupino's English films and were considering her for the lead role in their all-star production of *Alice in Wonderland*.[12] The film of Lupino's they had seen was titled *Money for Speed*. Lupino remembered the mix-up that got her to the American film capital:

> [In the film] I played a dual role. They only saw the section where I was this sweet little blond, not the part where I was the hooker.... When I finally got to Hollywood for the screen test, they said "What have we got here?"[13]

Actress Charlotte Henry (a natural blond) would go on to play Lewis Carroll's innocent Alice.

Said Lupino many years later: "*Alice in Wonderland* ... wouldn't have been right for me at all—I would have played her as a hooker and danced on the tabletops. Can you imagine, Alice in Wonderland as a tramp?"[14] Besides, Lupino added later, "They said my voice sounded more like the caterpillar."[15]

Regardless of that quickly lost role, Lupino was now under contract to Paramount Studios for $600 a week. With her mother and sister, she rented a house near the studio and began the usual studio build up: posing for cheesecake bathing-suit shots and going to popular Hollywood nightspots on the arms of other new, fresh faces.[16]

Slowly Ida Lupino began to gain some screen time in Paramount productions. She played spry young girls in films like *Search for Beauty*, starring Buster Crabbe, and in two comedy-dramas with Richard Arlen.[17] She also appeared in several forgettable films that happened to star unforgettable performers, including Bing Crosby, Ethel Merman, and Mary Pickford.[18] Basically, though, prominent roles were few. Lupino spent most of her time cooling her heels in her home swimming pool and hanging out with fellow Paramount contractee, actress Ann Sheridan.[19] Said Lupino of her early days in Hollywood, "All Annie and I did at Paramount was dance on tabletops while Buster Crabbe held us up. They let her go and we both wound up at Warner Brothers—in the same picture!"[20]

By 1937, after a victorious battle with polio, a fully recovered Lupino was ready for some changes. She had labeled her earlier film roles as "syrupy ingenue parts" and had grown hungry for something with more substance.[21] Lupino requested and was granted a release from her Paramount contract. Her first film as a freelance was in a weak RKO farce, *Fight for Your Lady*. After that, there were no acting roles for Lupino for one year.[22] Instead, she indulged other talents: radio performer, short-story writer, music composer. Her composition

IDA LUPINO

Aladdin Suite was performed by the Los Angeles Philharmonic during this period.[23] On the advice of friend Hedda Hopper, Lupino spent her down time letting her real hair color and eyebrows grow in, and brushing up on her acting.[24]

Ida Lupino took the first of her three trips down the aisle in 1938, at age twenty, when she married fellow actor Louis Hayward, a sleek matinee idol usually of second-billed features.[25] By 1939 Lupino had returned to screen acting in forgettable films with forgettable titles. To jump-start her career and finally get the kinds of roles she wanted, Lupino knew she would have to fight hard. She learned that respected director William Wellman was preparing a film version of Kipling's *The Light That Failed* back at her old stomping ground Paramount. The story concerned a painter's relationship with a young, Cockney street urchin who inspires him to paint his greatest work. After the painter goes blind, the young girl (Lupino) slashes the portrait in a fit of rage.[26] Lupino knew that this was her big chance. Legend has it that she learned the part, burst into Wellman's office, demanded an audition and gave an all-out performance to win him over.[27]

Though the film's costar, Ronald Colman, objected, Wellman cast Lupino.[28] Colman's objections might not have been without foundation; after the film was released, critics raved about Lupino's performance. Critic Graham Greene wrote, "He [Colman] was sometimes acted right off the set."[29] The *New York Times* said, "Lupino's Bessie is another of the surprises we get when a little ingenue bursts forth as a great actress."[30] Despite the acclaim, though, a time of relative inactivity followed for Lupino. Her husband's career flourished at this time while hers stood nearly still.[31]

That changed near the end of 1940 when Lupino was cast opposite old friend Ann Sheridan in the Humphrey Bogart/George Raft classic *They Drive by Night* at Warner Brothers. Lupino's role as a neurotic wife whose love for her husband drives her to murder and then to madness solidified her new rank as one of film's most gifted actresses. *Newsweek* said, "She stole the show."[32]

Now being discussed in the same breath as such actresses as Bette Davis, Lupino moved quickly from "A" picture to "A" picture. She starred opposite Bogart again in Walsh's *High Sierra* and played opposite John Garfield in Curtiz's *The Sea Wolf*, both in 1941.[33] That same year Lupino starred in her personal favorite among her films, *Ladies in Retirement*. In this grand ghoul exercise, Lupino was a housekeeper who kills to protect her two mentally ill sisters.[34]

One of Lupino's most notable film roles came in 1943. In *The Hard Way*, Lupino portrayed an ambitious, iron-willed older sister pushing her under-talented sibling to fame and fortune in showbiz. Ida Lupino tore into the role like a lion and for her efforts received the New York Film Critics' Award for best actress.[35] (Costarring with Lupino in the film *The Hard Way*, was another actress destined to find expanded opportunities later in television: Faye Emerson.)

The *New York Herald Tribune* wrote of Lupino's work at this time: "Ida Lupino ... is one of the great actresses of the screen."[36] Lupino has said about her acting philosophy: "I'm not a Method actress.... The only method I have goes, 'Dear God, I hope I make it today.'"[37] She also was not her best critic; Lupino said in 1975, "I walked out of a screening of *The Hard Way*. I hated my performance."[38]

Ida Lupino would go on to other films, some notable, most not. She acted with Paul Henreid in *In Our Time* (1944); was the best thing in a bad movie, *Devotion*, playing Emily Bronte (1946); worked opposite Errol Flynn in *Escape Me Never* (1947); and had a role in the cult favorite *Road House* with Cornel Wilde and Richard Widmark (1948).[39]

All in all Lupino's movie career was hit-and-miss. She said, "For about eighteen months back in the mid-1940s, I could not get a job in pictures as an actress." She filled up her spare time by working in radio.[40]

In 1945 Lupino divorced Louis Hayward. In 1948 she officially became a citizen of the United States.[41] Also in 1948, on August 5, Lupino married producer Collier Young, later a successful producer and then an executive assistant to Columbia Pictures' chief Harry Cohn.[42]

Bored with her acting career, Lupino began to write scripts that she hoped to produce, in her own words, "Free of [studio] front-office domination."[43] She said her goal was "to do high quality, low budget, independent films on provocative subject matter, to tell 'how America lives,' and be commercially successful at it."[44] Along with her new husband and Anson Bond, a TV producer and clothing store magnate, Lupino formed Emerald Productions, named after her mother.[45] Emerald's first film, *Not Wanted,* was the story of an unwed teenage girl who gives her baby up for adoption; it was a subject not usually dealt with in 1940s cinema. Lupino cowrote the script. The budget of the film was set at $153,000, and funding was obtained through a loan from the Chemical Bank of America.[46] Production began. All did not go smoothly.

Ida Lupino said in 1967, "I never planned to become a director. The fates—good and bad—were responsible."[47] Elmer Clifton, a longtime Hollywood workhorse of a director, was directing *Not Wanted* when, three days into production, he suffered a heart attack and later died. Remembers Lupino: "We were much too poor to afford another director so I stepped in and took over."[48] The film came out in 1949, crediting Clifton as director, but Lupino had directed virtually the entire project.[49]

The concept of a female film director was not totally foreign to Hollywood when Ida Lupino assumed her place behind the camera in the late 1940s. The legendary Lillian Gish once directed a silent short subject starring her sister Dorothy, and Lois Weber, a former social worker, directed numerous silent films with religious and conservative themes.[50] But by far, the most famous female film director before Ida Lupino was Dorothy Arzner. Arzner was the first woman ever admitted to the Director's Guild of America (Lupino would be the second), and throughout the 1930s and 1940s she directed more than a dozen studio-produced films, including *Christopher Strong*, with Katherine Hepburn, *The Bride Wore Red*, with Joan Crawford, and *Dance, Girl, Dance*, starring a young Lucille Ball.[51] Still, by the early 1940s, Arzner's career was over, and filmdom was without a woman director until Lupino came along.

Her move to the other side of the camera was not exactly planned, although, in retrospect, it should have been foreseeable. "I used to go and sit on the set when I was on suspension—which was a great deal of the time. Most of us were then," Lupino said.[52] Hanging around on film locations—with time on her hands—allowed her a chance to observe the process of movie-making:

> I never was one who woke up in the morning saying, "God, it's so great to be an actress!" I was always looking for ways to be less bored on the set, so I hung around the director and cameraman, asking them questions.[53]

Not Wanted came out on schedule and under budget; it would go on to gross $1 million at the box office, allowing Lupino's production company to go into the black. Partnership with Bond ended after that first film; Emerald Productions was dissolved.[54] Ida Lupino then formed a new company with husband Collier Young called The Filmakers (written, for no apparent reason, with only one "m").[55] At this time, when Lupino assumed her role as Hollywood's only female producer-actress-writer-director, she was thirty-three years old.

With Lupino as resident director and assistant screenwriter, Filmakers wasted no time in moving on to other projects. The company made two films in 1950. *Never Fear* (a.k.a. *The Young Lovers*) detailed the story of a young dancer suddenly stricken with polio. It was perhaps Ida Lupino's most autobiographical piece. *Outrage* addressed an equally unconventional and difficult subject: rape.[56]

Lupino divorced Collier Young in 1950 but The Filmakers and their partnership endured.[57] After the divorce Lupino took up with cartoonist-turned-actor Howard Duff. At the time of their first meeting he thought she was "phoney," and she thought he was "conceited." They were married on October 21, 1951.[58] Ida Lupino gave birth to her only child, Bridget, in 1952.[59]

The Filmakers' *Hard, Fast and Beautiful* came out in 1951 and was a less controversial story of a young tennis ace and her domineering mother. Perhaps Lupino's best directorial effort occurred next. *The Hitch-Hiker* (1953) told the story of two middle-class men who are tormented across the California landscape after they pick up a hitchhiker who turns out to be a psychotic killer.[60] This film was The Filmakers' most financially successful product.[61]

After the all-out action of *The Hitch-Hiker*, Lupino returned in her next film to her more typical human dramas. Cowritten by Lupino and Young, *The Bigamist* concerned a man who, through emotional need and a series of circumstances, finds himself married to two women at the same time. His first wife is a glamorous business woman played by Joan Fontaine, and the second is a down-on-her-luck waitress played by Ida Lupino.[62] Such characters had always attracted the actress, who said her films are about people who get lost, who really don't have a home anymore."[63] Two interesting side notes to *The Bigamist*: it is the only time Lupino ever directed herself on film, and, in a no-hard-feelings working relationship, Collier Young, now divorced from Lupino, was married to Ms. Fontaine at the time of the film's making.[64]

Ida Lupino would cowrite and produce one more film for The Filmakers, *Private Hell 36*. She also acted in it but, this time, left the directing to Don Siegel.[65]

The Filmakers came to an end in 1954, when the company's film distribution venture bankrupted them.[66] Though that period of Lupino's life, the life of an independent producer, had come to an end, she had made the time count. In just under five years of existence, her company had produced seven films, six of which Lupino directed herself.[67]

Ida Lupino's theatrical films have undergone an extraordinary amount of discussion. Many critics have found prefeminist feminism in her films.[68] Others have praised her documentary-like photography.[69] Still others have applauded her courage in addressing and dealing with topics not usually found in other Hollywood films of that time (illegitimacy, rape).[70] All have found quality. Critic Carrie Rickey has said, "She's unique in Hollywood ... because she treated delicate subjects unsensationally, with a restraint and intelligence."[71] Evaluating *The Hitch-Hiker*, Rickey said:

> No other director of her generation could shoot a movie on location in Mexico and not stereotype the Mexican actors.... Lupino respected all her characters, all their situations.[72]

And Wheeler Dixon, in his book *The "B" Movie Directors,* says Lupino's films constitute, "[a] significant, humane, and intelligent body of work."[73]

Lupino's first exposure with the television cameras came by way of friend David Niven in 1952. He invited her to act a role on the anthology he was cohosting, *The Four Star Playhouse.*[74] What was originally to be only a guest spot turned into a regular job. Along with David Niven, Charles Boyer, and Dick Powell, Lupino became one of the rotating hosts for this anthology program that ran weekly from 1952 until 1956.[75] In January of 1957 Lupino was before the cameras again, this time in her own television series. *Mr. Adams and Eve* starred Ida and husband Howard Duff in their very own weekly sitcom about two Hollywood stars who try to keep their home lives as "normal" and unglamourous as possible. For comedy's sake, they seldom succeeded.[76] Lupino was actress and star but left the directing of the episodes to someone else; *The Bigamist* aside, Lupino once said, "I can't direct myself."[77] The show was nominated for an Emmy Award before petering out after sixty-eight episodes.[78]

Lupino and husband Duff also guest starred on a June 8, 1959, installment of the *Lucy-Desi Comedy Hour.* This episode, "Lucy's Summer Vacation," had Lupino and Duff playing themselves and camping it up as self-centered movie stars sharing a cabin for a weekend with Lucy and Ricky Ricardo.[79]

Lupino's first directing assignment for television came in 1959. Ex-husband Collier Young, on to new producing challenges, asked her to direct a segment of the NBC series *On Trial* starring Joseph Cotten. Lupino remembers: "I hadn't directed for so long I was nervous, so nervous."[80]

As with motion pictures, a few women directors in television preceded Ida Lupino. Most notable was Lela Swift, who had already earned her place in the history books by being the only woman to direct weekly, live, prime-time dramatic anthologies. She helmed early productions for such series as *Suspense* and the *DuPont Show of the Week.*[81] Other than her however, no other woman had been able to carve out a niche for herself in the rough-and-tumble, "can't-get-behind-schedule" world of episodic television—no other woman, that is, until Ida Lupino.

Lupino said about the early days of her television directing career, "I was snobbish toward TV at first. But that changed fast. The pressure, the opportunities, the fantastic challenges—it's all fantastic, darling."[82] Her first directing project for TV, the *On Trial* episode, took Lupino only three days to research and three days to film.[83]

After *On Trial*, actor Richard Boone, star of the TV Western *Have Gun, Will Travel*, invited Lupino over to his show. Boone had been a fan of *The Hitch-Hiker* and admired Lupino's visual sense and skill for pacing and action. A script calling for a rape, eight murders, and a sandstorm had come up for an episode of *Have Gun*, and Boone wanted Lupino to direct.[84] Lupino would go on to do several episodes of *Have Gun, Will Travel*, and soon her ability to handle action, tough guys, guns, and crime gained her the reputation of being "blood-and-guts" Lupino.

Ida Lupino's ability to handle dramatic mayhem and madness earned her the industry nickname "the female Hitch," after the legendary master of suspense, Alfred Hitchcock.[85] She would be more directly associated with the master himself when he asked her to star in one of his weekly anthology programs. Lupino's response after reading the script: "I don't like the part. But I'd love to direct it."[86] She directed two episodes for *Alfred Hitchcock Presents*: "Sybilla," a story of an unhappy marriage, and "A Crime for Mothers," a story of adoption and kidnapping.[87] In her superb meditation on Ida Lupino's directing career, Louise Heck-Rabi points out an interesting paradox between Lupino's film and television careers: after years of creating films with a mostly female audience in mind, she was now, in television, working basically with male-written scripts and with all-male casts.[88]

Ida Lupino had a second flirtation with suspense beginning in 1961, when she was one of the primary directors for the series *Thriller*, hosted by Boris Karloff. These episodes, latter-day Hitchcock with touches of Poe, ran for two years on NBC and gave Lupino some of her most memorable moments on screen: her direction of the story "What Beckoning Ghost?" told of a woman who discovers a strange room prepared for her own funeral. Lupino filmed the episode in a dreamy, soft focus to emphasize visually the blurring of boundaries separating the world of the living from the world of the dead.[89] At the end of her time with *Thriller*, Lupino began a long association with the tough, gangster series *The Untouchables*.[90]

Besides Lupino's skill with action and suspense and her ability to spill blood with the best of them, she became quite famous for her creative transitions from one scene to another. In an episode of *The Untouchables*, Lupino let the screen fade from the distorted reflection of a gangster in a fun-house mirror to a normal mirror reflecting a young woman draping herself in fur.[91]

Lupino said of her reputation, "I did so many Westerns and action shows I was looked upon as a director who could not direct a man and woman story. For a long time I couldn't get a job directing a love story."[92] She finally got that opportunity a few years later when she helmed an episode of *General Electric Theater* starring Anne Baxter and Ronald Reagan.[93]

Though Ida Lupino oversaw mostly hard-boiled plots, her actual directing methods were the utmost in feminine coaching. Her sample directions to actors and crew were flowered with touching sentiments: "Peter, darling, hold the knife this way. And make sure we see that sweet meathook"; or "Darlings, mother has a problem. I'd love to do this. Can you do it? It sounds kooky but I want to do it. Now, can you do it for me?"[94] Perhaps her most memorable piece of direction was to an actor playing a death scene on *The Untouchables*: "Lovely bird, you've been shot in the belly. You must suffer, darling."[95] Ida Lupino said she was "not the kind of woman who can bark orders."[96]

> I don't ever say [to actors] "Do this. I want you to stand here. I want you to do that." Having been an actress, I know what it is like to be put into an uncomfortable position.[97]

Not surprisingly, everyone on Lupino's sets called her Mother. She said of her affectionate nickname:

> I love to be called Mother. For when I am working I regard my production company as a very special kind of family…. [W]e talk and feel and work things out together. We do everything together.[98]

Ida Lupino said about her role as a director:

> It keeps you in a constant state of first-night nerves. Got to make a little feature in five days. Will what you shoot today look odd in the morning? You may be terrified but you mustn't show it on the set. Nothing goes according to Hoyle…. Reshuffle your schedule. The script calls for a sunny day, [but] you can't shoot outdoors, it's raining…. Keep your sense of humor, don't panic. I sometimes wonder how anything ever gets on film.[99]

In 1964 Lupino steered before the cameras a startling episode of *The Twilight Zone*. In this episode, "The Masks," a group of greedy family members' faces begin mysteriously adopting mask-like aspects of their personalities and personal motivations. Earlier, she had acted in a *Twilight Zone* episode titled "The Sixteen-Millimeter Shrine," thus making her not only the only woman to ever direct a *Zone* episode but also the only individual to both direct and star in episodes during the course of that series' run.[100]

In 1965, while still an active and much-sought-after director for television, Lupino was called back to the big screen by Columbia Studios to direct *The Trouble with Angels*, a harmless comedy starring Rosalind Russell as a tough, but tender, Mother Superior and Hayley Mills as a rambunctious Catholic school girl.[101] Though Ida Lupino knew the film would not do much for her career, the opportunity to direct for the big screen and the access to big budgets and slightly more relaxed film schedules was too hard to turn down. The film also gave Lupino some opportunities for creative flair. She told Peter Bart:

> We are shooting it in color but the prevailing colors will be stark black and white and charcoal grey. Then there will be sudden slashes of bright color— a turquoise swimming pool, a green meadow. The possibilities of color are fantastic.[102]

After that assignment Lupino returned to her busy TV career. She would add episodes of *Bewitched*, *The Fugitive*, and *The Rogues* to her list of credits. One of her more challenging directorial duties came in 1966 on an episode of *The Virginian* titled "Deadeye Dick." Along with a cast of cowboys and fourteen horses, Lupino was forced to deal with the occasional interference of rattlesnakes and tarantulas that wandered onto the set. They were followed in later days by bees and an army of red ants. To add insult to injury, the show's leading actress fell from her horse, and unseasonal rain delayed the production. Despite it all, Lupino remained her "motherly" self, giving such gentle direction as:

> Now, Walter, baby, while we're here we might as well take the posse through. I want my camera here.... That's right. You read my mind, love.... OK, follow Mother, here we go kiddies![103]

Assignment led to assignment, job to job. Lupino for many years was one of the busiest directors working in television. By the end of her TV career, she had directed well over one hundred different projects—comedy, action, and drama—for the small screen, among them, episodes of *Dr. Kildare*, *Gilligan's Island*, and *The Big Valley*.[104]

No matter what property Lupino chose to direct, she usually got good results. Many critics consider her television work to be highly ambitious and technically advanced. Critic Barbara Scharres observed one bit of Lupino's direction for an episode of *Thriller* this way:

> In one continuous close-up shot [the actress] reaches for the sponge, her hand hovers over it in a moment of indecision, she reaches instead for the chocolates; just when you think she's safe, her hand darts back to the sponge, grasps it, and she is electrocuted. Comedy, suspense, and a tour-de-force display of Lupino's wittiness come together in one shot. In contrast to the often static camera work of fifties and sixties television, Lupino made extensive use of the moving camera.[105]

Lupino's last television directing assignment was an episode for a Bill Cosby sitcom in 1969. She said of that experience, "I was more like a visitor on that show, since Bill is a genius of a performer and does his own thing."[106]

Though primarily known as a director by now, Lupino remained active in front of the camera as well. She achieved a major comeback in 1972 in Sam Peckinpah's film *Junior Bonner*. She played the role of Steve McQueen's mother even though, in real life, she was only twelve years older than the actor. The next year, 1973, Lupino announced divorce plans from husband Howard Duff.[107]

Throughout the 1970s Lupino made numerous acting appearances in film and episodic television, her last being a guest spot on *Charlie's Angels*. She became increasingly reclusive in later years as she lived quietly in Southern California.[108] Her name entered the press from time to time: in 1983 it was reported that her business affairs had been turned over to her longtime manager;[109] and in 1991, though she did not attend, a retrospective of her directorial work, for both film and television, was staged by the Metropolitan Museum of Art.[110]

In June of 1995 it was reported that Lupino was suffering from colon cancer. A few months later, in August of 1995, she died of a stroke.[111]

In interviews over the years, Ida Lupino downplayed her role as film and television's most prominent female director. Repeatedly she said her emergence as a director came more from economic need than from creative impulse. Additionally, in 1972, she said, "It was more of a personal challenge.... I never felt like I was on a crusade for a cause." But, she added in that same interview, "I'd love to see more women working as directors and producers."[112]

Today, that has happened. Women directors (in film and television), while not exactly everyday and commonplace, are not by any means the rarity they once were. A host of names, well known and otherwise, in various media, have made a place for themselves. Directors of film and/or television like Penny Marshall, Barbra Streisand, Debbie Allen, Linda Day, Randa Haines, Betty Thomas, and others all owe a debt to women like Ida Lupino, women who paved the way, who made the films, who took the first steps and called the shots.

Ida Lupino

February 4, 1918	Born in London, England.
1931	Attended Royal Academy of Dramatic Arts.
Spring 1933	Made first film, *Her First Affair* in England.
August 1933	Arrived in Hollywood for movie screen test; received contract from Paramount studios; first film made in Hollywood, *Search for Beauty*, released later that year.
1938	Married Louis Hayward, actor.
May 11, 1945	Divorced Louis Hayward.
Fall 1947	Formed Emerald Productions to produce films.
June 25, 1948	Became citizen of the United States.
August 5, 1948	Married Collier Young, producer.
1949	First Emerald Productions' film release, *Not Wanted*, written and directed by Ida Lupino (uncredited).

January 1950	Joined Director's Guild of America, second woman to join union. Formed Filmakers production firm.
1950	Divorced Collier Young.
October 21, 1951	Married Howard Duff, actor.
September 25, 1952	Acted as regular on television series *Four Star Playhouse*.
Late 1952	Had daughter, only child, Bridget.
1953	*The Bigamist*, final Filmakers' film directed by Lupino released theatrically.
1954	*Private Hell 36*, final film from Filmakers produced and released.
January 4, 1957	*Mr. Adams and Eve*, sitcom, premiered.
September 23, 1958	Final episode of *Mr. Adams and Eve* aired.
1959	Episode of *On Trial*, Lupino's first directing assignment for television aired.*
1960	Directed episodes of *Have Gun, Will Travel* and *Alfred Hitchcock Presents*.
1961	Directed episodes of *Dick Powell Theatre*.
1962	Directed episodes of *Thriller, Hong Kong*, and *The Untouchables*.
1963	Directed episodes of *Mr. Novak* and *Breaking Point*.
1964	Directed episodes of *The Twilight Zone, Bewitched*, and *The Fugitive*.
1965	Final theatrical film directed by Ida Lupino, *The Trouble with Angels* opened; directed television episodes of *The Rogues*.
1966	Directed episodes of *The Big Valley* and *Gilligan's Island*.
September 14, 1969	Final directoral project for television, episode of *The Bill Cosby Show* aired.
1973	Divorced Howard Duff.
1976	Acted in final feature film, *The Food of the Gods*.
1977	Made final acting appearance in episode of *Charlie's Angels*.
February 1, 1991	Retrospective of directing work for film and television held at Museum of Modern Art in New York City.
August 3, 1995	Passed away in Burbank, California.* Television directing highlights; not a complete listing of credits for Ida Lupino.

Television directing highlights; not a complete listing of credits for Ida Lupino.

NOTES

1. "As Film Star, Director, Composer Ida Lupino Excels in Entertainment," *Box Office* (29 September 1975), P. SE-14.

2. Louise Heck-Rabi, *Women Filmmakers: A Critical Reception* (Metuchen, NJ: Scarecrow, 1984), p. 223.

3. *Current Biography* (1943), p. 467.

4. Ibid.

5. Ibid.

6. Jerry Vermilye, "Ida Lupino," *Films in Review* (May 1959), p. 266.

7. Gavin Lambert, "Ida Lupino in Brentwood: The Fiery Actress' Taste for the English Style," *Architectural Digest* (April 1994), p. 205.

8. John Wakeman, ed., *World Film Directors, Vol. II: 1945–1985* (New York: H.W. Wilson, 1988), p. 618.

9. Lambert, p. 206.

10. Vermilye, p. 266.

11. Graham Fuller, *Interview* (October 1990), p. 3.

12. *Current Biography*, p. 467.

13. Ally Acker, *Reel Women* (New York: Continuum, 1991), p. 76.

14. Fuller, p. 3.

15. "As Film Star, Director, Composer Ida Lupino Excels in Entertainment," p. SE-16.

16. *Current Biography*, p. 468.

17. Wakeman, p. 618.

18. Vermilye, p. 269.

19. Wakeman, p. 618.

20. "As Film Star, Director, Composer Ida Lupino Excels in Entertainment," p. SE-16.

21. *Current Biography*, p. 467.

22. Vermilye, p. 270.

23. Wakeman, p. 618.

24. Dwight Whitney, "Follow Mother, Here We Go Kiddies," *TV Guide* (8 October 1966), p. 16.

25. Vermilye, p. 271.

26. *Current Biography*, p. 468.

27. Wakeman, p. 618.

28. Ibid.

29. Ibid.

30. Vermilye, p. 271.

31. Ibid., p. 270.

32. *Current Biography*, p. 468.

33. Wakeman, p. 618.

34. *Current Biography*, p. 468.

35. Ibid.

36. Vermilye, p. 272.

37. Paul Gardner, "Ida Lupino in Comeback After 15 Years," *New York Times* (10 October 1972), p. 51.

38. "As Film Star, Director, Composer Ida Lupino Excels in Entertainment," p. SE-16.

39. Vermilye, p. 283.

40. Ida Lupino, "Me, Mother Directress," *Action* (May–June 1967), p. 15.

41. Wakeman, p. 618.

42. Vermilye, p. 276.

43. Helen Colton, "Ida Lupino, Filmland's Lady of Distinction," *New York Times* (30 April 1950), p. 5.

44. Heck-Rabi, p. 225.

45. Vermilye, p. 277.

46. Colton, p. 5.

47. Ibid., p. 9.

48. Ibid.

49. Heck-Rabi, p. 225.

50. Richard Lacayo, "Women in Hollywood," *People* (Spring 1991), p. 37.

51. Ephraim Katz, *The Film Encyclopedia* (New York: Perigee, 1979), p. 50.

52. "As Film Star, Director, Composer Ida Lupino Excels in Entertainment," p. SE-14.

53. Ginger Varney, "Ida Lupino, Director," *LA Weekly* (12–18 November 1982), p. 10.

54. Colton, p. 5.

55. Ibid.

56. Wheeler W. Dixon, *The "B" Directors: A Biographical Directory* (Metuchen, NJ: Scarecrow, 1985), p. 334.

57. Vermilye, p. 278.

58. Philip Minoff, "TV Personalities," *Family Circle* (March 1958), p. 24.

59. Vermilye, p. 278.

60. Heck-Rabi, p. 248.

61. Vermilye, p. 278.

62. Ibid.

63. Varney, p. 12.

64. Patricia White, "Ida in Wonderland," *Village Voice* (5 February 1991), p. 64.

65. Carrie Rickey, "Lupino Noir," *Voice* (29 October–4 November 1980), p. 44.

66. Varney, p. 10.

67. Rickey, p. 43.

68. Ibid., p. 44.

69. Heck-Rabi, p. 44.

70. Acker, p. 76.

71. Rickey, p. 43.

72. Ibid.

73. Dixon, p. 334.

74. Wakeman, p. 621.

75. Tim Brooks and Earle Marsh, *The Complete Directory to Prime Time Network TV Shows* (New York: Ballantine, 1981), p. 264.

76. Ibid., p. 497.

77. Lupino, p. 15.

78. Heck-Rabi, p. 243.

79. Bart Andrews, *Lucy & Ricky & Fred & Ethel: The Story of* I Love Lucy (New York: Fawcett, 1976), p. 341.

80. Lupino, p. 9.

81. Les Brown, *The* New York Times *Encyclopedia of Television* (New York: Times Books, 1977), p. 422.

82. Peter Bart, "Lupino, the Dynamo," *New York Times* (7 March 1965), p. 7.

83. Heck-Rabi, p. 241.

84. Ibid., p. 240.

85. "Television," *Time* (8 February 1963), p. 42.

86. Whitney, p. 18.

87. John McCarty and Brian Kelleher, *Alfred Hitchcock Presents* (New York: St. Martin's Press, 1985), pp. 196 and 200.

88. Heck-Rabi, p. 242.

89. Ibid, p. 241.

90. Ibid.

91. "Television," p. 42.

92. Lupino, p. 15.

93. Fuller, p. 3.

94. Ibid., p. 14.

95. Lacayo, p. 41.

96. Bart, p. 7.

97. Lupino, p. 14.

98. Ibid.

99. Whitney, p. 16.

100. Marc Scott Zicree, The Twilight Zone *Companion* (New York: Bantam, 1989), p. 378.

101. Bart, p. 7.

102. Ibid.

103. Whitney, p. 15.

104. Heck-Rabi, p. 249.

105. Acker, p. 74.

106. Judy Stone, "The Life of a Glamour Queen? Not for Lupino," *New York Times* (24 August 1969), p. 19.

107. Heck-Rabi, p. 246.

108. Richard Lamparski, *Whatever Became Of...?* (New York: Crown, 1986), p. 106.

109. "Ida Lupino," *Variety* (14–20 August 1995), p. 69.

110. "Ida Lupino Series Set for MoMA," *Variety* (28 January 1991).

111. "Ida Lupino," p. 69.

112. "Coast to Coast," *Hollywood Reporter* (16 November 1972).

Irna Phillips

In 1991 *TV Guide* published a special commemorative magazine celebrating its 2,000th issue. Included in its pages was a special section on television visionaries, "The Creators." Of the twenty names there (among whom were Pat Weaver, Norman Lear, David Sarnoff, William Paley, and Leonard Goldenson), only one belonged to a woman.[1] That woman was almost single-handedly responsible for creating one of the most enduring and most profitable television genres in history. As Dan Wakefield wrote in 1976, she "is to soap opera what Edison is to the light bulb and Fulton to the steamboat."[2] She founded the industry of the television soap opera and for over forty years was its single greatest writer, producer, guardian angel, and guiding light. The name? Irna Phillips.

Irna Phillips was born July 1, 1901, (some sources give 1903) in Chicago, Illinois, the tenth and last child of William S. and Betty Phillips (who was 42 years old when she gave birth to Irna). Few of her brothers and sisters survived to maturity. Her parents owned a small grocery store in Chicago and the family lived above it. Her father died when Irna was eight, and her mother took on the task of caring for the family; years later Phillips said of her mother, "[She] had the sturdiness befitting a pioneer."[3] By Phillips's own account, her childhood was a sad and lonely one. In 1965 she remembered herself as a "plain, sickly, silent child, with hand-me-down clothes and no friends," forced to sleep on a cot in the family's dining room because space was scarce. Phillips's only pleasure came from books and her own imagination, from which she fashioned cartons into stages and created make-believe families with large homes, wonderful clothes, and plenty of money.[4]

Irna's early schooling was uneven. She refused to go to school unless someone came in to dress her. Sometimes, as she remembered, no one bothered.[5] Nevertheless, she went on to graduate from Seen High School in Chicago in three years. After a short spell at Northwestern, Phillips transferred to the University of Illinois, where she indulged a love for acting. Though her professors thought her talented, she never landed a major role in a school production and was finally told she had neither "the looks nor the stature for professional success."[6]

Devastated by this news, Phillips, on her mother's advice, decided on a career in teaching. After graduation she taught for a year in a Fulton, Missouri, community college. Later she did graduate work at the University of Wisconsin, taking courses in speech, drama, and psychology. She then taught for five years in Dayton, Ohio.[7]

How Irna Phillips got back to Chicago is open to debate. Some sources say she returned to visit a newly born niece; others say that a tiff with a boyfriend sent her packing.[8] Others say she was only on vacation.[9] What *is* known is that she returned to the Windy City in 1930 and that she seldom left it again.[10] Exactly how Phillips got her first radio job is not known either. Two stories survive. In the first she was on a tour of WGN studios when someone mistook her for a radio actress applying for a job and handed her a script. Though they considered her voice too low for a woman, they were impressed enough with her reading of a poem by Eugene Field, "The Bowleg Boy," that they hired her.[11] The second story of Phillips's entrance into radio is that she walked into the station and asked point-blank for an audition. Either way, she ended up with a nonpaying job on WGN, broadcasting a daily trifle called *Thought for the Day*, which consisted of Phillips reading poetry and ad-libbing inspirational commentary.[12]

After two weeks Phillips was promptly let go only to be almost immediately rehired in a different capacity after she allegedly protested to her ex-boss. In her new job she was asked to write and act in a daily (six days a week) "radio strip," or serialized story. WGN had already been running the continuing story of *Gasoline Alley*, based on Frank King's comic strip about small-town America, and now wanted another daily show; this one "about a family."[13]

Irna Phillips responded with what many consider the first "soap opera." It was titled *Painted Dreams* and began on October 20, 1930, running in short, ten-minute installments.[14]

The show had six characters but only two actors. Phillips played the main character, Mother Monahan (a role based on Phillips's own mother), and the "mystery character," Kay. Actress Ireene Wicker (later "Kellogg's Singing Lady") played all the other parts—including the family's barking dog, Mikey. The two women got by without male voices by only referring to the men in their lives, never by having them present.[15]

Painted Dreams had run for two years on WGN when Phillips tried to create radio network interest in it. WGN refused the idea, saying that it owned the show outright and that it could not be moved to another broadcaster. Phillips quit the station and began what was to become a long, bitter court battle with the station over ownership of the series. The case dragged on in the courts for ten years, finally being decided against Phillips. By then, though, she had moved on to other things. She had also learned a lesson: All future shows and scripts she worked on would be copyrighted in her name alone.[16]

In 1932 Phillips bounced back with her second soap, titled *Today's Children*. It ran on WGN's chief rival WMAQ (at first unsponsored and with

IRNA PHILLIPS

Phillips footing all costs in order to retain ownership). It was a thinly disguised version of *Dreams*: Mother Monahan was now Mother Moran, and the other characters of the show were similarly redesigned. For a time Phillips acted in the serial but eventually found the dual work of acting and writing too taxing. She resigned herself to writing only.[17] Soon after, "the Phillips impulse" for creating new programs began. She created a short-lived soap, *Masquerade*—the story of a painter involved with different glamorous women. Devised as a way to sell the sponsor's cosmetics, it lasted three months.[18]

Today's Children ended in 1938, partly because the recent death of Phillips's mother made work on a mother-centered show too difficult for her emotionally, and partly because, as Phillips said, "I had exhausted all the problems of these people."[19]

These two failures and the demise of *Children* were balanced by two other Phillips creations that survived and prospered: *The Guiding Light* (debuting in 1937) and *The Road of Life* (debuting in 1938).[20]

Road of Life centered on the life of noble surgeon Dr. Jim Brent, who "mends broken legs and broken hearts with equal ease."[21] *Guiding Light* was the story of Dr. John Ruthledge, a small-town minister. The character was based on a friend of Phillips. Sometimes during the early years an entire fifteen-minute episode was devoted to a Ruthledge sermon. Collected into book form, the character's many sermons sold 290,000 copies nationwide.[22]

Irna Phillips also created another hospital-based drama around this time, *Woman in White*. And when a group of characters from *Guiding Light*, the Kransky family, developed enough, she spun them off into their own show, *The Right to Happiness*, in 1939. It ran until 1960.[23]

Along the way, creating, writing, and controlling her series, Phillips pioneered many of the staples of soap operas today. She was the first to incorporate professional people into her stories: lawyers, ministers, and doctors replaced minimum-wage, blue-collar workers as heroes.[24] Phillips was the first to use such soap devices as organ music (provided by Bernice Yanocek) for dramatic effect, and cliff-hanger endings to keep audiences coming back.[25]

Phillips was the first to bring a higher social consciousness to the world of soaps. In 1945, after using *The Guiding Light* to help sell war bonds and after realizing she had been "subconsciously" educating her listeners in various areas for years, Phillips decided to take a more uniform approach to the idea of "social significance." Phillips and staff sent letters to a variety of agencies around the country (the Red Cross, the American Legion), asking a simple question: "What is your problem and what can we do to help you with it on one of our programs?" From their responses, Phillips devised soap story lines intended to further those agencies' causes.[26]

Quite ingeniously, Irna Phillips also tailored her shows to her predominately housewife audience. She slowed the pace so that women doing housework could answer the door, vacuum, or see to the baby and still not miss anything. She rationed ideas and story lines by doing the same thing.[27]

Phillips, herself, was a highly eccentric woman, possibly more than any of the thousands of characters she created during her career. She consulted fortune tellers from time to time and changed the spelling of her name from the original Erna to Irna when a numerologist said it would ease her life.[28]

She was also a hypochondriac. She visited doctors nearly every day of her life. A physician who lived in her apartment building in Chicago stopped by several times a day to listen to her complaints and take her temperature.[29] Her trips to New York City were often mixed in with trips to different hospitals and specialists in Manhattan. Once, while staying in her suite at the Carlyle Hotel in Manhattan, she insisted that storm windows be installed to end the drafts. The windows are still there.[30] Frequently, she asked to be pushed around in a wheelchair.[31]

Not surprisingly, Phillips's preoccupation with illness and disease became evident in her work. Doctors and nurses as characters, hospitals as settings, and illnesses as subjects for drama were vintage Phillips characteristics.[32]

Phillips's treatment of the actors who worked on her shows was rather odd as well. She seldom bothered to learn the names of the performers, knowing them only as the characters they portrayed.[33] Actress Helen Wagner, who has played Nancy Hughes (now McClowsky) on *As the World Turns* since it premiered in 1956, was a friend of Irna's and remembers just how typical that was:

> I was always Nancy to her. Any reference to my husband always meant Chris, my on-screen husband, not my real-life husband. I never became "Helen" until very late in her career, after knowing her many, many years.[34]

Similarly, Phillips did not like the off-screen lives of her actors to interfere with the on-screen lives of their characters. Helen Wagner, whose character of Nancy was in the early days something of a homebody, was for many years denied a vacation from the show because it would mean writing the character out for a few weeks. Phillips told Ms. Wagner, "Nancy is a housewife, Nancy does not travel." It was several years before Nancy was allowed to go visit a sister out of state so that actress Helen Wagner could have a few days off.[35]

Like her characters' lives and her plots, Phillips rigidly controlled her home life and went to great lengths to keep it simple. She lived far away from the network TV industry in her Chicago apartment. Until she was in her late thirties, Phillips shared a bedroom with her mother, and she never learned how to drive. Though her sponsor once gave her a 1940 Plymouth to celebrate ten years in radio (and Phillips named it Sheila), it is doubtful she ever drove it.[36] Even her weekly menus were preset: on Sunday there was leg of lamb; Monday, chicken; Tuesday, steak; Wednesday, meatloaf; Thursday, lamb chops; Friday, spaghetti; and Saturday, stew.[37]

Phillips seldom had anything to do with the press, which she believed (perhaps rightly) dismissed soap operas as second-class subculture, snickering at her success and her fans' loyalty. She permitted few interviews during her entire career.[38]

Also not surprising was Phillips's flair for melodrama. In 1960 interviewer Peter Wyden related the story of the day Phillips's son Tom arrived late to meet her:

> She does not become just vaguely uneasy. Her concern is translated into imaginary but stark disaster—he's been run over, his body is lying at the curb, he is bleeding badly.[39]

Irna Phillips labeled herself a compulsive worrier and believed she would never get an ulcer because she turned all her worries into scripts.[40] "I do quite a bit of projecting," she told an interviewer.[41]

To oversee her programs, Phillips moved in 1940 to New York City. After seeing the toll the war was inflicting on the country in 1941, she fashioned the serial *Women Alone* to dramatize the plight of women left on the home front. Her experiences in New York also served as the model for yet another new drama, *Lonely Women*, which had a short on-air lifespan beginning in 1942 before Phillips recycled an old title and the show became known as *Today's Children* in 1943. After six months, though, New York was not to Phillips's liking, and she soon returned to Chicago. A similar move to California in 1943 did not work out either, and she returned to Chicago after only nine months.[42]

With so many shows on the air at one time, and wielding as much power as she did, Irna Phillips put forth a revolutionary idea for soap opera broadcasting in 1943. *The General Mills Hour*, as she foresaw it, would consist of three of her shows running back-to-back—each in different lengths, from fifteen to twenty minutes depending on plot—with characters from each occasionally overlapping and interacting. A narrating voice-over would navigate proceedings. It endured for a few months until Phillips abandoned the concept.[43]

By 1943, only a little over ten years after she began, Phillips was single-handedly responsible for five different daily dramas. Her total income from them was $250,000, and her literary output was estimated at two million words per year, the equivalent of forty novels.[44] She had established such a factory by this time that she found it necessary to have a lawyer and two doctors on retainer just to act as consultants.[45]

It was only later that Phillips reached the need for support writers, or "dialoguers," who filled out the basic story lines she devised. Many young writers who began with Phillips went on to successes of their own. In 1946 she hired a young recently graduated writer named Agnes Eckhardt, who later married and changed her name to Agnes Nixon.[46] Nixon would go on to create *All My Children* and *Loving*. Phillips also had a longtime collaborator in writer William Bell. After cocreating *Another World* with Phillips, he went on to found with his wife Lee Phillip Bell two of the most successful soaps of recent years, *The Young and the Restless* and, later, *The Bold and the Beautiful*.

Also in 1943, at near the same age her mother was when she herself was born, Phillips, unmarried and a career woman, adopted a child, Thomas Dirk. A year and a half later, Phillips adopted Katherine Louise.[47]

Throughout the 1940s Irna Phillips reigned as the undisputed queen of the radio soap opera. By the end of the decade a new medium was on the horizon and it would be that medium that Phillips (somewhat reluctantly) would conquer next.

By all accounts Irna Phillips was not anxious to move her shows from radio to television. With television, a fog horn could no longer substitute for the deck of a ship, and actors could no longer be brought in and replaced so easily. So reluctant was she to give up radio that after *The Guiding Light* debuted on television on July 30, 1952, the scripts were rebroadcast that same day on radio. The two *Guiding Light*s ran concurrently on the two media for several years until finally the incredible success of the television version made the radio outlet obsolete.[48]

Around this time Proctor and Gamble, the soap manufacturer and a longtime force in soap opera broadcasting, began its long association with Phillips. Phillips sold the ownership of her current TV dramas to Proctor and Gamble Productions. Between the two of them (Phillips and P & G) they formed the biggest, toughest alliance daytime television had ever seen.[49]

In 1956 Phillips, in association with Proctor and Gamble, stormed onto television with what was to become her most popular (and some say, personal favorite) creation, *As the World Turns*. The continuing story of the Hughes and Lowell clans of Oakdale, Illinois, began on April 2, 1956, as TV's first half-hour soap. It was produced live until 1975 when it was lengthened to an hour. The show revolutionized daytime drama by gaining more viewers than ever before in the history of the genre (sometimes as high as a fifty percent share of the audience), and it launched soapdom's first all-out lying, scheming villainess, Lisa Miller (later, after marriage[s], Lisa Hughes, then Coleman, then Mitchell, then others). She was played by actress Eileen Fulton, who continues on the show to this day. Fulton's and the show's fame were so intense in the mid-1960s that CBS created a nighttime spin-off titled *Our Private World*. It, however, would last only a few months.[50]

Irna Phillips's actual writing process for her series, radio and television, was rather unusual. Everyday at nine in the morning Phillips sat down at a rickety, brown card table—the same one she had used for years—and began to devise that day's scripts from projected story lines often set down months in advance. From there she would dictate dialogue to her secretary and close friend, Rose Cooperman. "I really don't think I write," she said "I act."[51] Occasionally sitting still and occasionally moving around the room, moving as the character would, Phillips assumed all the characters in the scene—male, female, adult, child—changing her voice to indicate a change in speaker.[52] This process worked so well for Phillips it was later adopted by many of her proteges, including William Bell.[53]

As Phillips would talk, "Rosie," her secretary, would take down every word, following the various characters by following changes in Irna's voice and gestures. Rosie filled in the punctuation along the way. Both women occasionally became so involved with the story line they were creating that they found themselves in tears.[54]

The average time for Irna Phillips to dictate a half-hour script was about an hour and forty-five minutes. It usually took longer to type the finished manuscript than it did for Phillips to dream it up.[55] During Phillip's "writing" she seldom lost her place or became confused. If she did, she could always consult one of the several genealogical charts she created for each show. They consisted of squares containing characters' names with solid lines connecting relatives, dotted lines connecting in-laws, and "X"'s over names of dead or missing family members.[56]

After the writing was fininshed Phillips would sit down and watch not only her shows but those of her competitors as well. While viewing her own shows, if she found something she did not like in script, performance, or production, it was switched immeidatly. This often meant a phone call to New York and a list of demands. A few times actors found themselves jobless after a phone call from Phillips. Not surprisingly, many actors, writers, and crew members feared Phillips's wrath. Once, when an actor playing what many thought an indispensable character asked for a raise in salary, Phillips refused and solved the whole problem by simply killing off the character. The show went on without him.[57] Don Hastings, who has played Dr. Bob Hughes on *As the World Turns* since 1960 (and wrote for the show for many years under the name J.J. Matthews), remembers Phillips as a tough but fair mother lion, ferocious in protecting her creation:

> She was very tough on her writers but would protect them if the network or the producers criticized them. She always said that if she okayed a script it was as good as her writing it herself.[58]

Though Irna Phillips could be difficult, and a great many lived in constant fear of her, nobody could deny her her skill. Don Hastings remembers a time when *As the World Turns*'s ratings had slipped. Owners Proctor and Gamble asked Phillips—then at work on another Proctor and Gamble show—to return and help *World*. "Can you bring us up to a thirty share by the end of the year?" they asked. Phillips delivered the thirty share in thirteen weeks.[59]

Additionally, Phillips was not as difficult on a personal level as she might first appear. Throughout her career she was instrumental in starting other writers in their careers. Agnes Nixon, Bill Bell, and many other names benefitted from her support and guidance. Phillips was also known to take many young actors under her wing, sheltering and encouraging them.

In her life in Chicago, Phillips had a small but tight-knit group of friends and a fiercely devoted household staff. They admired and respected her enough to overlook her dramatic nature and her many pseudo-illnesses. Producer Lee Bell, who with her husband Bill created *The Young and the Restless* and *The Bold and the Beautiful*, was a friend and coworker of Irna's for many years; she remembers an eccentric but likable person. "She was a genius," Bell said, "A brilliant, intelligent woman. You wanted to be around her. Whatever eccentricities [she had] didn't matter."[60]

In 1964 Phillips formulated a new series for NBC titled *Another World*. The title referred to the separate "psychological worlds" of its characters and the two separate economic worlds of the show's two major families. Not accidently, it also drew comparison with the previous Phillips creation *As the World Turns*.[61]

Another World was the first daytime soap to run one hour. It was also the first daytime show to address the topic of abortion.[62] Phillips invited controversy again in 1967 when she attempted to introduce an interracial story line into *Love Is a Many-Splendored Thing*, a show she was also writing at the time. When the network bosses balked at the idea, Phillips walked out. She abandoned the show, and it was canceled in 1973.[63]

Despite Phillips's forward thinking, however, she did not always approve of the direction daytime shows were taking. She said in 1972:

> The daytime serial is destroying itself, eating itself up with rape, abortion, illegitimacy, men falling in love with other men's wives, all of which is often topped by a murder, followed by a long, drawn-out murder trial.[64]

In 1964 ABC-TV put Irna Phillips, at age 63, on the payroll as a special consultant for its primetime soaper *Peyton Place*, the serialized twice-weekly program based on the book by Grace Metalious. By taking the *Peyton Place* job, Phillips achieved a very rare triple play: she now had her hand in, and was receiving paychecks from, shows running on all three major networks.[65]

In 1965 Phillips cocreated *Days of Our Lives* and composed what has since become arguably the most famous opening line for any show in television's history: "Like sands through the hour glass…"[66]

All did not always flow smoothly, however. The early years of *Another World* were filled with complications: major characters were thrown out with little explanation, and actors were replaced almost weekly. Frustrated, Phillips left *Another World* to concentrate on a show for ABC that she was cocreating with her daughter (and was based on Irna's own life). That show would only air for a few months when it premiered. Agnes Nixon was later brought into *Another World* as head writer to whip the show into shape.[67]

Since Irna Phillips had almost single-handedly created soap operas as a dramatic form many years ago in radio, they had begun to change. The incredible success of her own *As the World Turns* made daytime soap operas an important, highly profitable part of the network schedule. To gain viewers and therefore money, soaps became more and more sensational. Gradually they became more scandalous, sexual, and action-oriented; Irna Phillips's stories of women sitting around the breakfast table were becoming passe. Phillips found herself being left behind by the genre she had created. Allen Potter, who worked on *Another World* with Phillips during its first difficult years, summed up the problem: "She was from a different era. [She was] still writing kids going down to the malt shop."[68]

Phillips was asked to rejoin *As the World Turns* in 1972.[69] She simplified some of the plots but failed to turn the recent ratings dip around. Proctor and Gamble, the show's producer, fired Phillips in 1973. Back in Chicago she began work on an autobiography, but nothing was ever published.[70]

On December 23, 1973, Irna Phillips died in her sleep at her home in Chicago. She was seventy-two. In accordance with her wishes news of her death was kept from the press for several weeks.[71]

What made Phillips a success—the Queen of the Soaps, as she was often called—is somewhat difficult to answer. Helen Wagner recently explained it this way:

> We [*As the World Turns*] premiered the same day as *Edge of Night* [a now defunct mystery-based soap on ABC]. What was important on that show was the story. For *As the World Turns* what was important was the character.[72]

Phillips realized early in her career that the success of serialized stories depended on her audience becoming involved and knowledgeable about the characters on the show. She told *Broadcasting* in 1972:

> Characters have to be multidimensional. The story has to come from the characters, to the point where your viewers will get to know a character so well they can predict his or her behavior in a given dramatic situation.[73]

Phillips believed there were several reasons for her success, not the least of which was her self-described limited vocabulary ("my greatest asset"), which, she believed, made her programs universal. She also attempted in her writing to appeal to the basic instincts of self-preservation, sex, and family.[74]

Perhaps Phillips's greatest personal achievement, however, was creating a world, fully and believably, that she did not really know herself. Though for days, and then for decades, she celebrated the love of husband and wife, she never married; nor did she give birth; nor did she ever own a home. But somehow Irna Phillips knew enough about all those qualities to entertain millions for generations—to spin endlessly involving tales of day-to-day life; tales about the simple joys and daily dramas of paying the bills, raising children, belonging to a family, and falling in love.

Irna Phillips wrote in *McCall's* magazine in 1965, "None of us is different, except in degree. None of us is a stranger to success and failure, life and death, the need to be loved, the struggle to communicate...."[75]

Four of the programs Irna Phillips created—*As the World Turns, Guiding Light, Days of Our Lives*, and *Another World*—are still on the air today.

Irna Phillips

July 1, 1901	Born in Chicago, Illinois.
1922	Graduated with bachelor's degree in education.
1924	Graduated with master's degree in speech; began career teaching school in Missouri and, later, Ohio.
May 1930	Returned to Chicago; joined WGN as actress and ad hoc writer.

October 20, 1930	*Painted Dreams*, radio's first "soap opera" debuted; created by Irna Phillips.
June 16, 1932	*Today's Children*, second Phillips creation, premiered; departed WGN.
1934	*Masquerade* premiered.
1935	*Masquerade* aired last broadcast.
January 25, 1937	*The Guiding Light* premiered.
1938	*Today's Children* aired final broadcast; *Road of Life* and *Woman in White* premiered.
October 16, 1939	*The Right to Happiness* premiered.
1940	Phillips moved briefly to New York City; would return to Chicago after six months.
1941	*Women Alone* premiered; settled court suit with WGN.
June 29, 1942	*Lonely Women* (title later changed to *Today's Children*) premiered.
1943	Resided briefly in Los Angeles; adopted son, Thomas Dirk.
1944	Adopted daughter, Katherine.
Summer 1948	*Woman in White* aired last broadcast.
October 11, 1948	*The Brighter Day* premiered on radio.
January 31, 1949	*These Are My Children* premiered.
March 4, 1949	*These Are My Children* ended.
1950	Second incarnation of *Today's Children* ended on radio.
June 30, 1952	*The Guiding Light* debuted on television.
1956	*Brighter Day* ended on radio.
January 4, 1954	*The Brighter Day* premiered on television.
December 13, 1954	*Road of Life* premiered on television; show ended broadcasts on radio.
July 1, 1955	*Road of Life* aired last broadcast on television.
April 2, 1956	*As the World Turns* premiered.
November 25, 1960	*The Right to Happiness* ended on radio.
May 4, 1964	*Another World* premiered.
1964	Worked as consultant on primetime's *Peyton Place*.
May 5, 1965	*Our Private World*, *As the World Turns* spin-off, premiered in primetime.
September 10, 1965	*Our Private World* aired last episode.
September 28, 1965	*The Brighter Day* aired last broadcast on TV.
November 8, 1965	*Days of Our Lives* premiered.
September 18, 1967	*Love is a Many-Splendored Thing*, soap opera, premiered.
March 23, 1973	*Love is a Many-Splendored Thing* aired last broadcast.
Late 1973	Fired by Proctor and Gamble.
December 23, 1974	Passed away at home in Chicago.

NOTES

1. "The Creators," *TV Guide* (Commemorative Edition) (July 1991), p. 59.
2. Dan Wakefield, *All Her Children* (New York: Doubleday, 1976), p. 27.
3. *Current Biography* (1943), p. 590.
4. Irna Phillips, "Every Woman's Life Is a Soap Opera," *McCall's* (March 1965), p. 116.
5. Ibid.
6. Peter Wyden, "Madam Soap Opera," *Saturday Evening Post* (25 June 1960), p. 129.
7. Barbara Sicherman and Carol Hurd Green, *Notable American Women: The Modern Period* (Cambridge: Belknap, 1980), p. 542.
8. "Script Queen," *Time* (10 June 1940), p. 66.
9. Sicherman and Green, p. 542.
10. "Writing On: Irna Phillips Mends with Tradition," *Broadcasting* (6 November 1972), p. 75.
11. Madeline Edmondson and David Rounds, *The Soaps* (New York: Stein & Day, 1973), p. 43.
12. *Current Biography*, p. 590.
13. Sicherman and Green, p. 542.
14. Robert C. Allen, *Speaking of Soaps* (Chapel Hill, NC: University of North Carolina, 1985), p. 111.
15. "Writing On: Irna Phillips Mends with Tradition," p. 75.
16. Edmondson and Rounds, p. 44.
17. Allen, p. 112.
18. Wyden, p. 130.
19. Ibid.
20. *Current Biography*, p. 590.
21. "Queen of the Soaps," *Newsweek* (11 May 1964), p. 66.
22. Sicherman and Green, p. 543.
23. Wyden, p. 130.
24. Sicherman and Green, p. 259.
25. *Current Biography*, p. 519.
26. "With Significance," *Time* (11 June 1945), p. 46.
27. *Current Biography*, p. 519.
28. Wyden, p. 129.
29. Interview with Lee Bell (4 September 1991). All other information and quotes from Mrs. Bell in this chapter were taken from this interview.
30. Interview with Don Hastings (5 December 1991). All other information and quotes from Mr. Hastings in this chapter were taken from this interview.
31. Wyden, p. 129.
32. Robert LaGuardia, *Soap World* (New York: Arbor House, 1983), p. 20.
33. Wyden, p. 129.
34. Interview with Helen Wagner (10 October 1991). All other information and quotes from Ms. Wagner in this chapter were taken from this interview.
35. Ibid.
36. "Script Queen," p. 66.
37. Wyden, p. 129.
38. Wagner interview.
39. Wyden, p. 127.
40. Phillips, p. 117.
41. Wyden, p. 127.
42. Ibid., p. 130.
43. Ibid.

44. *Current Biography*, p. 591.

45. "Script Queen," p. 68.

46. Wakefield, p. 28.

47. Sicherman and Green, p. 543.

48. Wyden, p. 130.

49. Ibid.

50. Tim Brooks and Earle Marsh, *The Complete Directory to Prime Time Network TV Shows* (New York: Ballantine, 1981), p. 571.

51. Wyden, p. 129.

52. Phillips, p. 168.

53. Bell interview.

54. Wyden, p. 30.

55. Ibid., p. 129.

56. Phillips, p. 168.

57. *Current Biography*, p. 591.

58. Hastings interview.

59. Ibid.

60. Bell interview.

61. LaGuardia, p. 81.

62. Ibid.

63. Jean Rouverol, *Writing for the Soaps* (Cincinnati, OH: Writer's Digest Books, 1984), p. 11.

64. "Writing On: Irna Phillips Mends with Tradition," p. 75.

65. "Queen of the Soaps," *Newsweek* (11 May 1964), p. 66.

66. Rouverol, p. 11.

67. LaGuardia, p. 81.

68. Ibid.

69. "Week's Headliners," *Broadcasting* (17 January 1972), p. 9.

70. LaGuardia, p. 81

71. Landry, p. 71.

72. Wagner interview.

73. "Writing On: Irna Phillips Mends with Tradition," p. 75.

74. Sicherman and Green, p. 542.

75. Phillips, p. 116.

Judith Waller

For all that she accomplished in radio and television, her name remains one of the most obscure in broadcasting. Only of late, as the issue of educational media moves more toward the center of public awareness, has her career begun to be noticed, her life story recorded, her achievements celebrated. But it took more than a growing recognition of the importance of educational media to bring this woman's considerable accomplishments to light. It also required the determination of enterprising scholars (mostly female) who have researched their foremothers' history in an attempt to give voice to a past that is still largely silent. The collective research and writings of these post-women's movement scholars has added considerably to our understanding and appreciation not only of the field of women's history but of media history as well. And few women could be more deserving of such dedicated scholarship than Judith Waller.

Judith Cary Waller, a true pioneer in the fields of radio and television, was there at the birth of both media. And her vision for both was the same: entertainment tempered with education and community service. For her realization of that vision and her many programming "firsts," she gained, along with a long list of awards and honors, the moniker "First Lady of Radio."[1] When she left radio behind to help inaugurate the new marvel of television, she brought her own tough standards for broadcasting with her. On TV she oversaw the development of the first all-educational children's show and, after that, used television's unique technological abilities to spread her "media for education" message and mission even further.

In 1947, on WMAQ's twenty-fifth anniversary, Judith Waller wrote: "Do you remember? Well, maybe not—not all of you certainly. But there are views that come back to mind, like a kaleidoscope of time turned backward."[2]

Oak Park, Illinois, is a suburb of Chicago. At the time of Waller's birth on February 19, 1889, it was one of the most exclusive addresses in the Midwest.[3] Though her father, John Duke Waller, was a physician and her mother was the daughter of a college president, the family, consisting of Waller and her three younger sisters, was financially strapped. But Judith's aunt was a woman of considerable means and allowed Judith, on her graduation from Oak Park High School in 1908, to take a year's tour of Europe.[4]

On her return from the continent, Waller bypassed the high-society trappings expected of her in favor of business college and office work. "Business before debuts," she told *Ladies' Home Journal* in 1928.[5] She landed a series of secretarial jobs, eventually moving on to J. Walter Thompson Advertising Agency in Chicago and, later, in 1918, to their office in New York City. She returned to the Windy City in 1920.[6] Eventually she obtained a job as office manager of the Central Division of the American Red Cross, staying there for one year.[7] After leaving the Red Cross, she worked as an aid to a family friend for a few months.[8]

Judith Waller's broadcasting career began, inauspiciously enough, with a phone call in 1922. Walter Strong, a friend from Waller's trip to Europe, was now the business manager of the *Chicago Daily News* and Waller, with an eye on the journalism field, had applied to him for a job.

He said in their phone conversation, "I've just bought a radio station; come down and run it."

"I don't know what a radio station is, Walter," Waller replied.

"Neither do I. But come on down and we'll find out."[9]

Shortly thereafter, Judith C. Waller was named station manager (or "station director" or "master") of Chicago's second radio station, WGU.[10] It is believed Waller was the first woman, in any part of the United States, to hold such a position.[11]

Saddled with a radio station to run, Waller began to learn what there was to learn about radio, both as a technology and a business. She showed an early knack for programming. KYW, Chicago's other station, had already made jazz music its staple; Waller knew she had to counter-program to gain any sort of audience.[12] She approached opera diva Sophie Braslau backstage at the Chicago Symphony about performing on the then infant medium of radio.[13]

WGU (later to change its call letters to WMAQ) signed on the air on April 13, 1922.[14] That April day, Braslau sang her arias and the station was beset with technical problems. The station was shut down the next day due to mechanical difficulties.[15] No one was ever sure if anyone heard that first broadcast. (Despite the inaugural broadcast's less-than-stellar success however, classical music and grand opera would always remain a staple of WMAQ's programming under the guidance of station manager Waller. Soon it would be what the station was most known for in the city of Chicago.)[16]

Even after the station was up and running again, everything was catch-as-catch can. Any sound at all, any broadcast at all, any audience at all was considered a victory. The station was operating with little or already-outdated equipment, almost no budget (and no advertising revenues), and a paid staff of two, Waller and her engineer.[17]

With no money to pay performers, just filling the air was a full-time job. To attract talent Waller rang doorbells and made phone calls. She stopped

JUDITH WALLER

just short of kidnapping to get people in front of the then somewhat myste-
rious radio microphones.[18] If talent ran short, she herself often turned
announcer and, on more than one occasion, played a classical composition on
the song bells in order to fill airtime. From time to time she even found it
necessary to fill in playing the drums. Sometimes Waller often found herself
booking a program then rushing back to the *Daily News* office to write a
script and then back to the station to announce it.[19] Said Waller:

> One theatrical star after another came to broadcast for "publicity." Some were
> scared, like Sir Gilbert Parker who asked, after the broadcast, "This only
> went over to the Daily News Building, didn't it?" Ed Wynn reclined on the
> floor and Morris Gest was so exhausted after an appearance he had to lie down
> for half an hour. Rosa Raisa, the famous opera star, wanted to "sing one more
> 'leetle' song, it is 'sooch' fun" and Casella, the Italian pianist, wouldn't use our
> Mason and Hamlin—so his own was hauled in.[20]

Fortunately, at that time the station only broadcast two hours a day; that
meant only two hours of programming to dream up (something Waller was

soon doing very well). Due to the station's close affiliation with the *Daily News* newspaper, Waller felt a strong commitment to public service (and to utilizing the newspaper's resources). She asked the book editor to broadcast book reviews and the women's section editor to develop programming pertinent to women.[21] She also approached local groups and institutions—churches, civic organizations—about creating programs that suited their needs.[22]

In 1924 Waller filled air time by insisting on airing coverage of both national political conventions (later she broadcast President Coolidge's inaugural as well). Also in 1924 she hit on an idea and started an ongoing trend by producing the first play-by-play broadcast of a college football game.[23]

In 1926 a friend's son bemoaned the fact that, due to illness, he could not attend the local professional baseball games. That gave Judith Waller another idea.[24] Waller recalled: "I wondered why baseball couldn't go to him, and so, timidly, I approached Mr. Wrigley with the suggestion. Whether the humor of the situation or the new medium appealed to him, I never knew, but WMAQ became the first station to offer such a service to its listeners."[25] That year the Chicago Cubs ended the season dead-last in the league but with more ticket-buyers than ever before—baseball on radio attracted an audience no one had expected: women. Women began to attend the games and, financially, if not professionally, Chicago baseball had never been better.[26]

Sports and news were not Waller's only programming innovations, however. For culture and entertainment, she founded the WMAQ Players, radio's first organized drama company.[27]

Perhaps Waller's most historically important "discoveries" though, were comedians Charles Correll and Freeman Gosden, who began their program, *Sam 'n' Henry*, on rival Chicago station WGN in January 1926.[28] The duo and their show would evolve into one of the most popular radio and television properties ever, *Amos 'n' Andy*.

Today, *Amos 'n' Andy* is one of broadcasting's most legendary yet least fondly remembered programs; broadcasting's "two dirty words" as described by author Rick Mitz.[29] Correll and Gosden, both white ex-stage performers, created the characters out of the song and joke act they did on stage. In blackface and using a "black" dialect, their stage act and early radio broadcasts in the South proved popular with white audiences.[30] From 1926 until 1928 their *Sam 'n' Henry* show on WGN steadily gained a Chicago following. But as their popularity grew their relationship with WGN became strained over rights to sell and license both their show and their image. In early 1928 they approached Judith Waller about transferring their show to WMAQ.[31]

By all accounts Waller was not that eager to sign a minstrel act, no matter how successful, to her station. In addition, WGN claimed ownership of the title *Sam 'n' Henry*; if Correll and Gosden changed stations that meant changing the title of the show and possibly losing their audience in the confusion. A massive, expensive promotion would have to take place in Chicago to let listeners know that *Sam 'n' Henry* were now known by the names *Amos 'n' Andy*. Waller took the idea to associate Arthur Strong, saying at the time, "I don't particularly want them, but if you would give us $25,000 [for a] tremendous publicity campaign, then I'd be willing to take a chance."[32]

Amos 'n' Andy premiered on WMAQ on March 19, 1928. Almost instantly it became the biggest hit in the station's history. It also became such a powerful vehicle for the artists and the station that Waller was soon airing the show six nights a week—the first time in history that a nightly, stripped programming strategy had ever been tried.[33] Locally, the show was an unqualified success.

Soon, Waller was off to New York to interest the Columbia radio network in airing the show nationally. They weren't interested in the show, believing that a six-night-a-week serialized (as the show was then) "blackface act" would never attract an audience.[34] Said the CBS executive to Waller, "I think you'd better go back to Chicago. It's very plain that you know nothing about radio."[35]

(Waller's career was laced with such anecdotes: Jim and Marian Jordan, "Fibber McGee and Molly," worried over each script and were hesitant themselves about signing with a network since they saw no future in it.)[36]

Despite CBS's lack of interest, by August of 1929 WMAQ was feeding *Amos 'n' Andy* to the NBC Red network, which in turn broadcast it nationally.[37] The show soon became a national phenomenon unlike anything before and unlike anything since (except, perhaps, *I Love Lucy*): movie theaters stopped playing their features to break in with the broadcast for their audiences, bus lines and taxis noted drops in passengers when the show aired, and even city sewage departments noted that significant fewer toliets were flushed while the show was on.[38]

While the social and political climate of the 1990s bemoans the racist stereotypes that *Amos 'n' Andy* (on TV and radio) depicted, there is no argument over its place in broadcasting history. It survived and prospered on radio from 1926 until 1954, over a quarter of a century, making it the longest running radio program in history. Later, as a TV sitcom it ran from 1951 to 1953 and gave black actors their first regular, national jobs in television.[39]

But while Waller might have had a knack for entertainment, she had a passion for education. She said once, "It never seemed to me that radio's duty was primarily to broadcast dance music," and "a local commercial station [can] serve the community in a bigger way than an institutionally owned station ever hoped to."[40] Early on in its existence, Waller had the foresight to affiliate her station with area educational facilities; WMAQ became the broadcasting outlet for both the University of Chicago and Northwestern University.[41] Furthering her educational mission Waller also instituted a weekly Chicago newspaper feature. It was a weekly pictorial pullout meant to be a supplement to WMAQ's half-hour special radio talks by world travelers, scientists, and well-known lecturers. Thirty years before wide-spread commercial television (and forty-five before widespread color telecasting), Judith Waller combined sound with pictures.[42]

Waller was also instrumental in setting up the national radio program, *The American School of the Air*. Impressed with her work in the Windy City, CBS president William Paley asked Waller to come to New York and organize the project. She did, then returned to Chicago.[43]

Waller also founded at WMAQ the largest children's radio club in history. At its peak its membership consisted of 275,000 children. Its primary purpose was to assist area schools with their lessons; several times a week WMAQ carried children's radio programming specially designed to complement whatever subject was currently being taught. By 1928 over one hundred schools within a radius of fifty miles of Chicago were taking advantage of the service.[44] Waller put her thoughts on this subject in writing for the October 1937 issue of the journal *Education*. In her article, titled "What the Radio Has to Offer to Elementary School Children," she dismissed the lack of imagination originally used in creating education shows for school-room use: "The programs [were] usually a dull and stupid reading of a prepared geography, history or arithmetic lesson. The material broadcast would never have been presented in person before any class by any but a very inexperienced teacher." In place of this she proposed—and gave examples of—creatively produced radio programs uniquely suited to student and subject. Students, via radio, could benefit by hearing government officials discuss the political process or a professional theater guild performing a classic work of literature currently being studied by an English class.[45] "Radio does not enter the school as a substitute for the teacher," she wrote, "but as an added tool of efficiency."[46]

In 1931 NBC bought WMAQ in Chicago, and Waller willingly stepped down from the high post of station manager to take on the role of public affairs and education director.[47] It was a position she would hold for the next twenty-five years.

In 1931 Waller initiated the radio show *University of Chicago Roundtable*, which brought together the best scholars from the university for lively debates on philosophical issues. The program would air for more than twenty years nationally on the NBC network.[48]

Over the years, her zealous commitment to education earned her numerous awards and many distinguished achievements. In the 1920s she was part of the esteemed group picked by Secretary of Commerce Herbert Hoover to investigate the problems and possibilities of commercial broadcasting in the United States.[49] She was one of the founding members of the National Association of Broadcasters (the NAB).[50] She also served on the Federal Radio Education Committee and on the Educational Standards Committee of the NAB.[51] In 1942 she helped set up the NBC-Northwestern University Summer Radio (later Radio and TV) Institute, the first program of its kind, to provide professional instruction to students who wanted to enter the broadcasting industry. Waller frequently taught the course on public service broadcasting.[52]

In 1946 she published the first edition of her textbook, *Radio: The Fifth Estate*.[53] This book, which explored every aspect—technical to commercial—of a modern radio station, was frequently reprinted and used for years in college classes.[54]

As if all this activity was not enough, by the late 1940s television was on the horizon, and soon Judith Waller would be working in that medium as well. There, she would make some of the most significant contributions of her already legendary career.

Television's very first educational show for children was the brainchild of George Heinemann. One day he came across the fact that hundreds of baby-boom babies lived in the Chicago area and that there were not enough preschool facilities for them. Heinemann's big idea: why not bring the school to the children rather than the other way around. He resolved to create the world's first "nursery school of the air."[55] Heinemann put the idea into the capable hands of Judith Waller, whose Office of Public Affairs and Education would oversee the creation and implementation of a program that would provide a half hour of "simple, unpretentious" instruction for children under five.[56]

Waller and Reinhold Warrenrath Jr., a WMAQ director, then set out to find a simple, unpretentious host, the perfect kindergarten TV teacher. Word got back to them that a teacher named Horwach would be a good interview. A misspelling, however, sent them to Dr. Frances Horwich, dean of the Education Department at Roosevelt College.[57] Horwich had no television or radio experience but did have an extensive background in training kindergarten teachers, working in childhood education for the WPA, and editing magazines on child development.[58]

The spelling error was not discovered until well into the production of the pilot. By then, however, Waller and company had already decided that Frances Horwich, "Miss Frances" as she would soon be known, was the one for them and their show.[59]

Early on, an agreement was reached between Horwich and the producers: they would not question her pedagogical methods and she would not offer up any television advice.[60]

Creative thinking and a child's point of view, not economic limits, created a show that relied on one-to-one communication and not glamour trappings. Each show was opened straight on and without glitz with Miss Frances seated on a hassock three feet off the floor, looking down into the camera.[61] The camera was placed low to suggest a child's eye level. The pacing of the show—even Miss Frances's speech pattern—was purposely slow, patient, and filled with questions ("Wasn't that fun?" "Do you like to play games?").[62] Props were kept child-simple too: crayons, scissors, paper, and simple toys.[63]

The show's title was hit on one day when Peter Warrenrath, the son of producer Reinhold, saw the program's opening with its ringing hand-bell and simple theme: "I'm your school bell. Ding-dong-ding."[64]

As with Waller's first radio broadcast, *Ding Dong School* was not at first considered a technical, or programming, success, at least not by the people who put it together. NBC's Central Division Vice President, Jules Herbuveaux (the man most credited with creating the "Chicago School" of television), after viewing an early episode of the show said to a colleague, "I have either seen the worst television show ever created, or a roaring hit!"[65] Another executive reportedly said, "This will kill television. It will lead to nothing less than the revival of radio."[66]

So doubtful were station executives of the show's potential that they did little promotion for it and broadcast it that first day on October 2, 1952, as "secretly" as possible. The nay-sayers were wrong, and it became a roaring hit. Immediately after the broadcast the switchboard lit up with mothers and kids who loved Miss Frances and her simple, straightforward, motherly manner. They also loved her playful games and simple lessons about numbers and shapes.[67]

Along with games and lessons Miss Frances would, on occasion, read stories, lead sing-alongs, or play a record. From time to time, when she feared children's attention spans might be lagging, she led them in a short period of stretching and exercise.[68]

At the end of each episode, Miss Frances instructed the boys and girls to "run and get mother." She paused. Then a minute later she recounted the activities of the "school day" and gave helpful hints for further instruction and activities.[69]

Ding Dong School won the Peabody in 1952. The program went coast-to-coast beginning in March of 1953.[70] Carried on the NBC network, the show caught on nationally just as it had locally; soon it was enjoying a young captive audience of over two million viewers and their relieved mothers.[71] A young mother wrote in 1954, "I am learning to enjoy my child." Another wrote and said, "If you had a sponsor and that sponsor sold long underwear, I would buy a set each week just to make certain that your program stayed on the air."[72]

Ding Dong School was soon receiving 3,000 such letters a day and was spawning product runs at local stores. If Miss Frances suggested an activity with modeling clay or pipe cleaners one day, retailers could expect to be sold out of them within a week.[73]

In January 1954 the show's producer, Judith Waller, won *McCall's* magazine's Golden Mike award for outstanding contribution to television by women. She won for her "outstanding service primarily for youth" in the creation of *Ding Dong School.*[74] (Mildred Freed Alberg and Pauline Frederick would be singled out for the award as well.)

Ding Dong School ran nationally from 1952 until 1956, when NBC pushed it out to move towards a more "adult" Saturday morning schedule. Active syndicator ITC, however, revived the program—again with "Miss Frances"—in 1959. One hundred and thirty new programs were produced and marketed nationally as late as 1961.[75]

On April 30th of 1957, after being with the station for thirty-five years, Judith C. Waller's retirement from the station became official. But that did not mean she was leaving the world of mass communication, or education, behind. Two months after leaving the station she was named head of Purdue University's airborne television workshops. These workshop experiments attempted to transmit educational courses to a greater number of midwest schools by broadcasting them over a 250-mile radius from an airplane flying five thousand feet above Northern Indiana.[76]

Additionally, Waller continued to oversee the Northwestern University summer institute for many years and worked to expand the program to other colleges. In the fall of 1957 she taught as an adjunct at the school as well.[77]

When Judith Waller died at age eighty-four on October 28, 1973, in Evanston, Illinois, from a heart attack, the broadcasting industry lost one of its greatest visionaries, innovators, and unsung heroes. She was praised at the time of her death for her "wide-awake" attitude and for her "tough, original, critical mind and aversion to stuffiness."[78] She was praised, too, for her savvy programming skills and for her other, amazing contributions to the medium she helped form. Of course, she was praised and remembered for her unwavering commitment to using radio and television for education, for a common good.

Her work in radio and television was prolific, pioneering, and prophetic. Before thousands of dollars worth of government studies were initiated, three years before *Captain Kangaroo*, thirty years before *Sesame Street*, and decades before *Barney* and other lesson-oriented programs for children, before Channel One and other media-in-the-classroom projects, Waller's work, *Ding Dong School*, dared to treat children—and television—seriously. Unlike many of her contemporaries she realized the medium's inherent power and responsibility. At the time of *Ding Dong School* and Waller's other media/education endeavors there was no rule, no specific government legislation demanding programming of any sort for children. It was her initiative, her own sense of what radio and TV should and could be, that made her act. And it is in that regard that her influence remains immeasurable and incomparable.

Judith Waller

February 19, 1889	Born in Oak Park, Illinois.
February 1922	Named station manager of WGU, Chicago. First woman to hold such a position in radio.

April 13, 1922	WGU signed on air with opera performance.
Summer 1922	Participated in radio conferences in Washington, D.C., established by Secretary of Commerce Hoover.
1924	Aired national political conventions and local football games.
January 1926	*Sam 'n' Henry*, precursor to *Amos 'n' Andy*, began on WGN.
Summer 1926	Broadcast first regular season home games of a baseball team, the Chicago Cubs.
Spring 1928	Comedians Gosden and Correll approached Waller about transferring their show *Sam 'n' Henry* to WMAQ.
March 19, 1928	*Amos 'n' Andy* premiered on WMAQ radio.
August 19, 1929	NBC Red network aired *Amos 'n' Andy* for first time.
August 1931	WMAQ bought by NBC network; Waller stepped down as station manager; assumed role of Public Affairs and Education Director.
February 1931	Established *University of Chicago Roundtable* show on radio, for WMAQ.
October 1933	*University of Chicago Roundtable* aired nationally for first time.
June 1942	Founded NBC-Northwestern University Summer Radio Institute to educate students and professionals about broadcasting.
1946	First printing of *Radio: The Fifth Estate* by Judith C. Waller.
October 2, 1952	*Ding Dong School* premiered on WMAQ-TV.
March 1953	*Ding Dong School* aired nationwide for first time.
March 1954	*Ding Dong School* broadcast in color for first time.
June 12, 1955	Last *Chicago Roundtable* aired.
December 28, 1956	*Ding Dong School* aired final episode on NBC after being canceled by network.
April 30, 1957	Retired from NBC Midwestern Division and WMAQ.
June 1957	Named as head of the airborne Purdue television workshops.
Fall 1957	Taught as adjunct at Northwestern University.
September 15, 1959	*Ding Dong School* revived for nationwide broadcast, syndication by ITC.
November 25, 1960	Last incarnation of *Amos 'n' Andy* aired final radio broadcast.
Fall 1961	Second incarnation of *Ding Dong School* aired last episodes.
October 28, 1973	Passed away in Evanston, Illinois.

NOTES

1. "Judith Waller—First Lady of Radio," *NBC Chainbreak* (April 1947), p. 4.

2. Judith Waller, "Frightened Stars, Silent Nights All in 25- Years," *NBC Chainbreak* (April 1947), p. 3.

3. Interview with Judith Waller, transcript, Broadcast Pioneers Library (1 June 1951).

4. Barbara Sicherman and Carol Hurd Green, *Notable American Women: The Modern Period* (Cambridge, MA: Belknap Press, 1980), p. 716.

5. "Women in Business," *Ladies Home Journal* (December 1928), p. 125.

6. Waller interview.

7. "Women in Business," p. 125.

8. Waller interview.

9. "Judith Waller—First Lady of Radio," p. 4.

10. Sicherman and Green, p. 716.

11. Lois O'Neil-Decker, *The Women's Book of World Records and Achievements* (Garden City, NY: Anchor Press/Doubleday, 1977), p. 305.

12. "Women in Business," p. 125.

13. Waller interview.

14. "Judith Waller—First Lady of Radio," p. 4.

15. "Women in Business," p. 125.

16. Ibid.

17. Waller interview.

18. "Judith Waller—First Lady of Radio," p. 4.

19. Ibid.

20. Waller, "Frightened Stars," p. 3.

21. Waller interview.

22. Judith Waller, "Education and Public Affairs," speech transcript (Broadcast Pioneers Library, Washington, D.C., 1954).

23. Sicherman and Green, p. 716.

24. Fern Persons, oral history, in the collections of the Museum of Broadcast Communications, Chicago, Illinois (23 February 1993).

25. Waller, "Frightened Stars," p. 3.

26. Ibid.

27. "Judith Waller," *NBC Chimes* (May–June 1957), p. 11.

28. John Dunning, *Tune In Yesterday* (Englewood Cliffs, NJ: Prentice-Hall, 1976), p. 31.

29. Rick Mitz, *The Great TV Sitcom Book* (New York: Perigee Book, 1980), p. 27

30. Dunning, p. 31.

31. Waller interview.

32. Ibid.

33. O'Neil-Decker, p. 491.

34. Waller interview.

35. Ibid.

36. Waller, "Frightened Stars," p. 3.

37. Dunning, p. 33.

38. Ibid.

39. Mitz, p. 27.

40. Waller, "Education and Public Affairs."

41. "Women in Business," p. 125.

42. Ibid.

43. Williamson, p. 13.

44. "Women in Business," p. 125.

45. Waller, Judith C. "What the Radio Has to Offer to Elementary School Children, *Education* (October, 1937) pp. 70–71.

46. Waller, "Education and Public Affairs."

47. Sicherman and Green, p. 716.

48. Ibid.

49. "Judith Waller," *NBC Chimes* (May–June 1957), p. 11.

50. Sicherman and Green, p. 716.

51. Ibid., p. 717.

52. "Institute Opens June 28; NBC Employees May Enroll," *NBC Chainbreak* (April 1948), p. 7.

53. Judith C. Waller, *Radio: The Fifth Estate* (Boston: Houghton Mifflin Company, 1946).

54. O'Neil-Decker, p. 492.

55. George Heinemann, "Chicago, Chicago, That Television Town," *Television Quarterly* (Fall 1986), p. 46.

56. George W. Woolery, *Children's Television* (Metuchen, NJ: Scarecrow, 1985), p. 150.

57. Heinemann, p. 46.

58. *Current Biography* (1953) (Frances Horwich), p. 279.

59. Woolery, p. 150.

60. Heinemann, p. 46.

61. Woolery, p. 150.

62. Ibid.

63. "Seven Women in Radio and TV Win the *McCall's* Mike," *McCall's* (January 1954), p. 58.

64. Woolery, p. 150.

65. Heinemann, p. 46.

66. "Seven Women in Radio and TV Win the *McCall's* Mike," p. 58.

67. Heinemann, p. 46.

68. Woolery, p. 150.

69. Episodes of *Ding Dong School* can be viewed at the Museum of Broadcast Communications, Chicago, Illinois.

70. Woolery, p. 150.

71. *Current Biography* (1953) (Frances Horwich), p. 279.

72. "Seven Women in Radio and TV Win the *McCall's* Mike," p. 58.

73. Ibid.

74. Ibid.

75. Hal Erickson, *Syndicated Television* (Jefferson, NC: McFarland & Company, 1989), p. 75.

76. Waller interview.

77. "Judith Waller," *NBC Chimes* (May–June 1957), p. 11.

78. Sicherman and Green, p. 716.

Betty White

She is as enduring as she is endearing.

Like that other Betty, Betty Furness, she began in television right when television began. Like Gertrude Berg, she proved herself as savvy behind the scenes as in front of them. And like no one else, she has done it all: TV disc jockey, game show regular, game show emcee, commentator, variety show hostess, interviewer, and, of course, actress. Her Emmy-winning performance turns from early TV sitcom "perfect wife" on *Life With Elizabeth* to "neighborhood nymphomaniac" on *The Mary Tyler Moore Show* to wide-eyed innocent on *The Golden Girls* are classy, comic transformations that rank her as one of the most inspired and ingenious artists in the history of the television medium. Perhaps author Michael McWilliams said it best when, in his book *TV Sirens*, he wrote, "If Lucille Ball is the Queen of Television, then its Princess is Betty White."[1]

Betty Marion White was born in Oak Park, Illinois, (also the birthplace of Judith Waller) on January 17, 1922.[2] White was an only child and liked it that way; she remembers a blissfully happy childhood.[3] Her father Horace, a lighting company executive, and her mother, a homemaker, moved the family to Southern California when Betty was eighteen months old.[4]

Growing up in the then smog-free Los Angeles area, the Whites joyfully took in any stray animals that came their way and frequently took trips to the High Sierra Mountains.[5]

Betty attended Horace Mann Grammar School in Beverly Hills, where she gave up her early ideas of becoming a writer in favor of becoming an actress. Remembers White: "That's where the ham in me first showed. I wrote, directed, produced and starred in a tear-jerker called 'Land of the Rising Sun.' I could hardly wait to graduate and foist myself on a panting public."[6] Later at Beverly Hills High School she starred in a production of *Pride and Prejudice*. White remembers, "That's when the bug really bit."[7]

After graduation, White made the rounds of the movie studios, looking for work. They told her she was "unphotogenic,"[8] so she enrolled in the Bliss-Hayden Little Theater Group, which charged her $50 a week to learn her craft. Eventually she was "promoted" and allowed to work for free, playing the lead in a production of *Dear Ruth*.[9]

She also began to look for radio jobs, where being "photogenic" did not matter. She applied for a job on radio's *The Great Gildersleeve* only to find out from producer Fran Von Hartesveldt that they only hired union members. White remembers:

> We happened to ride down in the same elevator together, and he took pity on my disappointment. 'Would you like to join a union?' he asked. Of course, I told him 'yes.' 'It will cost you twice as much as the job will pay,' he said, but that was all right. I was grateful. It was a beginning.[10]

Her first radio jobs, reading commercials and playing bit parts, sometimes even doing crowd noises, on *The Great Gildersleeve*, *Blondie*, and *This is Your FBI*, got her her first paychecks, usually five dollars a show. "It was kind of nice," White has said. "I never had to worry about income tax."[11]

After getting her feet wet in radio, she moved into early LA television. She sang on a local special—a Dick Haynes "showcase"—for no money.[12] Later she made $10 per show for singing on the program *Tom, Dick, and Harry*. White recalls, "[They used to ask], 'Can you sing? In this show the gal has to sing.' I'd respond, 'Yes—a little.'"[13] She also made frequent appearances, always at $10 an appearance, on the local game show *Grab Your Phone*.[14] Of the latter White quipped, "My father used to say, 'Grab your what?'"[15]

One day in November 1949, as White recalls, Al Jarvis, a KLAC television personality, called her "out of the blue" and hired her to act as his on-air "girl Friday."[16] Jarvis took to the KLAC airwaves everyday and played records, just like on radio. Between songs he bantered with the camera and, in time, with Betty White. Her other duties included keeping the commercials straight (and often delivering them), rounding up interview subjects (sometimes right off the street), and answering viewer mail. Sometimes she even sang a song or two.[17] With the job came a major raise to $50 a week.[18]

White remembers the show:

> Five and a half hours a day, six days a week. I'd do songs, commercials, little sketches. I started out at $50 a week and made it up to $300. For thirty-three hours a week on television. The most commercials I ever did in one day then was fifty-eight. That was LIVE.[19]

Jarvis left in 1952 to be replaced by actor Eddie Albert for six months.[20] When Albert left to make a film, White, by that time the perfect blend of what one critic called "charm and enthusiasm,"[21] took over the show on her own for three more years.[22] One critic went on to call her "the female Arthur Godfrey."[23] But appearing on TV five days a week and working countless more hours preparing her show wasn't quite enough.

In 1952, with KLAC station manager Don Fedderson and George Tibbles, a writer/director, as equal partners, White formed Bandy Productions in order to produce her own self-starring sitcom.[24] The production company was named after one of White's animals at the time.[25]

BETTY WHITE

Life with Elizabeth, Betty White's first sitcom, was a direct outgrowth of her old KLAC antics. She and her costars often bantered some lines before singing songs. As *TV Guide* reported in 1954, "With time the lines got longer and the songs got shorter."[26]

Elizabeth was an unusual sitcom by 1950s standards (and even by today's standards) for several reasons beyond the fact that it was coproduced and co-owned by a twenty-eight-year-old woman who still happened to live with her parents. Not focusing on a single story, each half-hour show was made up of three incidents in the lives of Elizabeth and her husband Alvin (played by Del Moore). Each separate vignette illustrated the comic hijinks of "life with Elizabeth." White told TV critic Tom Shales in 1977 about some of *Elizabeth*'s plots: "We didn't worry about relevance in those days.... [Stories concerned] Elizabeth's biscuits not turning out."[27] White also recalls, "Usually the incidents were based on real life situations in the lives of George and Del and Betty ... and whomever."[28]

Stories always ended the same way too: announcer Jack Narz would break the third wall and ask, "Elizabeth, aren't you ashamed?" White, as Elizabeth, always turned toward the camera then, looking wide-eyed, quizzical, devilish, and shook her head rapidly side to side, signifying, in White's own words, "Nope."[29]

Beginning in 1953 Guild Films began to syndicate *Life with Elizabeth* to, eventually, 102 stations nationwide. During its lifespan, the program would go on to reach a very sizeable audience.[30] Critic Jack Gould in 1954 considered the program, with its gentle humor and sharp dialogue, on a level with, but different from, *I Love Lucy*.[31]

The program won White her first Emmy Award in 1952.[32]

Station manager Fedderson left KLAC (but not Bandy Productions) in late 1953 to go to NBC, who also hired Betty White away from her local KLAC daytime show. The network also bought the idea of a nationally broadcast daytime variety show starring White. The "female Godfrey" was soon readying for her first national exposure over a television network and was now making $750 a week.[33]

Premiering on February 8, 1954, *The Betty White Show* was described by writer Jack Lait:

> ... rolling along at an easy gait. Betty sings a song or two in an untrained but thoroughly competent voice. She interviews visiting celebrities, clowns with [bandleader Frank] DeVol ... and, all in all, seems to be enjoying herself every minute. The listener catches the same spirit, and the half hour is gone before you know it.[34]

For some time White was appearing in the two nationally broadcast shows simultaneously (*Elizabeth* and her daytime show) and worked an exhausting weekly schedule in order to do it. *Life with Elizabeth* was frequently rehearsed one night then filmed the next. Often filming ran into the next morning; often, as well, the finished film had to be sent for air on the same day it was shot.[35] No matter what, though, every weekday White was up at 4:30 A.M. to get ready for her daytime show.[36]

The two shows won White, along with the title "Honorary Mayor of Hollywood," her first measure of national fame.[37] Many reporters began to dub her "America's Sweetheart" around this time as well.[38]

In 1955, after 65 half-hour episodes, *Life with Elizabeth* came to an end. Its three-act format, however, made it marketable to stations that divided those episodes into 195 daily fillers; *Life with Elizabeth* had a long and highly profitable syndicated life years after it ceased production of new episodes.[39] Producer Fedderson would go on to become the driving force behind such TV hits as *Family Affair* and *My Three Sons*. A member of the show's crew, a man named Sam Peckinpah, also had a very successful career after *Elizabeth*.[40]

NBC's daytime *The Betty White Show* had ended after eleven months.[41]

Starting in 1955 White became part of producers/pioneers Goodson-Todman's extended family. She was a semiregular on *To Tell the Truth* and *What's My Line?*[42] From July to September of 1955, White was one of the four regular panelists on *Make the Connection*. Jim McKay was the host (later replaced by Gene Rayburn) as White and the others tried to guess what made two contestants' paths cross sometime in the recent past.[43]

Two years later White teamed again with partners Tibbles and Fedderson to produce her second sitcom *A Date with the Angels*, which starred White and Bill Williams as good-natured newlyweds Gus and Vicki Angel. (White explained sometime after, "The name Angel wasn't really intended for a play on words. I called my car 'Angel' and that's how we happened on the name.")[44]

ABC saw the pilot for *Angels*, liked it, and sold a sponsor on it. The sponsor signed White and company to a seventy-five episode contract specifying that the program would not be canceled for any reason until those seventy-five were filmed.[45] *Angels* premiered on May 10, 1957.[46]

Script meetings took place on Friday mornings, followed by rehearsals on Monday and Tuesday; Wednesday was camera rehearsal, and Friday was filming at the Desilu Studios before a studio audience of 300. Scripts usually revolved around schemes dreamed up by Vicki, who one critic described as a "smarter Gracie Allen."[47]

The program came to an end after only a six month run due to low ratings and was immediately replaced by a revamped *The Betty White Show*. A variety show with the accent on comedy, this new *Betty White Show* gave White the chance to play several different characters a week. It assumed the timeslot left vacant by *A Date with the Angels*.[48]

Again, something of a ratings disappointment, *The Betty White Show* was canceled by ABC in April of 1958.[49]

Disappointed and frustrated by her back-to-back cancellations, White concentrated during the next few years on being a freelance guest artist. She returned to regular panelist duties on *To Tell the Truth*, *I've Got a Secret*, *Match Game*, and *What's My Line?*[50] She was also a regular on *The Jack Paar Show* from 1959–62. Her bawdy barbs delivered with an innocent, apple-pie smile made her a favorite of late-night audiences.[51] Beginning in 1955 she hosted the telecasting of the Tournament of Roses Parade and would do so for the next twenty years; she hosted Macy's Thanksgiving Day Parade for ten.[52] And for a time in the 1960s, she had her own CBS radio show, *Ask Betty White* (formerly *Ask Betty Furness*).[53]

In 1961 White was on the new game show *Password*. It was hosted by Allen Ludden, a former school teacher, manager for Maurice Evans, TV programming director, and host of *G.E. College Bowl*.[54] White recalls: "He booked me on the third week of *Password*. I found out months later that that was the week his wife died, but he had to work through it."[55]

That chance game show booking would change White's life.

During the summer months, when Hollywood television production was shut down and reruns were on the airwaves, White toured actively in stage productions of *Brigadoon*, *South Pacific*, *Take Me Along*, *The King and I*, and others.[56] In 1962 she was reunited with Allen Ludden in a production of *Critic's Choice*. Ludden was by this time completely smitten with White. He courted her for over a year. White, "militantly single" in her own words, originally resisted his many marriage proposals: "I always said I'd never get married again ... but Allen out-numbered me. He started in and the children [Ludden had three teenagers at the time] joined in—and even the two poodles got in the act. And I surrendered—willingly."[57] The two were married in Las Vegas in 1963.[58]

An earlier marriage for White to casting director Lane Allen, which lasted from 1947 to 1949, was often ignored by reporters in the 1950s in order to cultivate White's "bachelor girl" image.[59] Said White of that first union, "... a wonderful fella [but] we never should have been married."[60]

White and Ludden set up their home in a 150-year-old farmhouse in Chappaqua, New York (while also maintaining a residence in LA).[61] Ludden continued hosting *Password*, and White, along with her annual parade duties, was a frequent guest on that and other programs. During the summer Ludden and White teamed to tour in stage plays, among them *Any Wednesday*, *Bells Are Ringing*, *Mr. President*, and *Guys and Dolls*.[62]

In 1964 Goodson and Todman were readying the game show *Get the Message* for NBC. They asked White to audition as hostess. The show sold, but Frank Burton got the emcee job.[63] Remembers White, "I did all the run throughs and tried to get the networks to say okay and they said no way, not a chance with a woman."[64]

In 1971 White parlayed her lifelong love of animals into a season's worth of syndicated programs called *The Pet Set*. In the show, produced by Media Syndication and Carnation Foods, White interviewed a different celebrity each week along with his or her favorite four-legged friend. The program also offered up pet-care tips.[65]

In 1973 White reentered primetime. She said once, "Once you get into the talk routine, producers don't want to trust you as an actress. They forget you started out as an actress."[66]

White and husband Ludden were longtime friends of actress Mary Tyler Moore and her then husband Grant Tinker, the two powerhouses behind the critical and commercial CBS hit *The Mary Tyler Moore Show*. It was something of an in-joke, then, when script #73 came along for *MTM* and called for an "icky sweet Betty White type." White remembers:

> Casting director Renee Valente said "Why not Betty White?" They said "no" because Mary and I were friends and if it didn't work out it would be awkward. After reading a dozen girls [though] no one was "sickening" enough. Renee said, "Call Betty"—and they did![67]

White got the part of Sue Ann Nivens, the man-crazy, tart-tongued "Happy Homemaker" of WJM-TV. Writer Michael McWilliams noted of White's performance: "When she sashayed onto the set of *MTM*, she brought with her the history of TV. Every leer, every twinkle, every wisecrack was attuned to the dynamics of video. She knew how to fill the box with expansive effect."[68] Writers Robert Alley and Irby Brown wrote of White's first appearance as Sue Ann, cradling a fallen souffle and crying "Oh, my poor *baby*!": "A bright new star of the Mary Tyler Moore stock company [had] emerged."[69]

White considers it one of the highlights of her professional career when she was told after that first show's taping that the writers were already planning to bring Sue Ann back for a second appearance.[70]

White has labeled her pre–Sue Ann television image exactly as "icky sweet," and part of what made her performance on *MTM* so successful (and funny) was her willingness to satirize her own small-screen persona. Sue Ann, on her fictional cooking show, was the definition of feminine passivity, but, when the camera was off, she was calculating, catty, and, in White's own words, "after anything in pants."[71]

Betty White made her first *MTM* appearance in 1973, the third year of the show's seven year run. Though never a series regular—the most shows she ever did out of a twenty-six show season was twelve[72]—White became as identified with the program as Mary tossing her hat into the air. She became so identified, in fact, that many viewers quickly forgot about the earlier TV incarnations of Betty White (a.k.a. "the perfect wife") as they accepted Sue Ann as a slightly exaggerated reflection of the actress. Allen Ludden often joked that "Betty's just like Sue Ann ... only Betty can't cook."[73]

For her work on *The Mary Tyler Moore Show* White won two back-to-back Emmys in the 1974–75 and 1975–76 seasons for outstanding supporting actress in a comedy.[74] She was part of the program's final show, which aired on September 3, 1977.[75]

After the demise of *MTM*, nearly all of the show's actors found themselves repackaged into spinoffs or new shows. Valerie Harper's Rhoda started the trend and Ed Asner's Lou Grant turned serious for a five-season run in his own hour-long dramatic show. Cloris Leachman starred in *Phyllis* beginning in 1975, and Gavin McLeod first assumed the captain's duties aboard *The Love Boat* in 1977.

Betty White too had her own starring sitcom. *The Betty White Show* began on CBS on September 12, 1977.[76] Like *Mary Tyler Moore*, the program had a self-reflexive show-within-a-show format. White played Joyce Whitman, an out-of-work actress who, as one reviewer put it, was "on the wrong side of middle age."[77] Whitman was attempting a TV comeback in a police series called *Undercover Woman*. Also like *Mary Tyler Moore*, *The Betty White Show* had a large ensemble cast. Georgia Engel (also a vet of *MTM*) costarred as White's/Joyce's out-of-work housemate (the two had supposedly met at the unemployment office). Pre–*Magnum, PI* costar John Hillerman played White's ex-husband, who, for comic effect, was also the director of *Undercover Woman*. Rounding out the cast were a nervous network executive, a young actress clawing her way to the top, and Joyce's very big and burly male stunt "double."[78]

The show premiered with advance critical praise. The *Daily News* called it "a winner,"[79] and *TV Guide*'s Robert MacKenzie called its leading lady "the mistress of a certain comedic territory.... Her way of delivering a sarcastic slice with a sunny smile is a lesson in comedy technique."[80]

But CBS placed the show on Monday nights against *ABC's Monday Night Football* and the *NBC Monday Night Movie*. In the ratings cellar at the time, CBS couldn't wait for shows to build an audience. It canceled the show in January of 1978. White acknowledged, "... there's a sadness in me I can't ignore—and a lot of embarrassment, too. You feel you promised so much and delivered so little."[81]

White kept busy on the small screen, though, in guest spots on daytime game shows and primetime hits and in TV movies such as *The Best Place to Be*, *The Gossip Columnist*, and *Before and After*. She devoted her private life to charities, mostly those concerned with animals.[82]

But concerns hit closer to home in 1979 when Allen Ludden was diagnosed with cancer. To spare friends, the Luddens kept Allen's illness private until near the very end, when the first people they told were Grant Tinker, Mary Tyler Moore, and Ludden's longtime secretary Gail Clark.[83] Said White, "When you know someone is ill, that death is present, it can create an awkwardness. But you live through it, you set that awkward thing aside."[84] The Luddens kept up work on the dream house they were building in Carmel, and Betty kept working.[85] Three days after moving into the house and three days shy of his and Betty's eighteenth wedding anniversary, in June of 1981, Allen Ludden died.[86] "My animals and work got me through it," White said; the week of her husband's death she had just finished up a guest spot on *Love Boat*.[87]

In 1983 Betty White came back. *Just Men!*, a *Match Game*–like game show, premiered on NBC on January 3, 1983. It showcased White as host and seven rotating prime-time "hunks" all trying to help two female contestants win new cars.[88]

White was not the first female game show emcee; Arlene Francis had taken a stab at it with *Blind Date* back in 1949 and White would not be the last (Elaine Joyce and Vicki Lawrence would follow).[89] But she does have the distinction of being the only "femcee" to win the Emmy Award as best TV game show host. Funny and unflappable as hostess, she won the statuette, beating out such old pros as Bob Barker and Dick Clark, in the fall of 1983. She remains to date the only female winner of that top honor.[90]

Just Men! lasted half a year.[91]

After *Just Men!*, it was back to primetime, where she supported Vicki Lawrence in her syndicated *Carol Burnett Show* spin-off, *Mama's Family*. She also made some memorable guest appearances on *The Tonight Show Starring Johnny Carson*, *The Love Boat*, *St. Elsewhere*, and other programs.[92] Said White once: "I've gotten to do everything there is to do in TV.... I always figured keep moving. It's hard to hit a moving target."[93]

In 1985, at age 63, Betty White returned to prime-time full-time with the biggest hit of her long career.

NBC's *The Golden Girls* premiered on September 14, 1985, with high hopes and high expectations. It brought back to series TV three of television's most respected comediennes: Bea Arthur, Rue McClanahan, and Betty White. From Broadway, it imported Tony-nominated Estelle Getty. The show was expected to shatter many TV taboos—about being over forty, about women over forty, and about who would watch a show about four women over forty.

White was originally cast as man-hungry Blanche (a variation on her Sue Ann role), but director Jay Sandrich and the actress thought better of it later and switched her role with Rue McClanahan's. White explained, "Because I had done Sue Ann, the audience wouldn't have expected too much from me as Blanche. Now, Rose was something else."[94] McClanahan became sassy Southern belle Blanche; Bea Arthur, the no-nonsense New Yorker Dorothy; and White, the low-wattage Rose. Getty played Sophia, Dorothy's irrepressible mother. White has described her Rose character as an innocent: "There's really nothing pretentious or conniving about her.... To Rose, life is a romantic musical, and she's waiting around to see how it all turns out. Meanwhile, she's humming her way through life."[95]

Crisply written and acted with panache by four veterans, *The Golden Girls* quickly shot into the ratings top ten, snagging 43 percent of the Saturday-night audience on its premiere and, in doing so, crossing generational lines. White frequently encountered little fans who could not quite pronounce her character's name but knew her anyway, "'Mommy,' they'd yell, 'It's Wose.'"[96]

At the close of the show's first season, all three leading actresses—White, Arthur, and McClanahan—found themselves nominated for Emmy Awards for best actress in a situation comedy. (Getty was nominated in the supporting category.) When the envelope was opened, the trophy went to Betty White. White said in her acceptance speech: "This is really for all four of us. We're a matched set. You can't split us up."[97]

Critics agreed. Marvin Kitman wrote of the "girls": "They are the Marx Brothers or Sisters of TV sitcoms today. They can do 'the look,' the double-take, the throwaway line. They know how to squeeze the juice out of every line and situation."[98]

After seven years of "Golden" moments (and Emmys won by all), Arthur grew tired of the weekly grind of sitcom work and wanted to get back to the stage. She left the series and *The Golden Girls* temporarily disbanded. The following season, however, White, Getty, and McClanahan reteamed to star in a variation on the series. Named *Golden Palace* the show had Rose, Blanche, and Sophia pooling their resources to buy a Miami hotel.[99] For spice Cheech Marin was added to the cast as the hotel's cook. The show premiered, this time on CBS, in August of 1992. It aired for one season.

A lifelong animal lover, White served for three years as President of the Morris Animal Foundation, an animal health organization. One of the foundation's projects was building a laboratory in Rwanda to carry on the work of the late Dian Fossey.[100] White has also been on the board of the Los Angeles Zoo for over twenty years. She also supports the Fund for Animals, the American Humane Society, Actors and Others for Animals, and Pet Pride.[101] Allen Ludden often said of his wife's animal passion, "Animals are her real work. Acting is just her hobby."[102]

Betty White always keeps busy.

Her first book, *Betty White's Pet Love*, came out in 1983. Her second, a collection of autobiographical reflections titled *Betty White—In Person*, was published in 1988. One reviewer said of the book, "It's as exactly as endearing and funny as you might expect it to be." Her third, *The Leading Lady: Dinah's Story,* is about blind performer Tom Sullivan's seeing eye dog.[103]

In 1990 White was toasted by the Museum of Broadcast Communications in Chicago, which staged a black-tie gala in her honor and screened hundreds of hours of her programs from *Life with Elizabeth* up to *The Golden Girls*. A return engagement occurred in September of 1993, when she was part of a leading ladies luncheon (along with Gale Storm and Jane Wyatt) that kicked off an exhibition looking at the images of women on primetime television.

In 1994 White was again back on the airwaves, and back to some of her old Sue Ann ways, on *Bob*, Bob Newhart's third, self-named series. In it she played the rather coldhearted head of a greeting card company. *Bob*, despite a game cast and good notices, did not survive the season. Betty White, however, was quickly back on the box a few months later in commercials for Tropicana Twister. In them she played a tight-lipped prude, fearful of the decadent pleasures of citrus punch. As with Sue Ann, she was once again brilliantly sending up her "goody two-shoes" image, an image resurrected with her portrayal of Rose.[104]

But for Betty White the activities of 1994 were only a hint of things to come. In mid–1995 it was announced that White was among the six most recent inductees into the Academy of Television Arts & Sciences' Television Hall of Fame. Inducted along with such luminaries as Jim McKay, Dick Van Dyke, and Bill Moyers, White is the tenth woman to be so honored.

Nineteen ninety-five also saw the publication of White's long-awaited auto-biography *Here We Go Again: My Life in Television*.[105]

That same year, it was also announced that White would be returning to series television. *Maybe This Time*, a Disney-produced, Saturday-night sit-com costarring actress/singer Marie Osmond, premiered in September.[106]

Said Betty White in a 1993 interview: "I don't do movies or Broadway. I'm a TV actress. That's what I do."[107] By being a "TV actress" for forty years she has gained (besides a fistful of Emmys) a host of nicknames and identities: "Angel," "Happy Homemaker," "Golden Girl," and one that started early and stuck, "America's Sweetheart." She's garnered some titles behind the scenes too: producer, personality pioneer. She has earned the respect of an industry she helped build and the devotion of the fans who have watched it over the years.

Television viewers always recognize the natural graciousness evident in all of White's performances, and they probably detect a trace of gutsiness too. That comes across whether she's being the "perfect wife," the "neighborhood nymphomaniac," or simply herself.

As she continues to work, crafting ever-more effervescent performances for the small screen, Betty White also continues to reinvent herself—as another character, another archetype, another new comic identity.

For Betty White, what's past is prologue; we have not heard the last from her.

Betty White

January 17, 1922	Born in Oak Park, Illinois.
Late 1940s	Had first jobs in radio and early Los Angeles television.
1947	Married Lane Allen, casting director.
1949	Divorced Lane Allen.
November 8, 1949	Hired by Al Jarvis as a regular on local Los Angeles television.
1952	After departure of Eddie Albert, assumed full hosting duties on KLAC show; *Life with Elizabeth* premiered as local show on KLAC in Los Angeles.
October 1953	*Life with Elizabeth* began being shown in first-run syndication.
Febuary 8, 1954	First broadcast of NBC's *The Betty White Show*.
December 1954	Final broadcast of *The Betty White Show* on NBC.
1955	After end of *Life with Elizabeth*, appeared as regular or semi-regular on game shows for Goodson-Todman Productions including *Make the Connection*, *What's My Line?* and *To Tell the Truth*. Began hosting Tournament of Roses Parade.

May 10, 1957	*A Date with the Angels* premiered.
January 29, 1958	Last episode of *A Date with the Angels* aired.
February 5, 1958	*The Betty White Show*, variety program, premiered.
April 30, 1958	Final broadcast of *The Betty White Show*.
1959-1962	Performed as regular on *The Jack Paar Show*.
June 14, 1963	Married Allen Ludden, television performer.
1971	Hosted syndicated show *The Pet Set*.
September 15, 1973	Made first appearance as Sue Ann Nivens on *The Mary Tyler Moore Show*.
September 3, 1977	Final episode of *The Mary Tyler Moore Show* aired.
September 12, 1977	Debuted in *The Betty White Show* on CBS.
January 9, 1978	Last episode of *The Betty White Show* aired.
June 1981	Suffered death of husband Allen Ludden.
January 3, 1983	First episode of game show *Just Men!* premiered.
April 1, 1983	Final *Just Men!* broadcast.
September 14, 1985	*Golden Girls* premiered.
July 1992	*Golden Girls* aired last episode.
August 1992	*Golden Palace* premiered on CBS.
August 1993	Last episode of *Golden Palace* aired.
1994	Acted in *Bob* on CBS.
June 19, 1995	Inducted into Academy of Television Arts & Sciences' Television Hall of Fame (announced).
August 1995	Published autobiography, *Here We Go Again: My Life in Television*.
September 1995	*Maybe This Time* premiered.

NOTES

1. Michael McWilliams, *TV Sirens* (New York: Perigee, 1987), p. 77.
2. Jack Lait, "TV *Is* Going to the Dogs," *Pictorial Review* (20 June 1954), p. 10-P.
3. Betty White, *In Person* (New York: Doubleday, 1987), p. 126.
4. *Celebrity Register* (New York: Times Publishing Group, 1986), p. 538.
5. Carolyn See, "Why No One Will Knock Betty White," *TV Guide* (17 December 1986), p. 16.
6. Liza Wilson, "Betty White, TV's Cinderella," *American Weekly* (15 August 1954), p. 13.
7. Betty White, letter to author (24 August 1995).
8. May Okon, "Life with Betty," *Los Angeles Sunday News* (20 November 1955), p. 4.
9. See, p. 16.
10. Edmund Leamy, "A Break for Betty," *World Telegram* (New York) (27 August 1955), p. 10.
11. Wilson, p. 13.
12. White letter.
13. Leamy, p. 10.
14. *Current Biography* (1987), p. 601.

15. *Larry King Live*, Cable News Network (9 November 1988).

16. White letter.

17. Richard Dyer MacCann, "Television's Betty White," *Christian Science Monitor* (11 May 1954), p. 32.

18. Wilson, p. 13.

19. See, p. 16.

20. Roland E. Lindbloom, "Betty White Stays in Black," *New York Herald Tribune* (11 June 1957), p. 81.

21. Okon, p. 4.

22. Wilson, p. 13.

23. John Crosby, "Radio and Television," *New York Herald Tribune* (24 May 1954), p. 22.

24. Lait, p. 10-P.

25. Ibid.

26. Ibid.

27. *Current Biography*, p. 601.

28. White letter.

29. Episodes of *Life with Elizabeth* can be viewed at the Museum of Broadcast Communications, Chicago, Illinois.

30. Wilson, p. 13.

31. Jack Gould, "Television in Review," *New York Herald Times* (24 March 1954), p. 58.

32. White letter.

33. Ibid.

34. Lait, p. 10-P.

35. Ibid.

36. Lait.

37. Lindbloom, p. 81.

38. "Betty White's 'Life with Elizabeth,'" *TV Guide* (23 April 1954), p. 16.

39. Hal Erickson. *Syndicated Television: The First Forty Years, 1947–1987.* (Jefferson, NC: McFarland & Company, 1989), p. 60.

40. Ibid.

41. *Current Biography*, p. 601.

42. White letter.

43. Tim Brooks and Earle Marsh, *The Complete Directory to Prime Time Network TV Shows* (New York: Ballantine, 1992), p. 475.

44. Lindbloom, p. 81.

45. Ibid.

46. Brooks and Marsh, p. 186.

47. Tony Slide, "Betty White: Life After Sixty," *Emmy Magazine* (September–October 1985), p. 69.

48. Brooks and Marsh, p. 85.

49. Ibid.

50. *Current Biography*, p. 601.

51. Ricki Fulman, "Ask Betty White," *New York Daily News* (19 November 1967), p. S13.

52. *Celebrity Register*, p. 538.

53. Fulman, p. S13.

54. Wally Burke, "Death of TV Host Ludden," *New York Post* (10 June 1981), p. 94.

55. See, p. 20.

56. "Betty White Bio" (Columbia Broadcasting System, 1975), p. 1.

57. *Current Biography*, p. 602.

58. Burke, p. 94.

59. *Current Biography*, p. 602.

60. See, p. 16.

61. Fulman, p. S13.

62. *Current Biography*, p. 602.

63. White letter.

64. Jefferson Graham, *Come On Down!!!: The Game Show Book* (New York: Abbeville, 1988), p. 79.

65. Erickson, p. 239.

66. Jerry Buck, "No Mr. Nice Guy for Betty White," *New York Post* (31 October 1977), p. 35.

67. White letter.

68. McWilliams, p. 77.

69. Robert S. Alley and Irby B. Brown, *Love Is All Around: The Making of* "The Mary Tyler Moore Show" (New York: Delta, 1987), p. 142.

70. Lynn Hoogenboom, "New Shade of White in 'Chance of a Lifetime,'" *TV Shopper* (16 November 1991), p. 1.

71. *Current Biography*, p. 602.

72. See, p. 18.

73. Karen Croke, "Betty White: Life Is Rose-y," *Close Up* (June 1987), p. 5.

74. *Current Biography*, p. 602.

75. Brooks and Marsh, p. 493.

76. Ibid.

77. Slide, p. 69.

78. Brooks and Marsh, p. 76.

79. Kay Gardella, "Betty White a Winner," *New York Daily News* (12 September 1977), p. 64.

80. Robert MacKenzie, "Review By Robert MacKenzie" (*The Betty White Show*), *TV Guide* (25 November 1977), p. 36.

81. *Current Biography*, p. 602.

82. Mara Neville, "Betty's Animal Instincts," *New York Daily News* (8 April 1988), p. 62.

83. See, p. 20.

84. Ibid.

85. Burke, p. 94.

86. Ibid.

87. See, p. 20.

88. David Schwartz, Steve Ryan, and Fred Wostbrock, *The Encyclopedia of TV Game Shows* (New York: Zoetrope, 1987), p. 256.

89. Graham, p. 78.

90. Schwartz, Ryan and Wostbrock, p. 256.

91. Ibid.

92. Programs from every phase of Ms. White's career can be seen at the Museum of Broadcast Communications, Chicago, Illinois.

93. Alan Carter, "A Rose By Any Other Name," *City Lights* (8 February 1987), p. 27.

94. Croke, p. 5.

95. *Current Biography*, p. 603.

96. Watson, Mary Ann, "From 'My Little Margie' to 'Murphy Brown': Women's Lives on the Small Screen," *Television Quarterly* (Winter 1994), p. 23.

97. *Current Biography*, p. 603.

98. Ibid.

99. Gardella, p. 77.

100. Neville, p. 62.

101. White letter.

102. *Current Biography*, p. 603.

103. White letter.

104. Ibid.

105. Betty White, *Here We Go Again: My Life in Television* (New York: Scribner, 1995).

106. Ibid., p. 233.

107. *Show Biz Today*, Cable News Network (1 November 1993).

Appendix:
Other Notable Women

As a definitive study and evaluation of important women in the history of television, this book is woefully incomplete.

A comprehensive record and summary of all the notable accomplishments made by women since the beginning of television broadcasting would easily run a thousand pages and, even then, would probably not encompass everyone. The justification of subjects alone could never be adequately handled: Who should be included? Who should be excluded? What criteria should, or could, be used?

The fifteen women whose lives are profiled here were not alone when they were working during the formative years of the television medium. The following list of women are some—though not all—of their fellow visionaries who have also created lasting impressions on the television medium and who deserve to be remembered and appreciated for their own special accomplishments and achievements.

As poet Anne Sexton wrote, "Many women are singing together of this...."

• Fran Allison was the human member of the trio *Kukla, Fran & Ollie*. She began with the Chicago show in 1947 and would remain with the show, through various incarnations, until it was finally put to rest in 1976. Before hooking up with Burr Tillstrom's puppets, Kukla and Ollie, she had been a vocalist and radio actress. Later she was seen frequently in commercials and on quiz shows. In the early 1980s, she had a talk show for senior citizens in Los Angeles.

• Wendy Barrie, like Faye Emerson, was a prominent early TV "personality." A former film actress, she hosted a handful of early New York–based children's shows and talk shows, most of which featured celebrities who stopped by to talk to the glamorous Miss Barrie. Her program, *The Wendy Barrie Show*, ran from 1949 until 1950. Her happy sign off: "Be a good bunny!"

• Mili Bonsignori was an Emmy award–winning film editor long associated with Edward R. Morrow and Fred Friendly on their program *See It*

Now and other hard-hitting *CBS Reports* specials. She became a freelance editor in the late 1960s and gained further recognition in the assembling of such films for television as *Anatomy of a News Story* and *Hunger in America*. She received an Emmy for the latter.

• Carol Burnett, legendary actress and comedienne, began her career on TV in 1955 on a children's show but had her first taste of fame as a guest star on several variety shows. She gained a regular job in 1959 on *The Garry Moore Show*. *The Carol Burnett Show* premiered in 1967 and endured until 1979. She has scored additional successes over the years in various TV comedy and drama productions. She was the second woman inducted into the Television Hall of Fame.

• Imogene Coca, brilliant comic foil to Sid Caesar on the classic television program *Your Show of Shows*, was a TV veteran by the time the show began in 1950. She made her first television appearances in 1939. Coca remained as part of the *Show of Shows* ensemble until it ended in 1954. She has remained a consistent presence on television in series and guest appearances.

• Madelyn Pugh Davis was, along with Bob Carroll, Jr. and Jess Oppenheimer, one of the original writers for *I Love Lucy*. Earlier, she had written for Lucille Ball's radio hit *My Favorite Husband*. She would follow Lucy to her second comedy series *The Lucy Show*.

• Nancy Dickerson, hired as CBS-TV's first female news correspondent in 1960, later found greater visibility working for NBC, where in 1963 she became the first woman to have her own daily newscast, *Nancy Dickerson with the News*. She also holds the distinction of being the first woman to report from the floor of a national political convention.

• Elma Farnsworth, wife of Philo T. Farnsworth, one of the recognized inventors of modern all-electronic television, was his assistant and coworker. Her work with her husband made the work of all other women—and men— in this medium possible.

• Arlene Francis is one of the most famous, enchanting, and unsinkable early TV talk-show hosts. She began making regular TV appearances, as a host and game show panelist, in 1949. Later she hosted her own daytime talk show, the *Home* show, from 1954 until 1957. She is perhaps best remembered as a longtime member of the *What's My Line?* panel of questioners.

• Dorothy Gordon, a former radio commentator, took her well-received "Youth Forums" to television in 1953. The shows, in which she served as moderator, brought high school and college students together (sometimes with adults as well) to discuss a wide selection of issues. She told *Current Biography* in 1955, "When we encourage a flow of ideas between young people … we are planting the seeds of democracy."

• Virginia Graham is a vivacious former talk-show host of such programs as *Girl Talk* (1956–1961) and *The Virginia Graham Show* (1970–1972). She has been a tireless worker for cancer research (she battled the disease herself at age 37) and for elderly and widows' rights. She now writes, lectures, and occasionally makes television appearances.

• Dr. Frances Horwich was "Miss Frances" of TV's *Ding Dong School.* The dean of the Education Department at Roosevelt College when she was tapped to become TV's first video teacher, Horwich was with the show from its beginning in 1952 until its end in 1959. She produced children's specials for WMAQ after the program ended and then retired to the Southwest.

• Lisa Howard, a former actress, was, along with Pauline Frederick, one of television's first women reporters. Her greatest claims to fame came in the forms of exclusive one-on-one interviews with Khrushchev and Fidel Castro.

• Lucille Kallen, a talented comedy writer of early television, began her career in 1949 on the *Admiral Broadway Revue.* In 1950 she became one of the three primary writers on *Your Show of Shows* and would remain there until the show ended in 1954. She would go on to share writing credits for that show with such names as Sid Caesar and Mel Brooks.

• Virginia Marmaduke was a renowned newspaperwoman from the Windy City. Nicknamed "the Duchess," she found a second niche for herself in Chicago-based television. Her talk show, *A Date with the Duchess,* began in 1958. Later she gave advice to the lovelorn over WGN-TV under the alias Ruth Jamieson.

• Helen Marmor was the first woman to be named an executive in a TV network news organization. She was named manager for NBC News Program Services in 1970, overseeing a staff of fifty reporters, technicians, and cameramen. Later she was named manager of the *NBC Weekend News.*

• Agnes Nixon began her career with soap queen Irna Phillips. She struck out on her own in 1968 and went on to create two of television's most popular daytime serials: *One Life to Live,* and her trophy piece *All My Children.*

• Helen Parrish is the nearly forgotten hostess of television's first variety show—and first major network show—*Hour Glass,* which hit the airwaves in 1946. The show, which at that time could be seen by only a few thousand people, lasted for one year. Ms. Parrish, a former child actress, later continued her career as an actress on several television series throughout the 1950s.

• Martha Rountree, one of the first and most innovative women in television news, was a former freelance writer who helped develop the format for television's *Meet the Press,* the longest running regular series on network television. It began on the air in 1947. For a time, she also served as the show's moderator.

• Marlene Sanders, one of television's most respected reporters and documentary filmmakers, became the first female television network news vice-president in 1976 when ABC appointed her as head of their documentary unit. She was also in 1972 the first woman to anchor a network evening newscast.

Since leaving network news, she has become an outspoken advocate for women working in broadcast journalism.

• Lela Swift, a director of live dramas in the early 1950s, is the only woman to have achieved that distinction. She began her directing career with play anthologies like *Studio One* and *Suspense*. Later she moved into directing episodes of daytime's *Dark Shadows* and *Ryan's Hope*, the latter for which she won several Emmys.

• Liz Trotta, tough, go-getting reporter first for NBC News, holds the distinction of being the first full-time female foreign correspondent for a major network. She reported from Vietnam in 1968, 1969, and 1971. During her career she also covered events such as the India-Pakistan war and the release of the first American POWs.

• Barbara Walters—world famous reporter, anchor, and interviewer with a long list of achievements and firsts—began with CBS but quickly jumped to NBC, where she was a writer for the *Today* show. In 1963 she became an on-air personality for that show. Ultimately she worked up to the rank of cohost. In 1976 she was hired away by ABC News for $1 million a year and the chance to be television's first regular female evening news anchor. After that assignment she assumed duties on *20/20* and on her own highly rated interview specials. The current generation of newswomen recognize her, more than any other, as their forebear.

• Peggy Wood was the lead actress of one of television's very first sitcoms—*Mama*, a series based on the play *I Remember Mama*. It was broadcast, live, on CBS from 1949 until 1956.

Bibliography

Many of the magazine and newspaper articles cited in this book were supplied to the author by libraries, archives, businesses, and private citizens. In a few cases the material's exact page number is missing. Effort has been made to find or verify the page numbers of those works. Unfortunately, many of the works have come from publications which have never been indexed, have a very limited circulation, or are now defunct; record of the article's original page number has, therefore, been lost.

Introduction

Allen, Robert C. *Speaking of Soaps*. Chapel Hill, NC: University of North Carolina Press, 1985.

Arden, Eve. *The Three Phases of Eve*. New York: St. Martin's Press, 1985.

Barnouw, Erik. *The Golden Web*. New York: Oxford, 1968.

_____. *The Image Empire*. New York: Oxford, 1970.

_____. *A Tower in Babel*. New York: Oxford, 1966.

Berg, Gertrude. *Molly and Me*. New York: McGraw-Hill, 1961.

Bliss, Edward. *Now the News*. New York: Columbia University Press, 1991.

Brady, Kathleen. *Lucille: The Life of Lucille Ball*. New York: Hyperion, 1994.

Brown, Les. *The New York Times Encyclopedia of Television*. New York: Times Books, 1977.

Burnett, Carol. *One More Time*. New York: Random House, 1986.

Dickerson, Nancy. *Among Those Present*. New York: Random House, 1976.

Francis, Arlene. *A Memoir*. New York: Simon and Schuster, 1978.

Fuldheim, Dorothy. *A Thousand Friends*. Cleveland, OH: Cleveland World Press, 1974.

_____. *I Laughed, I Cried, I Loved*. Cleveland, OH: Cleveland World Press, 1966.

Gelfman, Judith. *Women in Television News*. New York: Columbia University Press, 1976.

Graham, Virginia. *There Goes What's Her Name*. New York: Avon, 1965.

Hammond, Charles Montgomery, Jr. *The Image Decade: Television Documentary 1965–1975*. New York: Hastings House, 1981.

Hart, Kitty Carlisle. *Kitty*. New York: Doubleday, 1988.

Head, Sydney W., and Christopher H. Sterling. *Broadcasting in America*. Boston: Houghton Mifflin, 1982.

Heck-Rabi, Louise. *Women Filmmakers: A Critical Reception*. Metuchen, NJ: Scarecrow, 1984.

Higham, Charles. *Lucy: The Real Life of Lucille Ball*. New York: St. Martin's Press, 1986.

Israel, Lee. *Kilgallen*. New York: Dell, 1979.

LaGuardia, Robert. *Soap World*. New York: Arbor House, 1983.

Lewis, Tom. *Empire of the Air: The Men Who Made Radio*. New York: HarperCollins, 1991.

Martin, Linda, and Kerry Segrave. *Women in Comedy*. Secaucus, NJ: Citadel Press, 1986.

Meadows, Audrey. *Love, Alice: My Life as a Honeymooner*. New York: Crown, 1994.

Moody, Kate. *Growing Up on Television*. New York: Times Books, 1980.

Morella, Joe, and Edward Z. Epstein. *Forever Lucy: The Real Life of Lucille Ball*. New York: Berkley, 1990.

O'Neil-Decker, Lois. *The Women's Book of World Records and Achievements*. Garden City, NY: Anchor Press/Doubleday, 1977.

Oppenheimer, Jerry. *Barbara Walters*. New York: St. Martin's Press, 1990.

Palmer, Edward L. *Children in the Cradle of Television*. Lexington, MS: Lexington Books, 1987.

Polsky, Richard. *Getting to "Sesame Street": Origins of the Children's Television Workshop*. New York: Praeger, 1974.

Sanders, Marlene, and Marcia Rock. *Waiting for Prime Time*. Chicago: University of Illinois Press, 1988.

Savitch, Jessica. *Anchorwoman*. New York: Putnam, 1982.

Schilpp, Madelon Golden, and Sharon M. Murphy. *Great Women of the Press*. Carbondale, IL: Southern Illinois University Press, 1983.

Trotta, Liz. *Fighting for Air: In the Trenches with Television News*. New York: Simon & Schuster, 1991.

White, Betty. *Here We Go Again: My Life in Television*. New York: Scribner, 1995.

Mildred Freed Alberg

Alberg, Mildred Freed. Telephone interview. 9 Dec. 1991.

_____. "Our Fight Against TV Taboos." *Saturday Evening Post* 21 Mar. 1959: 28+.

"Hallmark Hall of Fame: The First 40 Years." UCLA Film and Television Archive. 1991.

Marill, Alvin H. *Movies Made for Television*. New York: Baskin, 1987.

"Mildred Freed Alberg." NBC News Release. 20 Sept. 1960.

"Mildred Freed Alberg." Screen Gems Biography. 1973.

Pelegrine, Louis. "Hot Millions." *Film and Television Daily* 5 Sept. 1968.

Shanley, J. P. "Distaff TV Executive: Mrs. Mildred Alberg Talks of 'Hans Brinker' and a Studio Canal." *New York Times* 9 Feb. 1958: 13.

"She Takes the Good and Makes It Popular, Rather than Taking the Popular and Making It Good." NBC Feature. 22 Oct. 1959.

"Somer Alberg." *Variety* 15 June 1977.

Sturcken, Frank. *Live Television*. Jefferson, NC: McFarland, 1990.

Lucille Ball

Andrews, Bart, and Thomas J. Watson. *Loving Lucy*. New York: St. Martin's Press, 1980.

Brady, Kathleen. "The CEO of Comedy." *Working Woman* Oct. 1986: 92+.

Brooks, Tim, and Earle Marsh. *The Complete Directory to Prime Time Network TV Shows*. New York: Ballantine, 1981.

Current Biography 1952: 34+.

Current Biography 1978: 31+.

Darrach, Brad. "All the World Loved This Clown, Lucille Ball." *People* 8 May 1989: 47+.

"Death of Lucille Ball, The." *Broadcasting* 1 May 1989: 39+.

Gilbert, Lucille. "World's Best-Loved Redhead Lucille Ball Is Dead at 77." *Variety* 27 Apr. 1989: 1+.

Harris, Warren G. *Lucy & Desi*. New York: Simon & Schuster, 1991.

Henry, William A. "A Zany Redheaded Everywoman." *Time* 8 May 1989: 101.

Hirschberg, Lynn. "I Love Lucy." *Rolling Stone* 23 June 1983: 27+.

"Immortals, The." *TV Guide* (Commemorative Edition) July 1991: 19+.

Katz, Ephraim. *The Film Encyclopedia*. New York: Perigee, 1979.

Kroll, Jack. "Everybody Loved Lucy." *Newsweek* 8 May 1989: 75.

"Lucy Has Grown Up a Lot." *US News & World Report* 22 Sept. 1986: 80.

"Lucy: The Life Behind the Laughter." *People* 14 Aug. 1989: 66+.

Martin, Linda, and Kerry Segrave. *Women in Comedy*. Secaucus, NJ: Citadel, 1986.

Mitz, Rick. *The Great TV Sitcom Book*. New York: Perigee, 1983.

"Real Story of Desi and Lucy, The." *People* 18 Feb. 1991: 84+.

Richmond, Ray. "In the Beginning There Was the Tube, and On the Tube Was Lucy." *Los Angeles Herald Examiner* 2 Mar. 1986: sec. E, p. 10+.

Robbins, Fred. "Life with Lucy Gets Better ... and Better." *Fifty Plus* Dec. 1986: 44+.

_____. "Who Me? Funny?" *Redbook* Dec. 1986: 120+.

Rosenberg, Howard. "She Set the Standard for Situation Comedy." *Los Angeles Times* 27 Apr. 1989: sec. 6, p. 1+.

Velocci, Tony. "The Real Lucille Ball." *Nation's Business* Oct. 1981: 75+.

"We Love Lucy." *US News & World Report* 8 May 1989: 14.

Gertrude Berg

Berg, Gertrude. *Molly and Me*. New York: McGraw-Hill, 1961.

Bordman, Gerald. *The Oxford Companion to American Theatre*. Oxford: Oxford University Press, 1984.

Brooks, Tim, and Earle Marsh. *The Complete Directory to Prime Time Network TV Shows*. New York: Ballantine, 1981.

Current Biography 1960: 26+.

Denton, Charles. "Mrs. B. Comes to Hollywood." *Los Angeles Examiner* 1 Oct. 1961: 4+.

Dunning, John. *Tune in Yesterday*. Englewood Cliffs, NJ: Prentice-Hall, 1976.

Edmondson, Madeline, and David Rounds. *The Soaps*. New York: Stein & Day, 1973.

Franklin, Joe. *Joe Franklin's Encyclopedia of Comedians*. Secaucus, NJ: Citadel Press, 1979.

Freedman, Morris. "The Real Molly Goldberg." *Commentary* Apr. 1956: 359+.

"Gertrude Berg Conquers Japan." *Life* 9 Mar. 1959: 50+.

"Gertrude Berg, Molly of 'The Goldbergs,' Dead." *New York Times* 15 Sept. 1966: 43.

Harmon, Jim. *Great Radio Comedians*. New York: Doubleday, 1970.

Humphrey, Hal. "So What's New with Molly?" *Los Angeles Mirror* 9 Sept. 1961: 9.

"Inescapable Goldbergs, The." *Time* 23 June 1941: 55+.

Landry, Robert J. "Gertrude Berg Dead at 66; 'Goldbergs,' Etc., Star Had 'Instinctive Showmanship.'" *Variety* 21 Sept. 1966.

Leonard, William. "Molly Goldberg's 30 Wonderful Years." *Chicago Tribune* 29 Oct. 1961.

"Make a Wish." *Variety* 25 Aug. 1937: 17.

Martin, Linda, and Kerry Segrave. *Women in Comedy.* Secaucus, NJ: Citadel, 1986.

"Milestones." *Time* 23 Sept. 1966: 97.

Mitz, Rick. *The Great TV Sitcom Book.* New York: Perigee, 1983.

"Molly." *Look* 27 Feb. 1951: 20+.

Poling, James. "I'm Molly Goldberg." *Redbook* Aug. 1950.

Seldes, Gibert. "The Great Gertrude." *Saturday Review* 2 June 1956: 26.

Sicherman, Barbara, and Carol Hurd Green. *Notable American Women: The Modern Period.* Cambridge: Belknap, 1980.

Stevenson, Isabelle, ed. *The Tony Awards.* New York: Crown, 1980.

"Unsinkable Molly Goldberg, The." *TV Guide* 25 Nov. 1961: 23+.

Waters, Harry F., and Janet Huck. "Networking Women." *Newsweek* 13 Mar. 1989: 48+.

Peggy Charren

"Ban TV Ads Aimed at Children?" *US News & World Report* 16 Jan. 1978: 47+.

"Barring the Schoolhouse Door." *Advertising Age* 23 Jan. 1989: 16.

"Champion of Children's TV." *NEA Today* Oct. 1990: 9.

Charren, Peggy. Telephone interview. 10 June 1992.

Charren, Peggy. "What's Missing in Children's TV." *World Monitor* Dec. 1990: 3+.

Dominick, Joseph, Barry L. Sherman, and Gary Copeland. *Broadcasting/Cable and Beyond.* New York: McGraw-Hill, 1990.

Harris, Paul. "Charren's 20-Year Fight for Children's TV Rights Nears Finish Line." *Variety* 30 July 1990: 9.

Halonen, Doug. "Charren Draws Praise as ACT Plans to Fold." *Electronic Media* 13 Jan. 1992: 2+.

"A Harsh Critic of Kid's TV." *Business Week* 29 May 1978: 52.

"If a Bunny Answers, Hang Up." *US News & World Report* 20 May 1991: 13.

Lawson, Carol. "Guarding the Children's Hour on TV." *New York Times* 24 Jan. 1991: sec. C, p. 1+.

Moody, Kate. *Growing Up on Television.* New York: Times Books, 1980.

O'Leary, Noreen. "ACT's Peggy Charren: A Mother's Work Is Never Done." *Adweek* 20 Feb. 1989: 32+.

Palmer, Edward L. *Children in the Cradle of Television.* Lexington, MS: Lexington Books, 1987.

_____ and Aimee Dorr. *Children and the Faces of Television.* New York: Academic Press, 1980.

"Peggy Charren." Action for Children's Television. 1992.

"Reflections." *Life* Spring 1990: 73.

Schneider, Cy. *Children's Television.* Chicago, IL: National Textbook Company, 1987.

Seligman, Daniel. "The Commercial Crisis." *Fortune* 14 Nov. 1983: 39.

Waters, Harry F. "The Ms. Fixit of Kidvid." *Newsweek* 30 May 1988: 69.

Who's Who in America. Wilmette, IL: Macmillan, 1988.

Zeidenberg, Leonard. "FCC's Puzzler: Should It Move on Children's TV?" *Broadcasting* 20 Nov. 1972: 52+.

Zoglin, Richard. "Ms. Kidvid Calls It Quits." *Newsweek* 20 Jan. 1992: 52.

Joan Ganz Cooney

"Allied Fields." *Broadcasting* 17 Feb. 1975: 62.

Barnouw, Erik. *Tube of Plenty.* New York: Oxford University Press, 1982.

"Bio Sketch: Joan Ganz Cooney." Children's Television Workshop News, 1991.

"Boss Is Better." *Forbes* 1 June 1975: 43+.

Brown, Les. *The New York Times Encyclopedia of Television.* New York: Times Books, 1977.

"CTW's Big Act That No One's Followed." *Broadcasting* 20 Nov. 1972: 50+.

Current Biography 1970: 97+.

Dominick, Joseph, Barry Sherman, and Gary Copeland. *Broadcasting/Cable and Beyond.* New York: McGraw-Hill, 1990.

Dreibelbis, Gary. "A Case Study of Joan Ganz Cooney and Her Involvement in the Development of the Children's Television Workshop." Ph.D. diss. Northern Illinois University, 1982.

"First Lady of 'Sesame Street,' Joan Ganz Cooney." *Broadcasting* 7 June 1991: 67.

"Forgotten 12 Million." *Time* 14 Nov. 1969: 96+.

"From an Idea to an Institution." Children's Television Workshop News, 1991.

Gilbert, Lynn, and Gaylen Moore. *Particular Passions.* New York: Crown, 1981.

Hellman, Peter. "Street Smart." *New York* 23 Nov. 1987: 49+.

Heuton, Cheryl. "TV Learns How to Teach." *Channels* 22 Oct. 1990: 64+.

"Joan Ganz Cooney." Academy of Television Arts and Sciences. 1989.

Kalter, Joanmarie. "Survival Isn't Child's Play." *TV Guide* 25 July 1987: 36+.

Kramer, Michael. "A Presidential Message from Big Bird." *US News & World Report* 13 June 1988: 19.

Lloyd, Kate Rand. "America's Secret Weapon." *Working Woman* Nov. 1986: 158+.

Mifflin, Lawrie. "Maker of 'Sesame Street' Lays Off 12% of Its Staff." *New York Times* 7 June 1995: sec. B, p. 3..

_____. "Nonprofit Muppet Going to Commercial TV." *New York Times* 21 June 1995: sec. B, p. 2.

Moreau, Dan. "Change Agents." *Changing Times* July 1989: 88.

Morris, Michele. "The St. Joan of Television." *Working Woman* May 1986: 70+.

Robinson, Ray. "Big Bird's Mother Hen." *Fifty Plus* Dec. 1987: 24+.

Schneider, Cy. *Children's Television.* Chicago, IL: National Textbook Company, 1987.

Sedulus (pseud.). "Sesame Street." *New Republic* 6 June 1970: 23+.

"Sony Gets Many 'Sesame St.' Rights." *Publishers Weekly* 1 May 1995: 16.

Sweeney, Louise. "Joan Cooney's Preschool TV Workshop." *Christian Science Monitor* 26 Apr. 1968: 30.

"TV's Switched-On School." *Newsweek* 1 June 1970: 68+.

Tyler, Ralph. "Cooney Cast Light on Vision." *Variety* 13 Dec. 1989: 63+.

Faye Emerson

Adams, Val. "Glamour Girl of the Television Screen." *New York Times* 19 Feb. 1950: 11.

Brooks, Tim, and Earle Marsh. *The Complete Directory to Prime Time Network TV Shows.* New York: Ballantine, 1981.

"Call Elliott in Faye's Wrist Slashing." *Daily News* (Los Angeles) 28 Dec. 1948: 1+.

Crosby, John. "Faye Emerson's Now Columnist." *Daily News* (Los Angeles) 12 Sept. 1953: 16.

Current Biography 1951: 184+.

Current Biography 1954 (Frederick, Pauline): 293.

"Divorce to Faye Emerson." *New York Times* 18 Jan. 1959: 33.

"Faye and the Six Wise Men of Broadway." *Life* 24 May 1948: 85.

"Faye Emerson Announces Betrothal on TV Show." *Los Angeles Times* 8 Nov. 1950.

"Faye Emerson." *Variety* 16 Mar. 1983.

"Faye's Décollete Makes TV Melee." *Life* 10 Apr. 1950: 87+.

"Faye Emerson Quits Films to Be with Elliott." *Los Angeles Times* 4 Mar. 1946.

"Faye Joins List of Ten Best-Dressed." *Daily News* (Los Angeles) 1 Jan. 1951.

"Faye Sheds a Husband, Sees a Fight." *Life* 23 Jan. 1950: 39.

Flynn, Joan King. "How Faye Emerson Got Into Television." *Los Angeles Examiner* 1 Apr. 1951: 25.

Gould, Jack. "Faye Emerson Officiates on New Video Program on CBS—Cab Driver, Bill Green, Guest." *New York Times* 29 Sept. 1950: 54.

Hamburger, Philip. "Shall We Dance?" *New Yorker* 8 Apr. 1950: 101+.

Hartt, Julian. "Ceremony Performed in Ranger Station on Brink of Gorge." *Los Angeles Examiner* 4 Sept. 1944: 1.

Kendall, John. "Faye Emerson, Actress, FDR Daughter-in-Law, Dies at 65." *Los Angeles Times* 11 Mar. 1983: 3.

Lamparski, Richard. *Whatever Became Of...?* New York: Crown, 1968.

Martin, Pete. "The Blond Bombshell of TV." *Saturday Evening Post* 30 June 1951: 24+.

McNeil, Alex. *Total Television*. New York: Penguin Books, 1980.

Myers, Deb. "Faye Emerson." *Cosmopolitan* Aug. 1950: 34+.

"Not Too Heavy." *Time* 24 Apr. 1950: 57+.

"Roosevelt Case Dropped." *New York Times* 30 Dec. 1948: 21.

Roosevelt, Elliott, and James Brough. *Mother R.* New York: Putnam, 1977.

Shayon, Robert Lewis. "Two Bravos and One Raspberry." *Saturday Review* 11 Aug. 1951: 32.

Shulman, Arthur, and Roger Youman. *The Golden Age of Television*. New York: Bonaza, 1979.

"Transition." *Newsweek* 21 Mar. 1983: 82.

Pauline Frederick

Bendel, Mary-Ann. "Topic: Women on the Air." *USA Today* 14 Jan. 1985: 9-A+.

Blair, Gwenda. *Almost Golden*. New York: Simon & Schuster, 1988.

Blau, Eleanor. "Pauline Frederick, 84, Network News Pioneer, Dies." *New York Times* 11 May 1990: sec. D, p. 18.

Current Biography 1954: 291+.

Frederick, Pauline. *Ten First Ladies of the World*. New York: Meredith Press, 1967.

Gelfman, Judith. *Women in Television News*. New York: Columbia University Press, 1976.

"Highest Honor." *Broadcasting* 7 July 1980: 70.

"Is the Lady Reporter 'For Women Only'?" *New York Mirror* 1 Dec. 1960: 20.

MacLennan, Nancy. "Only One of Her Kind." *New York Times* 5 Dec. 1948: 15.

Matusow, Barbara. *The Evening Stars*. New York: Ballantine, 1983.

"New from NPR." *Broadcasting* 17 Jan. 1977: 41.

Oliver, Myrna. "Pauline Frederick Dies at 84; Helped to Open Broadcast Journalism to Women." *Los Angeles Times* 11 May 1990: sec. A, p. 34.

"Pauline Frederick, 84; Veteran Broadcaster Helped Women in News." *Philadelphia Inquirer* 12 May 1990.

"Pauline Frederick Works Almost Non-Stop Covering UN Crises —With Little Time 'To Get Your Hair Washed for TV.'" NBC Biography. 27 July 1960.

Sanders, Marlene, (newswoman/author). Letter to author. 2 July 1991.

_____, and Marcia Rock. *Waiting for Prime Time*. Chicago: University of Illinois Press, 1988.

"Seven Women in Radio and TV Win the *McCall's* Mike." *McCall's* May 1956: 74+.

"She Scorns 'The Feminine Approach.'" *TV Guide* 4 May 1957: 22+.

"Spinster at the News Mike." *Newsweek* 27 Oct. 1947: 66.

Talese, Gay. "Perils of Pauline." *Saturday Evening Post* 26 Jan. 1963: 20+.

Willens, Doris. "Pauline Frederick: Only Woman Who...." *Editor & Publisher* 23 July 1949: 42.

Yamada, Gayle K., and David H. Hosley. "Pauline Frederick: Broadcast News Pioneer." *Communicator* Aug. 1990: 18+.

Dorothy Fuldheim

Condon, Maurice. "She Keeps the Citizenry Seething." *TV Guide* 22 Oct. 1966: 42+.

"Congratulations." *Cleveland Plain Dealer* 2 Mar. 1956.

Cook, Russell. "Dorothy Fuldheim's Activist Journalism and the Kent State Shootings." Unpublished paper. E.W. Scripps School of Journalism, Athens, Ohio, 1992.

Dolgon, Robert. "City's Grande Dame Going Strong at 81." *Cleveland Plain Dealer* 12 Jan. 1975.

"Dorothy Fuldheim." *Scripps-Howard News* 7 Nov. 1983: 7+.

"Dorothy Fuldheim Was Forever Asking 'Why?'" *Cleveland Plain Dealer* 27 Nov. 1929: 9.

Fuldheim, Dorothy. "Dorothy's First 25 Years Were the Hardest." *Cleveland Press* 13 July 1973.

Fuldheim, Dorothy. *I Laughed, I Cried, I Loved*. Cleveland, OH: Cleveland World Press, 1966.

_____. "I would like to thank ..." WEWS Commentary. 1 Dec. 1980.

Gallagher, Nancy. "Here's Dorothy Fuldheim!" *Cleveland Press* 8 Aug. 1959.

Gordon, Bill. "Dorothy." *Cleveland Magazine* Feb. 1990: 22+.

Gray, Nancy K. "Before Barbara Walters There Was Dorothy Fuldheim." *Ms.* Dec. 1976: 43+.

Hickey, William. "Dorothy Fuldheim Gets 3-Year Contract." *Cleveland Plain Dealer* 30 Mar. 1983.

_____. "The Redhead Sets a Record." *Cleveland Plain Dealer* 1 Oct. 1972: sec. F, p. 6.

"'The House' Dorothy Lives In—An Encore, The." *Cleveland Press* 26 June 1979.

Kerekes, Julius (friend of Ms. Fuldheim's). Letter to author. 19 July 1991.

Kingsley, Barbara. "Bash to Honor Fuldheim." *Cleveland Plain Dealer* 21 June 1983.

Kvet, Jerry. "Fuldheim Pie Throwers Get 60 Days, $500 Fine." *Cleveland Press* 20 June 1980: sec. B, p. 5.

Larronde, Suzanne. "At 89, She's Still a TV News Queen." *Modern Maturity* Dec. 1982–Jan. 1983: 58.

"Lecturer Finds Dictatorships Equally Cruel." *Cleveland Plain Dealer* 5 Oct. 1936.

"Miss Fuldheim Returns Home." *Cleveland Plain Dealer* 6 Mar. 1955.

Minch, John J. "Decisive Dorothy Salts City TV." *Cleveland Plain Dealer* 15 July 1965.

"Non-Retiring Ways of a Nonagenarian Newswoman, The." *Broadcasting* 4 July 1983: 103.

Sammon, Bill. "Dorothy Fuldheim: The Woman Behind the Famous Face." *This Week* (Cleveland, OH) 3 Sept. 1982: 6+.

Seifullah, Alan, and Mary Strassmeyer. "Dorothy Fuldheim, TV News Legend, Dies." *Cleveland Plain Dealer* 4 Nov. 1989: sec. A, p. 1+.

Seltzer, Bob. "Heart in Her Work." *Cleveland Press* 21 Feb. 1975.

Sharkey, Mary Anne. "The End of the Fuldheim Era." *Cleveland Plain Dealer* 4 Nov. 1989: sec. B, p. 6.

Strassmeyer, Mary. "A Monument Named Dorothy." *Sunday Cleveland Plain Dealer Magazine* 9 May 1976: 6+.

Taubman, Charlotte. "Mike Maids." *Cleveland Press* 20 Feb. 1954.

Waters, Harry F. "The First Lady of TV News." *Newsweek* 11 June 1979: 91.

Winfrey, Clintie. "She Startled Clubwomen." *Cleveland Plain Dealer* 23 June 1939.

WEWS News Release. 25 Jan. 1962.

WEWS News Release. 11 Mar. 1985.

Betty Furness

"100 Days of Betty Furness, The." *New Republic* 5 Aug. 1967: 10+.

Adams, Val. "Betty Furness Quitting? You Can Be Sure." *Los Angeles Times* 11 Nov. 1960: 15.

"Betty Furness." *Newsweek* 26 July 1971: 11.

"Betty Furness Bio." Westinghouse, Inc., 1957.

"Betty Furness, Broadcaster and Longstanding Member of CU's Board, Dies." *Consumer Reports* June 1994: 370+.

Brooke, Jill. "NBC Pulls the Plug on Betty Furness." *New York Post* 9 Mar. 1992: 20.

Brooks, Tim, and Earle Marsh. *The Complete Directory to Prime Time Network TV Shows*. New York: Ballantine, 1992.

Brown, James. "Summer Job for Betty Furness." *Los Angeles Times* 7 June 1976: 14+.

"Can Betty Furness Help the Consumer?" *Consumer Reports* May 1967: 258+.

Carswell, Sue. "Gritty Woman." *People* 14 Apr. 1994: 74+.

Chamberlin, Anne. "And Now, for the Consumer, Miss Betty Furness!" *Saturday Evening Post* 18 June 1967: 26+.

Current Biography 1968: 134+.

Dalmas, Herbert. "Betty Furness: No. 1 Saleswoman." *Coronet* Oct. 1953: 38+.

Gilbert, Lynn, and Gaylen Moore. *Particular Passions*. New York: Crown, 1981.

Gross, Amy. "Betty Furness: Consumer Reporter/Advocate, Breaking the Age Barrier—With Wit, Wisdom and Style." *Vogue* Oct. 1979: 380+.

Halberstam, David. *The Fifties*. New York: Villard, 1993.

Hernandez, Raymond. "Betty Furness, 78, TV Reporter and Consumer Advocate, Dies." *New York Times* 3 Apr. 1994: 27+.

Hilliard, Robert L., and Michael C. Keith. *The Broadcast Century*. Boston: Focal Press, 1992.

Humphrey, Hal. "Betty Furness All Burned Up." *Los Angeles Times* 22 July 1994.

Katz, Ephraim. *The Film Encyclopedia*. New York: Perigee, 1979.

"Kitchen Riches." *Newsweek* 12 Jan. 1953: 70.

Klemesrud, Judy. "Can She Be a Ralph Nader on TV?" *New York Post* 9 Mar. 1992: 15.

McNeil, Alex. *Total Television*. New York: Penguin, 1980.

Matusow, Barbara. *The Evening Stars*. Boston: Houghton Mifflin, 1983.

Memorial Service for Betty Furness, Studio 8-H, NBC, New York, NY (18 April 1994).

Midgley, Leslie. Telephone interview. 25 Oct. 1994.

"Miss Furness Named to N.Y. Consumer Post." *Los Angeles Times* 31 Mar. 1973: 10.

Morehead, Albert. "America's Top Saleswoman." *Cosmopolitan* Feb. 1953: 136+.

"New 'Shopper' for LBJ." *US News & World Report* 20 Mar. 1967: 21.

Oliver, Myrna. "Betty Furness; Ad Star, Consumer Advocate." *New York Times* 4 Apr. 1994: 26+.

Ramsey, Betty Jo. "Betty Furness: Quick-Change Artist." *Good Housekeeping* June 1960: 30+.

Ruch, Charles A. (Westinghouse Historian). Letter to author. 14 Oct. 1994.

Russell, Lisa. "Passages." *People* 23 Mar. 1992: 70.

Satz, Rita. Telephone interview. 1 Nov. 1994.

Shelton, Elizabeth. "Betty Furness: One Year on the Job." *Washington Post* 5 May 1968: 17.

Shever, Steven. *Who's Who in Television and Cable*. New York: Facts on File, 1983.

Springer, John. *They Had Faces Then: Superstars, Stars and Starlets of the 1930s*. Secaucus, NJ: Citadel, 1974.

"Star in Consumer Role." *New York Times* 6 Mar. 1967: 37.

Whitcomb, Meg. "You Can Be Sure If It's Betty Furness." *Fifty Plus* Aug. 1980: 49.

Frieda Hennock

Barnouw, Erik. *The Golden Web*. New York: Oxford University, 1968.

_____. *Tube of Plenty*. New York: Oxford University Press, 1982.

Brown, Les. *The New York Times Encylopedia of Television*. New York: Times Books, 1977.

"Commissioner Frieda B. Hennock." Federal Communications Commission. 6 July 1948.

Current Biography 1948: 278+.

Eklund, Laurence C. "Portia on the FCC." *Milwaukee Journal* 2 Sept. 1948.

"First Fifty Years of Broadcasting, The." *Broadcasting* 23 May 1981: 101.

"First Woman Member of FCC Makes Impression on Senators with Frankness." *Washington Post* 6 July 1948: 2.

"Flunked." *Broadcasting* 5 Feb. 1973: 74.

"Frieda Hennock Simons Dead; Lawyer, 55, Had Been on FCC." *New York Times* 21 June 1960: 2.

Gross, Lynne Schafer. *Telecommunications*. Dubuque, IA: William C. Brown, 1986.

Hennock, Frieda B. "The 3 R's on TV." *Variety* 3 Jan. 1951.

Hennock, Frieda B. "TV—Problem Child or Teacher's Pet?" *New York State Education* Mar. 1951: 397+.

Krasnow, Erwin, Lawrence D. Longley, and Herbert A. Terry. *The Politics of Broadcast Regulation*. New York: St. Martin's Press, 1982.

MacLeod, John. "Woes and Triumphs of a Lady Advocate." *American Weekly* 5 Sept. 1948.

Millspaugh, Martha. "Miss Commissioner Hennock." *Hamilton Sun* 8 Aug. 1948: 5.

"Miss Hennock's Warpath." *Pathfinder* 12 July 1950.

"Never Underestimate ..." *Fortune* Oct. 1949: 22.

"Our Respects To—Madame Commissioner." *Broadcasting* 31 May 1948: 44.

Paglin, Max (former legal counsel to the FCC). Telephone interview. 26 Oct. 1991.

Sicherman, Barbara, and Carol Hurd Green. *Notable American Women: The Modern Period.* Cambridge: Belknap, 1980.

Sterling, Christoper H., and John M. Kittross. *Stay Tuned.* Belmont, CA: Wadsworth, 1990.

Thayer, Mary Van Resselaer. "Washington's Most Influential Women." *Parade* (*Washington Post*) 31 July 1949: 6.

"TV Color's Future: 7 Who Rule." *US News & World Report* 27 Oct. 1950: 34+.

"Wanted Woman." *Time* 19 July 1948: 56.

Welch, Mary Scott. "Donna Quixote." *Look* 17 July 1951: 76.

"Woman in a Man's World." *Talks* Jan. 1949: 37.

"Woman Nominated as Member of FCC." *New York Times* 25 May 1948: 6.

Lucy Jarvis

Campbell, Robert. *The Golden Years of Broadcasting.* New York: Rutledge, 1976.

Current Biography 1972: 240+.

DeBell, Jeff. "Sophisticated Lady." *Roanoke Times & World News* 12 Apr. 1989: 1+.

The Forbidden City (motion picture). National Broadcasting Company, 1973.

Gilbert, Lynn, and Gaylen Moore. *Particular Passions.* New York: Crown, 1981.

Giniger, Henry. "Art for TV's Sake." *New York Times* 27 Oct. 1963: 13.

Hammond, Charles Montgomery, Jr. *The Image Decade: Television Documentary 1965–1975.* New York: Hastings House, 1981.

Humphrey, Hal. "TV's Other Lucy." *Los Angeles Mirror* 22 Dec. 1961: 17.

"Inside China with NBC." *Broadcasting* 21 Aug. 1972: 35.

Jarvis, Lucy. Letter to author. 16 July 1992.

Kremlin, The (motion picture). National Broadcasting Company, 1963.

Louvre, The (motion picture). National Broadcasting Company, 1964.

"Lucy Jarvis." National Broadcasting Company. Apr. 1981.

"Lucy Jarvis—JTFP Bio." Jarvis Theatre & Film Production. 1992.

"Mission: Impossible." *Time* 12 Jan. 1968: 52+.

Robinson, Jeffrey. *Bette Davis ... Her Film and Stage Career.* London: Proteus, 1982.

Ryback, Timothy W. "East Woos West in a Romantic Soviet Rock Opera." *New York Times* 7 Jan. 1990: 25+.

Shanley, John P. "Woman Producer Conquers Kremlin." *New York Times* 19 May 1963: 17.

Ida Lupino

Acker, Ally. *Reel Women.* New York: Continuum, 1991.

Andrews, Bart. *Lucy & Ricky & Fred & Ethel: The Story of* I Love Lucy. New York: Fawcett, 1976.

"As Film Star, Director, Composer Ida Lupino Excels in Entertainment." *Box Office* 29 Sept. 1975: SE-14+.

Bart, Peter. "Lupino, the Dynamo." *New York Times* 7 Mar. 1965: 7.

Brooks, Tim, and Earle Marsh. *The Complete Directory to Prime Time Network TV Shows.* New York: Ballantine, 1981.

Brown, Les. *The New York Times Encyclopedia of Television.* New York: Times Books, 1977.

"Coast to Coast." *Hollywood Reporter* 16 Nov. 1972.

Colton, Helen. "Ida Lupino, Filmland's Lady of Distinction." *New York Times* 30 Apr. 1950: 5.

Current Biography 1943: 467+.

Dixon, Wheeler W. *The "B" Directors: A Biographical Directory*. Metuchen, NJ: Scarecrow, 1985.

Fuller, Graham. *Interview* Oct. 1990: 3.

Gardner, Paul. "Ida Lupino in Comeback After 15 Years." *New York Times* 10 Oct. 1972: 51.

Heck-Rabi, Louise. *Women Filmmakers: A Critical Reception*. Metuchen, NJ: Scarecrow, 1984.

"Ida Lupino." *Variety* 14–20 August 1995: 69.

Katz, Ephraim. *The Film Encyclopedia*. New York: Perigee, 1979.

Lacayo, Richard. "Women in Hollywood." *People* Spring 1991: 35+.

Lupino, Ida. "Me, Mother Directress." *Action* May-June 1967: 14+.

McCarty, John, and Brian Kelleher. *Alfred Hitchcock Presents*. New York: St. Martin's Press, 1985.

Minoff, Philip. "TV Personalities." *Family Circle* Mar. 1958: 24+.

Rickey, Carrie. "Lupino Noir." *Voice* 29 Oct.4–Nov. 1980: 43+.

Stone, Judy. "The Life of a Glamour Queen? Not for Lupino." *New York Times* 24 Aug. 1969: 19+.

"Television." *Time* 8 Feb. 1963: 42.

Varney, Ginger. "Ida Lupino, Director." *L.A. Weekly* 12–18 Nov. 1982: 10+.

Vermilye, Jerry. "Ida Lupino." *Films in Review* May 1959: 266+.

Wakeman, John, ed. *World Film Directors, Vol. II: 1945–1985*. New York: H.W. Wilson, 1988.

White, Patricia. "Ida in Wonderland." *Village Voice* 5 Feb.1991: 64.

Whitney, Dwight. "Follow Mother, Here We Go Kiddies." *TV Guide* 8 Oct. 1966: 14+.

Zicree, Marc Scott. *The* Twilight Zone *Companion*. New York: Bantam, 1989.

Irna Phillips

Allen, Robert C. *Speaking of Soaps*. Chapel Hill, NC: University of North Carolina, 1985.

Bell, Lee (television producer). Telephone interview. 4 Sept. 1991.

Brooks, Tim, and Earle Marsh. *The Complete Directory to Prime Time Network TV Shows*. New York: Ballantine, 1981.

"Creators, The." *TV Guide* (Commemorative Edition) July 1991: 56+.

Current Biography 1943: 590+.

Edmondson, Madeline, and David Rounds. *The Soaps*. New York: Stein & Day, 1973.

Hastings, Don (actor/writer). Telephone interview. 5 Dec. 1991.

LaGuardia, Robert. *Soap World*. New York: Arbor House, 1983.

Phillips, Irna. "Every Woman's Life Is a Soap Opera." *McCall's* Mar. 1965: 116+.

"Queen of the Soaps." *Newsweek* 11 May 1964: 66+.

Rouverol, Jean. *Writing for the Soaps*. Cincinnati, OH: Writer's Digest Books, 1984.

"Script Queen." *Time* 10 June 1940: 66+.

Sicherman, Barbara, and Carol Hurd Green. *Notable American Women: The Modern Period*. Cambridge: Belknap, 1980.

Wagner, Helen (actress). Telephone interview. 10 Oct. 1991.
Wakefield, Dan. *All Her Children*. New York: Doubleday, 1976.
"Week's Headliners." *Broadcasting* 17 Jan. 1972: 9.
"With Significance." *Time* 11 June 1945: 46+.
"Writing On: Irna Phillips Mends with Tradition." *Broadcasting* 6 Nov. 1972: 75.
Wyden, Peter. "Madam Soap Opera." *Saturday Evening Post* 25 June 1960: 30+.

Judith Waller

Current Biography 1953 (Frances Horwich): 279+.
Dunning, John. *Tune in Yesterday*. Englewood Cliffs, NJ: Prentice-Hall, 1976: 31+.
Erickson, Hal. *Syndicated Television*. Jefferson, NC: McFarland & Company, 1989.
Heinemann, George. "Chicago, Chicago, That Television Town." *Television Quarterly* Fall 1986: 46+.
"Institute Opens June 28; NBC Employees May Enroll." *NBC Chainbreak* Apr. 1948: 7.
"Judith Waller." *NBC Chimes* May–June 1957: 11.
"Judith Waller—First Lady of Radio." *NBC Chain Break* Apr. 1947: 4.
Mitz, Rick. *The Great TV Sitcom Book*. New York: Perigee Book, 1980.
O'Neil-Decker, Lois. *The Women's Book of World Records and Achievements*. Garden City, NY: Anchor Press/Doubleday, 1977.
Persons, Fern. Oral history. Chicago, IL: Museum of Broadcast Communications, 23 Feb. 1993.
"Seven Women in Radio and TV Win the *McCall's* Mike." *McCall's* Jan. 1954: 58+.
Sicherman, Barbara, and Carol Hurd Green. *Notable American Women: The Modern Period*. Cambridge, MA: Belknap Press, 1980.
Waller, Judith. "Education and Public Affairs." Speech transcript. Washington, D.C.: Broadcast Pioneers Library, 1954.
_____. "Frightened Stars, Silent Nights All in 25-Years." *NBC Chainbreak* Apr. 1947: 3.
_____. Interview transcript. Washington, DC: Broadcast Pioneers Library, 1 June 1951.
_____. *Radio: The Fifth Estate*. Boston: Houghton Mifflin Company, 1946.
Waller, Judith C. "What the Radio Has to Offer to Elementary School Children." *Education* Oct. 1937: 70+.
"Women in Business." *Ladies Home Journal* Dec. 1928: 125.
Woolery, George W. *Children's Television*. Metuchen, NJ: Scarecrow, 1985: 150+.

Betty White

Alley, Robert S., and Irby B. Brown. *Love Is All Around: The Making of* "The Mary Tyler Moore Show." New York: Delta, 1987.
"Betty White Bio." Columbia Broadcasting System, 1975.
"Betty White's 'Life with Elizabeth.'" *TV Guide* 23 Apr. 1954: 16+.
Brooks, Tim, and Earle Marsh. *The Complete Directory to Prime Time Network TV Shows*. New York: Ballantine, 1992.
Buck, Jerry. "No Mr. Nice Guy for Betty White." *New York Post* 13 Oct. 1977: 35.
Burke, Wally. "Death of TV Host Ludden." *New York Post* 10 June 1981: 94.
Carter, Alan. "A Rose By Any Other Name." *City Lights* 8 Feb. 1987: 27.

Celebrity Register. New York: Times Publishing Group, 1986.

Croke, Karen. "Betty White: Life Is Rose-y." *Close-Up* June 1987: 5.

Crosby, John. "Radio and Television." *New York Herald Tribune* 24 May 1954: 22.

Current Biography 1987: 601+.

Erickson, Hal. *Syndicated Television: The First Forty Years, 1947–1987.* Jefferson, NC: McFarland & Company, 1989.

Fulman, Ricki. "Ask Betty White." *New York Daily News* 19 Nov. 1967: S13.

Gardella, Kay. "Betty White a Winner" *New York Daily News* 12 September 1977: 64.

Gould, Jack. "Television in Review." *New York Herald Tribune* 24 Mar. 1954: 58.

Graham, Jefferson. *Come On Down!!!: The Game Show Book.* New York: Abbeville, 1988.

Hoogenboom, Lynn. "New Shade of White in 'Chance of a Lifetime.'" *TV Shopper* 16 Nov. 1991: 1.

Lait, Jack. "TV *Is* Going to the Dogs." *Pictorial Review* 20 June 1954: 10-P.

Larry King Live. Atlanta, GA: Cable News Network, 9 Nov. 1988.

Leamy, Edmund. "A Break for Betty." *World Telegram* (New York) 27 Aug. 1955: 10.

Lindbloom, Roland E. "Betty White Stays in Black." *New York Herald Tribune* 11 June 1957: 81.

MacCann, Richard Dyer. "Television's Betty White." *Christian Science Monitor* 11 May 1954: 32.

MacKenzie, Robert. "Review By Robert MacKenzie." *TV Guide* 25 Nov. 1977: 36.

McWilliams, Michael. *TV Sirens.* New York: Perigee, 1987.

Neville, Mara. "Betty's Animal Instincts." *New York Daily News* 8 Apr. 1988: 62.

Okon, May. "Life with Betty." *Los Angeles Sunday News* 20 Nov. 1955: 4.

Schwartz, David, Steve Ryan, and Fred Wostbrock. *The Encyclopedia of TV Game Shows.* New York: Zoetrope, 1987.

"Show Biz Today." Atlanta, GA: Cable News Network, 1 Nov. 1993.

See, Carolyn. "Why No One Will Knock Betty White." *TV Guide* 17 Dec. 1986: 16+.

Slide, Tony. "Betty White: Life After Sixty." *Emmy Magazine.* Sept.–Oct. 1985: 69.

Watson, Mary Ann. "From 'My Little Margie' to 'Murphy Brown': Women's Lives on the Small Screen." *Television Quarterly* Winter 1994: 23.

White, Betty. *Here We Go Again: My Life in Television.* New York: Scribner, 1995.

_____. *In Person.* New York: Doubleday, 1987.

_____. Letter to author. 24 August 1995.

Wilson, Liza. "Betty White, TV's Cinderella." *American Weekly* 15 Aug. 1954: 13+.

Index

241